KT-556-733

BCP
Council

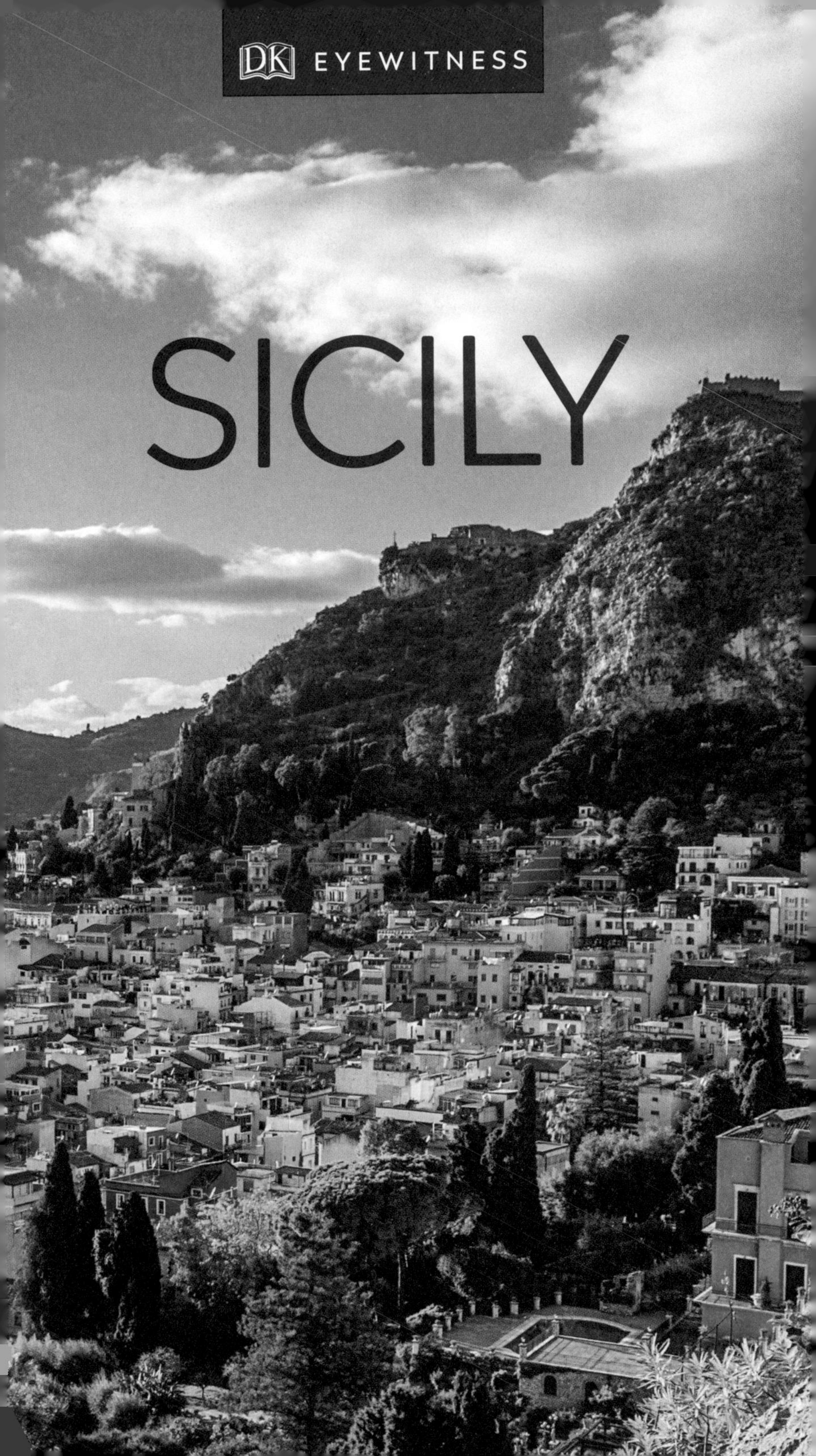
DK
EYEWITNESS
SICILY

CONTENTS

DISCOVER SICILY 6

EXPERIENCE PALERMO 58

EXPERIENCE SICILY 106

NEED TO KNOW 232

Left: Decorative ceramics made in Sicily
Previous page: Picturesque Taormina and Mount Etna
Front cover: A fishing boat by Cefalù's harbour

DISCOVER

The pretty town of Cefalù by the coast

WELCOME TO SICILY

Breathtaking natural wonders and miles of heart-stirring coastline. Extraordinary architecture and legendary Greek and Roman ruins. Steaming volcanoes and storybook villages. Sicily promises to deliver all this and more. Whatever your dream trip to these breathtaking islands entails, this DK Eyewitness travel guide is the perfect companion.

1 The colourful wheel of a traditional Sicilian cart.

2 The spectacular hilltop town of Ragusa.

3 A freshly prepared Sicilian-style lunch.

4 A rocky beach near the village of Scopello.

Rising out of shimmering cyan seas, sun-kissed Sicily and its satellite islands are some of the most beautiful in the Mediterranean. Sitting just to the west of Italy's boot, Sicily itself is endowed with its own distinct identity, one shaped by a patchwork of cultures and civilizations echoing back to the Greeks. The endless coastline – made up of pebble-strewn coves, sandy beaches and rugged cliffs – encircles a landscape of rolling farmland, dramatic salt pans, windswept mountains and amber-and-green-hued vineyards fed by rich volcanic soil. Magnificently dominating the island's east is the tempestuous, fiery peak of Mount Etna, the highest volcano in Europe.

Scattered across the island are countless pretty villages and captivating cities. Among them is bustling Palermo, Sicily's architecturally eclectic capital, dotted with Greek, Arab and Norman buildings. There's also hilltop Ragusa, beach-side Cefalù, beautifully Baroque Noto and timeless Syracuse, home to maze-like streets and expansive piazzas. Wherever you are, there's mouthwatering cuisine to be sampled, including freshly caught seafood, super-sweet *cannoli* and, of course, creamy *gelato*.

So, where to begin? Our guide breaks Sicily down into easily navigable chapters, with detailed itineraries, expert local knowledge and colourful, comprehensive maps to help you plan your perfect trip. Whether you're visiting for a weekend, a week, or are taking a grand tour of Sicily and it's beautiful islands, this DK Eyewitness travel guide will ensure that you see the very best the islands have to offer. Enjoy the book and enjoy Sicily.

REASONS TO LOVE SICILY

Spectacular food and wine, mystifying archaeological sites, secluded beaches and picturesque fishing villages - there are so many reasons to love Sicily. Here, we pick some of our favourites.

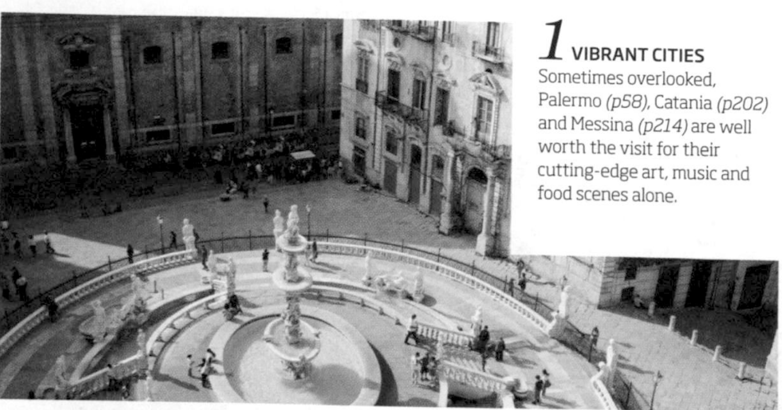

1 VIBRANT CITIES

Sometimes overlooked, Palermo *(p58)*, Catania *(p202)* and Messina *(p214)* are well worth the visit for their cutting-edge art, music and food scenes alone.

FESTIVALS GALORE 2

Whether it's historical re-enactments, musical concerts in town squares, or *sagres* (local food festivals), Sicilians know how to celebrate.

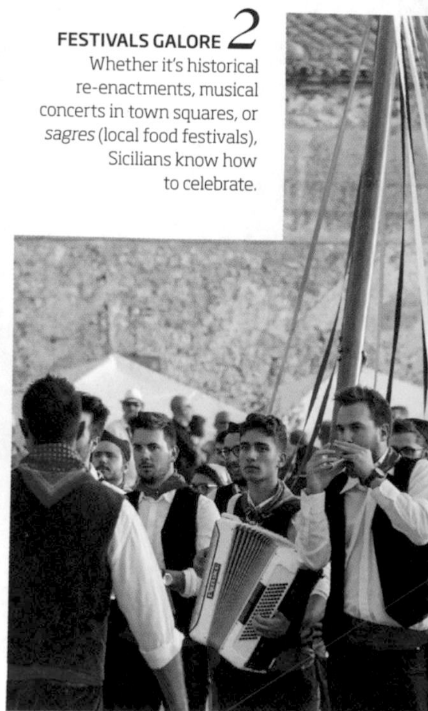

3 THE COFFEE BAR

Visit a coffee bar for a Sicilian breakfast of espresso or cappuccino with brioche - swap the coffee for *granita* in the warmer months. Stand at the counter to feel like a local.

COASTAL ESCAPES 4

Relax on secluded coves, go off the grid on a family-friendly beach or set sail and find a beautiful sunset. Get away from it all along Sicily's vast and varied shoreline.

THE ANCIENT WORLD 5

Shrouded in legend, Sicily's archaeological remains beg to be explored. Wander ancient Segesta *(p122)*, Selinunte *(p126)* and the Valle dei Templi *(p150)*; the latter is spectacular at night.

HOME COOKING SICILIAN STYLE 6

Bite into an *arancina* tinged with saffron, or gorge on a plate of tangy couscous, first introduced by Sicily's North African neighbours.

ISLAND ADVENTURES 7

Sicily provides activities for the audacious and the bold. Whether your thing is hiking, diving, caving or soaring through the air, Sicily will take you there.

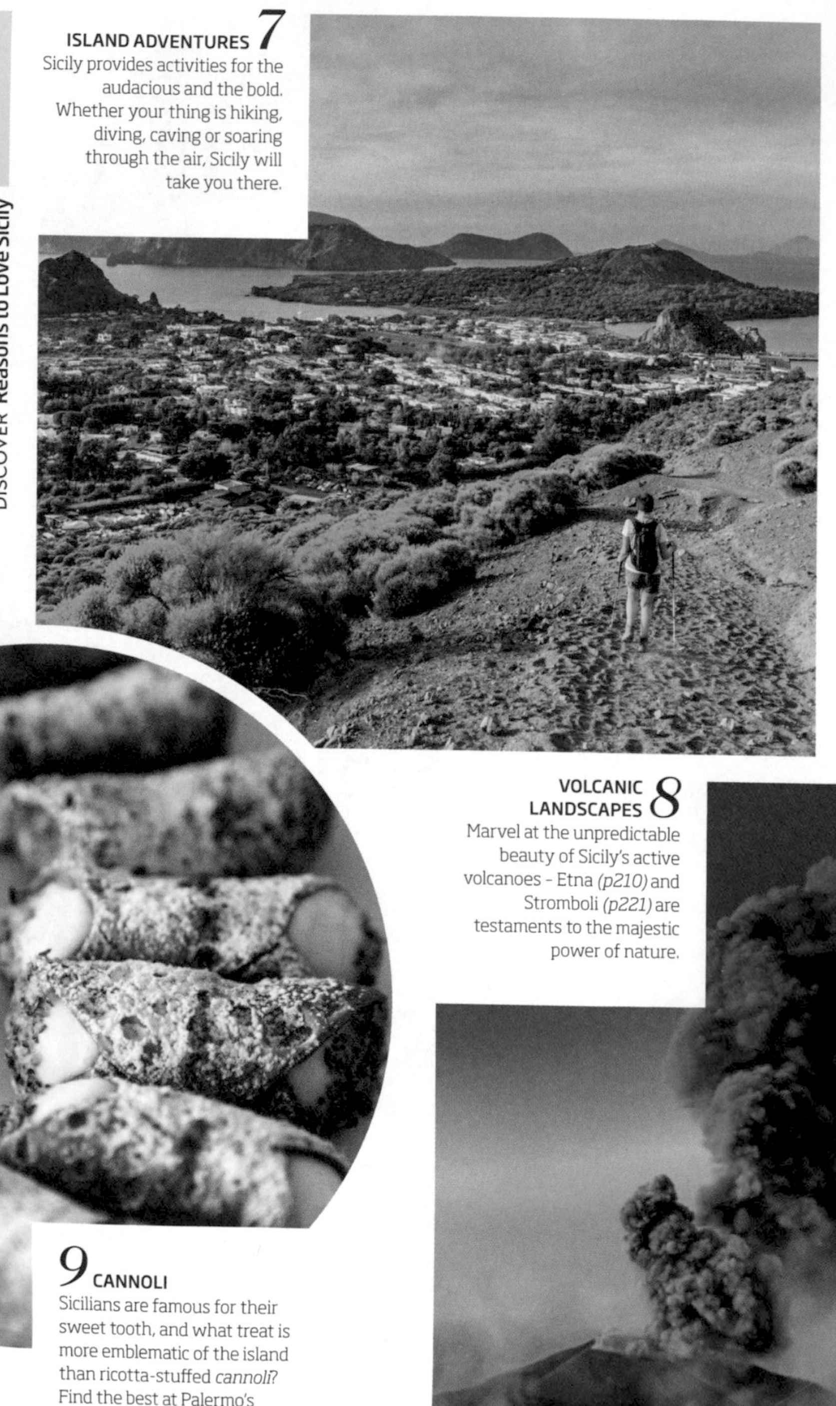

VOLCANIC LANDSCAPES 8

Marvel at the unpredictable beauty of Sicily's active volcanoes – Etna *(p210)* and Stromboli *(p221)* are testaments to the majestic power of nature.

9 CANNOLI

Sicilians are famous for their sweet tooth, and what treat is more emblematic of the island than ricotta-stuffed *cannoli*? Find the best at Palermo's Cannolo Festival *(p53)*.

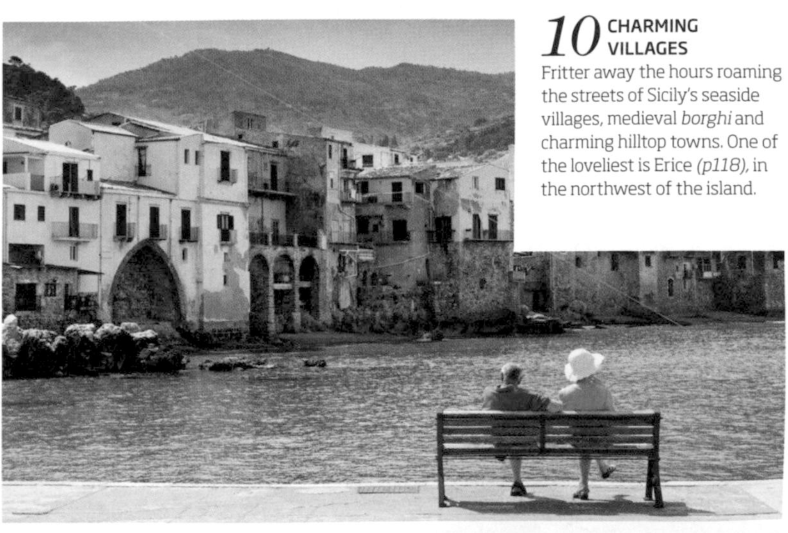

10 CHARMING VILLAGES

Fritter away the hours roaming the streets of Sicily's seaside villages, medieval *borghi* and charming hilltop towns. One of the loveliest is Erice *(p118)*, in the northwest of the island.

TEATRO DEI PUPI 11

Using traditional marionettes, the Opera dei Pupi (Opera of the Puppets) is unique to Sicily. Watch heroes battling villains in Palermo *(p101)*.

SICILIAN WINES 12

Cellars in Noto *(p178)*, Etna *(p210)* and Marsala *(p130)* are producing terrific vintages, impressing consumers and connoisseurs alike.

EXPLORE SICILY

This guide divides Sicily into five colour-coded sightseeing areas, as shown on this map. Find out more about each area on the following pages.

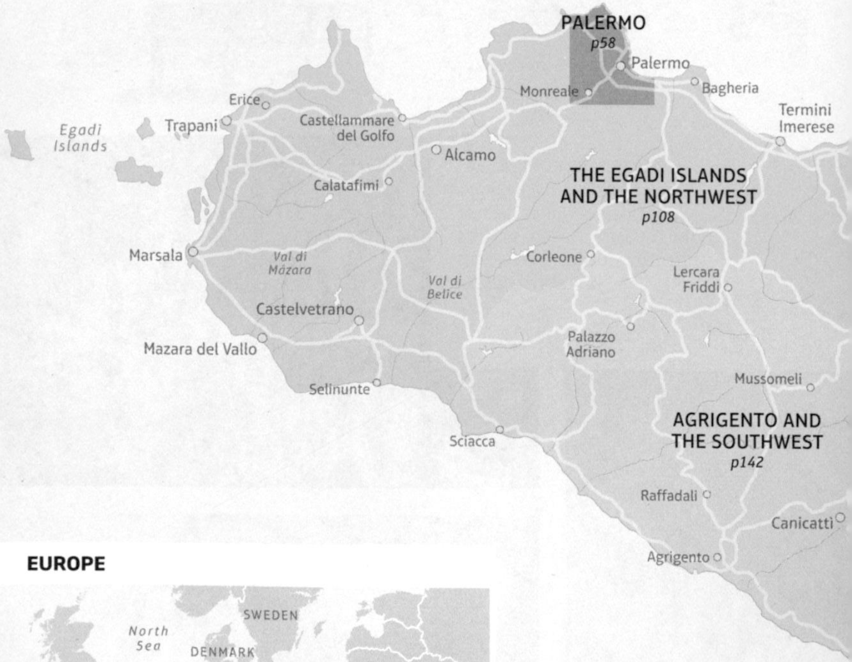

PALERMO
p58
Palermo
Monreale
Bagheria
Termini Imerese
Egadi Islands
Erice
Trapani
Castellammare del Golfo
Alcamo
Calatafimi
THE EGADI ISLANDS AND THE NORTHWEST
p108
Marsala
Val di Mázara
Val di Belice
Corleone
Lercara Friddi
Castelvetrano
Mazara del Vallo
Palazzo Adriano
Selinunte
Mussomeli
Sciacca
AGRIGENTO AND THE SOUTHWEST
p142
Raffadali
Canicattì
Agrigento

EUROPE

SWEDEN
North Sea
DENMARK
IRELAND
UNITED KINGDOM
BELARUS
POLAND
GERMANY
CZECH REP.
UKRAINE
SLOVAKIA
AUSTRIA
HUNGARY
FRANCE
SWITZ.
ROMANIA
CROATIA
SERBIA
BULGARIA
ITALY
SPAIN
Sicily
GREECE
TURKEY
Mediterranean Sea
MOROCCO
TUNISIA
ALGERIA
LIBYA
EGYPT

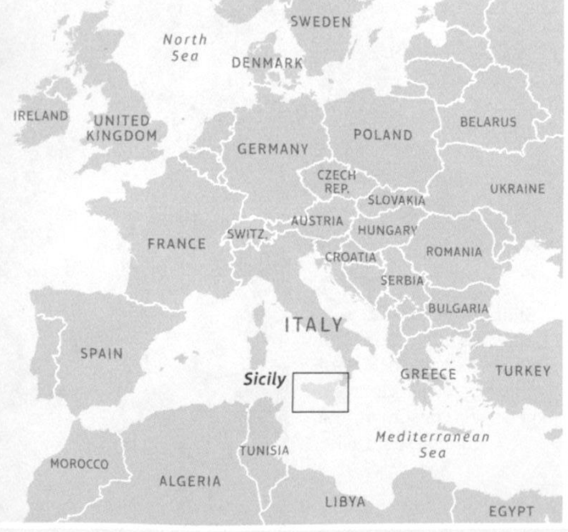

Aeolian Islands
Tyrrhenian Sea
Golfo di Patti
Milazzo
Messina
Tindari
Sant'Agata di Militello
Monti Peloritani
Reggio di Calabria
Cefalù
Milianni
MOUNT ETNA, THE AEOLIAN ISLANDS AND THE NORTHEAST
p198
Ali Terme
Castelbuono
Monti Nebrodi
Randazzo
Taormina
Monti Madonie
Bronte
Fiumefreddo di Sicilia
Castellana Sicula
Nicosia
Mount Etna
Adrano
Leonforte
Acireale
Paternò
Enna
Aci Castello
Catania
Caltanissetta
Gerbini
Golfo di Catania
Barrafranca
Piazza Armerina
Lentini
Caltagirone
Monti Iblei
Augusta
Golfo di Augusta
SYRACUSE, VAL DI NOTO AND THE SOUTH
p168
Licata
Gela
Syracuse
Palazzolo Acreide
Golfo di Gela
Val di Noto
Ragusa
Comiso
Noto
Modica
Golfo di Noto
Scicli
Ispica
Marina di Ragusa
Pozzallo
Pachino
Mediterranean Sea

GETTING TO KNOW SICILY

The diverse region of Sicily is made up of the main island and a clutch of smaller islands. Ringed by a trio of ultramarine seas, these sun-drenched islands have a rugged landscape blanketed by mountains, volcanoes, and vineyards and orchards, as well as cultural cities and picturesque towns.

PAGE 58

PALERMO

Dubbed *Conca d'Oro* (golden basin), Sicily's capital is a colourful and dynamic port city that lies pinched between Mount Pellegrino, Aspra and the Tyrrhenian Sea. Here, a spiderweb of streets lead to countless Baroque and Gothic churches, while the city's eye-catching Liberty-style *palazzi* are upstaged only by its splendid Cathedral and gilded Cappella Palatina. Scattered across Palermo are a hodgepodge of lively piazzas, bustling outdoor markets and crumbling neighbourhoods strung with fluttering laundry, alongside vibrant up-and-coming restaurants and cafés.

Best for

Arab-Norman architecture, browsing open-air markets and eating delicious cannoli

Home to

Palazzo Abatellis, Palermo Cathedral, Cappella Palatina, Duomo di Monreale

Experience

Attend an opera at Teatro Massimo

PAGE 108

THE EGADI ISLANDS AND THE NORTHWEST

A great many civilizations left their footprints on the northwest of Sicily. Today ancient settlements such as Segesta, Selinunte and Solunto sit alongside picture-postcard resort towns like Cefalù and Bagheria. The area's rugged coastline is home to little fishing villages, beautiful beaches and the Riserva Naturale dello Zingaro, while further inland are mountainous uplands. Numerous islands are also scattered off the coast, from tiny Ustica to the rocky Egadi Islands.

Best for
Strolling through medieval fishing villages and discovering Norman castles

Home to:
Cefalù, Riserva dello Zingaro, Erice, Segesta, Egadi Islands, Selinunte

Experience
Take a drive along the Salt Road

PAGE 142

AGRIGENTO AND THE SOUTHWEST

Unforgettable for its classical skyline of Olympian deities, the Valley of the Temples' garland of colonnades tumble across a crest of land near the hilltop city of Agrigento. Further east, the well-preserved mosaics of Villa del Casale at Piazza Armerina offer a unique window into everyday Roman life. Hilly interiors of green-and-yellow vineyards and olive groves contrast with jagged cliffs facing the far-off Pelagie islets – mere droplets in the balmy Mediterranean.

Best for
Exploring Greek temples and Roman ruins

Home to
Agrigento, Piazza Armerina: Villa Romana del Casale

Experience
Dine on traditional dishes such as pollo alla Marsala *made with capers from Pantelleria*

PAGE 168

SYRACUSE, VAL DI NOTO AND THE SOUTH

Tremendous contrasts characterize this end of Sicily, making it a treat for the senses. Here, limestone gorges cut through a landscape blanketed by carpets of wildflowers, while bluffs curve over sandy beaches. The area is also home to several historic cities that contain UNESCO World Heritage Sites, including the Baroque Noto, Greek-influenced Syracuse and fairy-tale Ragusa, while eastward you'll discover scores of scenic villages.

Best for
Outdoor amphitheatres, Baroque churches and ceramics shopping.

Home to
Syracuse, Ortigia, Noto, Ragusa, Caltagirone

Experience
Listen to amplified sounds inside the Ear of Dionysius

PAGE 198

MOUNT ETNA, THE AEOLIAN ISLANDS AND THE NORTHEAST

The northeast quadrant of Sicily offers an array of unique travel experiences. Here you will encounter pine-forested highlands, a romantic volcanic archipelago, a coastal stretch of dreamy holiday resorts, noisy cities and pretty fishing hamlets, all set against the awe-inspiring backdrop of capricious Mount Etna.

Best for
Fresh seafood, active volcanic craters

Home to
Catania, Taormina, Mount Etna, Messina, Aeolian Islands

Experience
Cool off with a slushy Granita *on the island of Salina*

1

2

3

4

1 Palermo's skyline.

2 Admiring Chiesa del Gesù.

3 Walking through the Duomo di Monreale's courtyard.

4 White snails for sale at a street food market.

Sicily brims with travel opportunities, from a weekend in the capital to island-hopping. These itineraries will inspire you to make the most of your visit.

2 DAYS

in Palermo

Day 1

Morning For a taste of all that Palermo has to offer, start the day with a cappuccino and *granita con brioche* at a local bar then wander over to Mercato di Ballarò *(p93)*, the oldest and most rollicking street market in the city. Next, walk west on Via Casa Professa, popping into Chiesa del Gesù *(p90)*, a 16th-century Baroque jewel of marble inlays and impressive stuccowork. Afterwards, treat yourself to a gourmet lunch at Al Fondaco Del Conte *(www.alfondacodelconte.it)* set in a historic palazzo.

Afternoon After lunch, plot a course for Palazzo dei Normanni *(p89)*, a palace built by the Arabs and expanded by a Norman king. Don't miss Cappella Palatina's *(p86)* astonishing mosaics – a highlight of any visit. Next, set out along Villa Bonanno *(p88)* towards Palermo's lofty Cathedral *(p84)*, a true bastion of the city, its geometric exteriors juxtaposed with Neo-Classical interiors. Afterwards, a walk down Via Maqueda provides a momentary distraction, offering plenty of shopping and places for an afternoon *aperitivo*.

Evening For something on the lighter side, tuck into a crispy, wood-fired pizza at Ristorante Pizzeria Italia *(www.ristorantepizzeriaitalia.it)* for dinner. Not far off the palm tree-studded Piazza Castelnuovo is the avant-garde Bolazzi *(Piazzetta Francesco Bagnasco 1)*, a late-night club where you can dance to live music performed by Italian artists.

Day 2

Morning It's a one-hour bus journey from Piazza Indipendenza to the Duomo di Monreale *(p98)*. Spend the morning gazing at its striking Romanesque towers and 12th- and 13th-century mosaics narrating the Old Testament, before refuelling with an espresso at a bar-bistro on Piazza Guglielmo. Catch the bus back to town and disembark at Palazzo Reale. Walk down Corso Vittorio Emanuele and turn left onto Via Roma until you stumble upon the bustling Mercato della Vucciria *(p76)*. Grab a bite to eat from one of its renowned street food vendors.

Afternoon After you've had your fill of Palermo's flavourful treats, spend the afternoon exploring the area around the old and "new" parts of the city. Weave your way down to San Francesco d'Assisi *(p72)*, an austere building with a lovely rose window and carved Gothic doorway. Stop at Palazzo Mirto *(p70)* for a guided tour of this 18th-century nobleman's mansion containing original furnishings. Hug the road along the water passing Castello a Mare, the ancient fortress guarding the harbour. Your final stop is Via Principe di Belmonte, the pedestrian area in the Borgo Vecchio quarter, where you can take a well deserved break.

Evening Have a leisurely dinner in one of the many friendly *trattorie* in the Borgo Vecchio. As the day comes to an end, join the evening *passegiatta* where people-watching becomes an art form.

→

1 Boats docked in Trapani.

2 Cycling down Corso Vittorio Emanuele in Trapani.

3 A vineyard near Marsala.

4 Ancient finds at Museo Archeologico Baglio Anselmi.

5 DAYS

on the trail of salt and wine in western Sicily

Day 1

Arrive in the port city of Trapani *(p128)* to embark on a viticultural adventure. Once you've checked into La Gancia *(www.lagancia.com)*, stroll through Trapani's maze of winding streets with its endless succession of churches. The Cathedral of San Lorenzo is a particularly enduring example of Baroque architecture. In the afternoon, take your pick of the wine bars that line the Via Torrearsa and sip a local varietal – alfresco of course. End your day with a leisurely dinner in the courtyard of Ai Lumi *(Corso Vittorio Emanuele 75/77)*, weather permitting.

Day 2

After breakfast, drive down the Salt Road (SP21) to the Museo del Sale *(p129)*, where a fascinating guided tour retraces the steps of the centuries-old salt extraction techniques. A quick lunch in the museum café gives you plenty of time for a spin around the glistening salt pans nearby before embarking south to Marsala *(p130)*. En route, pull into Baglio Cudia Resort *(Contrada Spagnola 381)* to enjoy a swim in the late-afternoon sun. Linger at Baglio Cudia's in-house restaurant for dinner and end the day with a stroll along the banks of the lagoon.

Day 3

Boat across the Stagnone *(p129)* to the former Phoenician colony of Mothya on Isola San Pantaleo. Explore the austere beauty of the archaeological site then tour the Museo di Mozia, which houses a remarkable statue of a Greek boy from the 5th century BC, before heaing back to the mainland. For an afternoon treat, book a winery tour and tasting at Cantine Florio *(Via Vincenzo Florio 1)*, the makers of sweet Marsala wine. Relax on the terrace as you savour a fine glass of wine accompanied by unforgettable Mediterranean views. As evening approaches, check into Agriturismo Donnafranca *(www.donnafranca.it)*: a wine estate that produces organic red and white varietals.

Day 4

Spend the morning exploring the colourful history of Marsala. The Museo Archeologico Baglio Anselmi is the place to start, home to reconstructed remains of a Punic warship. After a seafood lunch, head to Risinata Forest near Sambuca di Sicilia, where the remains of a 4th-century BC building indicate Sicily's wine economy may have existed even back then. Return to Marsala in time for a sundown toast and a fancy dinner at Osteria Il Gallo e L'innamorata *(Via S. Bilardello 18)* – less than a 10-minute walk from Hotel Carmine *(www.hotelcarmine.it)*.

Day 5

Hit the road early and make a beeline for the upscale resort of Baglio Soria *(www.firriato-baglio-soria-trapani.it)*. Check in and stake out a sunlounger by the panoramic pool and order a snack from the bar. Reserve the afternoon for a wine course to learn about production and tasting techniques from grape to glass. After, head to the sophisticated wine bar for a practical application of your newfound knowledge. A spectacular spot for an *aperitivo*, the elevated Sky Lounge has sweeping views of the coast and beyond: the perfect end to your trip.

7 DAYS

island hopping in the Aeolian archipelago

Day 1

Board a hydrofoil from Milazzo *(p230)* to the small island of Vulcano *(p220)* and kick off your day with a climb to the Gran Cratere for unobstructed panoramas. If the smell of sulphur is overwhelming, opt for a swim in the Jacuzzi-like *acque calde* (warm waters) bubbling near the rock stack before a picnic on the beach. Once satiated, relax in the mud baths around Porto di Levante before catching a hydrofoil from Vulcano's main port to Lipari *(p219)*, the main island in the archipelago. Enjoy a fresh seafood dinner at trendy Kasbah Café *(www.kasbahlipari.it)* here, washed down with a glass of the island's famous wine, Malvasia delle Lipari.

Day 2

Rent a bicycle and ride to the Spiaggia Bianca where the waters are emerald from the pumice once mined nearby. Pedal over to Marina Corta for a long lunch looking out over its enchanting fishing harbour and then journey back in time at the Museo Archeologico Eoliano *(p219)*, which contains a great collection of Neolithic, Greek and Roman artifacts. After dinner participate in the town's nightly *passeggiata*, a snail's pace stroll that sees the streets swell with people.

Day 3

Catch the hydrofoil from Lipari to the town of Santa Maria on the twin-peaked island of Salina *(p220)*. Have a bite to eat in the coastal town of Lingua, saving room for a refreshing *granita* at Bar Alfredo *(Via Alfieri)* on the seaside piazza. Hop on the bus to the town of Pollara and stroll along the coastal road down to Perciato di Pollara, where you can do some snorkelling in the bay's shallow waters. Have a nightcap at one of Lipari town's bars along Corso Vittorio Emanuele which throng with holidaying Italians in the summer months.

Day 4

Book a private boat excursion with Aeolian Islands *(www.eoliana.net)* departing from Marina Corta to the exclusive island of Panarea *(p220)*, a

3

4

5

[1] Boats by the harbour in Lipari. ↑
[2] The idyllic Panarea island.
[3] Fresh food in Lipari.
[4] Impressive views from Vulcano.
[5] Crystal-clear waters of Salina.

haven for the rich and famous. Gaze at the ruins at Cala Junco then drop anchor in the port of car-free San Pietro, where you can comb the charming streets for a trattoria in which to have a leisurely late lunch. Take the ferry back to Lipari in time for sunset drinks and dinner.

Day 5

Take a boat over to Stromboli *(p221)* and spend the morning lazing on the beach, taking a break from sunbathing for lunch under the shady pergola at La Lampara *(Via Vittorio Emanuele)*. Arrange a guided hike to the summit of the iconic volcano for the afternoon. It's best to arrive just before sunset for impeccable views of the glowing magma. Enjoy a seafood dinner at Ristorante Punta Lena *(Via Marina 8)* and stay at La Sirenetta Park Hotel *(www.lasirenetta.it)*, a little slice of luxury across the road from the beach.

Day 6

A boat tour of Filicudi *(p221)*is the best way to see its Faraglione della Canna rockstacks and nature reserve – and the perfect way to start the day. Then cruise over to La Sirena *(p219)* for a gourmet lunch overlooking the beach. Continue by boat to remote Alicudi *(p219)* where there are no paved roads, only a peaceful network of mule paths and steps waiting to be explored. Once back to civilization on Stromboli, take a coffee break in one of the bars that line the port. Catch the hydrofoil back to Lipari and opt for the catch of the day at Da Filippino *(p220)* for a fresh dinner.

Day 7

After breakfast at the hotel, do some last-minute souvenir shopping at Fratelli Laise *(Via Vittorio Emanuele 188)* where you can pick up local products and a bottle of Malvasia di Lipari to take home with you. Have a light lunch at a sidewalk café before taking a final spin around town, stopping for some *gelato* as you amble through the streets. Catch the hydrofoil or ferry back to Milazzo before the sun sets to begin your journey home and end your island-hopping adventure.

1

2

2 WEEKS

A grand tour of Sicily

Day 1

Start your journey in the hilltop town of Taormina *(p206)*, a train ride from Catania. After a visit to the Palazzo Corvaja *(p206)*, cool off with a dip in the sea at Isola Bella *(p209)* and dry off with lunch surfside. Stroll along the glamourous, boutique-lined Corso Umberto I *(p207)* before heading to the magnificent Greek Theatre *(p206)*, set against the stunning backdrop of Mount Etna. As evening draws in, enjoy sunset cocktails under the clock tower on Piazza IX Aprile *(p207)* before catching the train back to Catania.

Day 2

Catch an early bus from Catania's railway station to Etna's base camp at Rifugio Sapienza *(www.rifugiosapienza.com)*, where you'll be whisked up to the volcano by cable car, and hike to the lava flows that surround the crater. Make your way down this lunar-like surface for a high-altitude coffee at the *rifugio*. Return to Catania for a burger at Fud Bottega Sicula *(Via Santa Filomena 35)* before a nightcap at Bohème *(www.bohememixologybar.com)*.

Day 3

Spend the morning immersed in the life of the renowned Italian composer Vincenzo Bellini at the Museo Civico Belliniano *(p203)*. After you've had your fill of his original scores and instruments, grab lunch at a café on Via Etnea *(p204)*, then stop for afternoon Catanese puppet theatre at Marionettistica Fratelli Napoli *(p41)*. Continue your cultural day with an evening concert at Teatro Bellini *(p203)*, arriving early for a pre-show *aperitivo* on Piazza Bellini. After the show, dine at Mè Cumpari *(www.mecumparituriddu.it)*, a bistro-style eatery serving seasonal dishes.

Day 4

Hire a car and drive to ancient Syracuse *(p172)*. Take your time exploring the ruins of the Roman and the Greek amphitheatres at Parco Archeologico Neapolis, sauntering over to experience the Ear of Dionysius in the Latomia del Paradiso area. After lunch at a family-run eatery, walk over to Museo Archeologico Regionale Paolo Orsi *(p173)* to check out antiquities excavated from Southern

1 Exploring Piazza Duomo in Ortigia. ↑
2 Taormina's Palazzo Corvaja.
3 The lush centre of Ortigia.
4 Traditional Sicilian puppets.
5 Catania's city centre.

Sicily. Bed down in Ortigia *(p176)* at the Hotel Gutkowski *(www.guthotel.it)* after dinner at their terrace restaurant.

Day 5

Start the day cruising round Ortigia's bustling morning market, then stroll from Duomo to Fonte Aretusa along Lungomare Alfeo, which has a wonderful terrace overlooking a pond. Enjoy a picnic on the water's edge with an assortment of foods from the market. After an hour ducking in and out of boutiques along Corso Matteotti, take a break at A Putia *(www.aputiadellecosebuone.it)*, a wine bar off Via Roma. Set aside the evening for dinner and drinks near Castello Maniace, where you'll find restaurants and bars all along the sea wall. After your meal, walk to Piazzetta San Rocca to experience Ortigia's buzzing nightlife.

Day 6

Depart for Noto *(p178)*, with a pause en route for lunch in the picturesque town of Avola, famous for its robust red wine. Take your time marvelling at Noto's superlative architecture and golden Baroque skyline, especially along Corso Vittorio Emanuele. Climb the steps that link to upper Noto Antica where ruins of the pre-earthquake old town remain. As evening approaches, dine on nouvelle cuisine at Ristorante Crocifisso *(www.ristorantecrocifisso.it)*, heading to Caffè Sicilia *(p179)* for a *gelato* dessert.

Day 7

The next stop is the tuna-fishing village of Marzamemi *(p196)*. Seek out the main piazza where La Cialoma *(Piazza Regina Margherita 16)* sets up outdoor tables on the public square. After lunch, continue to Modica *(p190)*, world-famous for its chocolate. Take a tour of Antica Dolceria Bonajuto *(p41)*, the oldest confection factory here, then head on to the Museo del Cioccolato di Modica *(Corso Umberto I 149)* to learn about the history of chocolate dating back to Columbian times. Dine on Sicilian dishes at Taverna Nicastro *(p191)* before settling in at B&B L'Orangerie *(www.lorangerie.it)*.

1

3

2

Day 8

Set out for the two-tiered town of Ragusa *(p184)*, beginning at the main piazza of Ragusa Ilba (lower town) where the impressive Duomo di San Giorgio *(p186)* can be admired. Work up an appetite souvenir shopping before finding a cosy bar that prepares food to go, to enjoy on a shady bench or grassy patch nearby. Walk over to the steps connecting Ragusa's lower and upper sections to find the lovely Santa Maria delle Scale *(p185)*. If time permits, drive across the tallest viaduct in Europe to experience the views from the upper town, before splashing out on a two Michelin-starred dinner at the fabulous Ciccio Sultano Duomo *(p187)*.

Day 9

Enjoy breakfast at Pasticceria di Pasquale *(Corso Vittorio Veneto, Ragusa Superiore 104)* before leaving for Caltagirone *(p188)*. Take a detour to Vittoria *(p191)*, renowned for its Cerasuolo di Vittoria wine, and buy a bottle from an artisanal shop in the historic centre. Then drive to Chiaramonte Gulfi *(p191)* to enjoy a relaxing lunch and see antique looms in the textile museum *(Museo del Ricamo e dello Sfilato, Via Laurea 4)*. Upon arrival in Caltagirone, seek out a hotel in the historic centre before heading out for some drinks.

Day 10

Avoid the queues and head to the popular Regional Ceramics Museum *(Via Giardini Pubblic)* early before prowling the shops in search of the perfect handmade pottery creations (arrange to ship home). Veer off onto a side street to discover an inconspicuous *trattoria* for a quiet lunch. No trip to Caltagirone is complete without climbing the majolica-tiled stairs up to Santa Maria del Monte *(p189)*, and the view from the top is worth the effort. Reward yourself with the ricotta puff pastries at Dolceria Scivoli *(Viale Mario Milazzo 121)* before a fresh seafood dinner at Il Locandiere *(Via Luigi Sturgo 55)*.

Day 11

Head to Piazza Amerina, home of the exquisite Villa Romana del Casale *(p152)*.

1 Santa Maria delle Scale, Ragusa.

2 A church in Caltagirone.

3 Decorating pottery in Caltagirone.

4 The ancient Valle Dei Templi.

5 Exploring Scala dei Turchi.

Take your time exploring this remarkable UNESCO World Heritage Site, then begin your journey to Agrigento *(p146)*, making a quick detour to survey Morgantina *(p155)*: the site of a Greek and Roman settlement. Back on the motorway, make a pit stop at the inland town of Enna *(p154)* for lunch. Pull into Agrigento and perk up with an espresso at Caffè Concordia *(p147)* before strolling around Piazza Vittorio Emanuele *(p148)*. For dinner, dine at Accademia del Buon Gusto *(www.accademiadelbuongusto.it)*. Ask for a table on the terrace for the best view of the Temple of Concord *(p151)*, part of the the Valle dei Templi.

Day 12

Get up close to the Valle dei Templi *(p150)* and avoid the mid-day heat with a morning tour, followed by a visit to the Archaeological Museum *(p151)*. Have lunch at the museum's cafeteria then drive out to the coast to view the mystical and surreal Scala dei Turchi. Head back and dine in the centre of Agrigento, then make your way to the San Leone district for live music until the small hours.

Day 13

Visit the remains of Selinus Acropolis at Selinunte *(p126)*, a heap of toppled Doric columns scattered around eight temple sites. Head over to nearby Castelvetrano, parking on a side street and continuing on foot to the main square for lunch. Next, take the coast road to the enchanting hilltop town of Erice *(p118)*, which towers high above the port of Trapani. Visit the Norman Castello di Venere *(p119)* at the mountain's crest and the Cyclopean walls *(p118)* edging the northern side of town. Spend the late afternoon roaming the tiny patterned streets, zigzagging past houses hiding secret flowering courtyards. After dinner, sip a *passito*: a sweet dessert wine produced in the surrounding hills.

Day 14

Drive to Segesta *(p123)* to witness the awesome, freestanding limestone temples and ancient amphitheatre. Stop at sleepy Mondello *(p101)* for a swim and lunch on the beach before ending your journey in nearby Palermo *(p58)*.

Nature Reserves

Sicily's zigzagging coast is strewn with protected open spaces. Explore the wonders of Riserva dello Zingaro *(p116)* and Vendicari *(p192)*, laced with hiking trails atwitter with birdlife – binoculars and a birding guide are a must. Even more outdoor activities await on the sylvan peaks of the Nerbrodi, Peloritani and Madonie. These glorious mountains are perfect for trekking, camping, kayaking and skiing. Just pick an outdoor adventure and go.

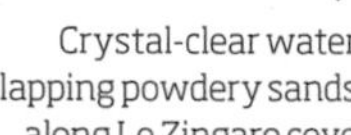

Crystal-clear water lapping powdery sands along Lo Zingaro cove

SICILY FOR NATURAL WONDERS

Sicily's wild natural beauty is the stuff of legends. Mother nature has lavished this glittering gem in the Mediterranean Sea with snow-capped mountain crests, rumbling volcanoes, crystalline sapphire surf and verdant rolling farmland as far as the eye can see.

Mighty Volcanoes

Sicily is home to some of the continent's most active volcanoes. Towering Mount Etna *(p210)* regularly emits plumes of ash and oozing streams of lava from 3,350 m (10,990 ft). Out to sea, Stromboli *(p221)*, Mount Etna's baby cousin, sits on an Aeolian island of the same name. Join a guided trek with Il Vulcano a Piedi *(www.ilvulcanoapiedi.it)* and climb to the summit to feel the peak rumble beneath your feet as the sun rises.

A brave few on the trail through whisping steam near Stromboli's summit

Into the Rock

The rushing waters at the bottom of Gole dell'Alcantara, formed by lava flowing down from Mount Etna, cut a swathe through black basalt rock. Descend public steps down to the basin to wade through a 150-m (500-ft) riverbed to explore unexpected caves - rubber boots recommended. On the Egadi Islands *(p124)*, enter the caves of Levanzo *(p124)* to marvel at paintings of animals hand-daubed by Paleolithic and Neolithic artists.

← Scaly basalt cliffs and a hidden cave at the bottom of Alcantara gorge

↑ A pastel rainbow as the sun sets over windmills and briny saltpans

Saltpans

Lapping seawater, shallow plains and unrelenting heat create conditions ideal for the saltpans of Mozia *(p131)*. Head to the Museo del Sale *(www.museodelsale.it)* outside Trapani *(p128)* to learn about local traditions of extracting and processing salt, practised here since the time of the Phoenicians. Then get up close with a cycle along the saltpans on the sun-beaten stretch between Trapani and Marsala *(p130)*. Bring your camera to snap gently whirling 16th-century windmills reflected in the shallow puddles of seawater.

PICTURE PERFECT
Scala Splendour

Stand in front of the blinding-white cliffs of La Scala dei Turchi for a snap that will make your social media followers green with envy.

What's on Tap?

A wave of Sicilian *birrifici* (microbreweries) are creating world-class artisanal brews inspired by their northern neighbours. Stop by Ballarak tap room *(www.ballarak.it)* in Palermo to quaff their own doppelbock, using ingredients drawn from the island's rich heritage. Time your visit with Beer Catania *(www.beer catania.it)*, and tour the island glass by glass.

←

Opening a refreshing bottle of fine Sicilian craft beer

SICILY RAISE A GLASS

In a country where wine flows like water, drinking is a celebration of the everyday. The Sicilians have turned the *aperitivo* into an art form – but that's not all. Say "*Cin cin*" to beguiling artisanal *birra*, vivacious wines and carefully crafted spirits.

KEEPING IT REAL

In 1962, Italy legislated measures to ensure the quality of its wines, and protect indigenous grapes and cultivation practices. Only certified bottles can be labelled DOCG (controlled and guaranteed designation of origin) and DOC (controlled designation of origin). Cerasuolo di Vittoria is currently Sicily's only DOCG wine. Produced in Ragusa *(p184)* using native Sicilian grapes *frappato* and *nero d'avola*, it has become a Sicilian oenological symbol.

High Spirits

After the plates are cleared, try one of Sicily's iconic *digestivi*. Amaro Averna is a palate-cleansing elixir of bitter botanicals based on Benedictine traditions. In the shadow of Mount Etna, choose *liquore di fichi d'india* (prickly pears), poured over *gelato*. Try an ice-cold glass of *mandarinecello* – made with sweet mandarins – after espresso, an ideal *ammazzacaffè* (coffee killer).

→

Cloudy *limoncello* garnished with perfect round orange slices

Summer rosé and a spread of nibbles at an *aperitivo* party

TOP 5 SICILIAN WINES

Marsala
This amber fortified wine has lingering notes of apricot and tamarind.

Nero D'Avola
One of Sicily's oldest grapes, this full-bodied ruby red is to Sicily what Malbec is to Argentina.

Bianco d'Alcamo
Indigenous Catarratto and Grillo grapes create this refreshing, straw-green Sicilian white.

Passito di Pantelleria
Dessert wine harvested late and dried on cane mats for an intensely sweet flavour.

Novello
This "new wine", produced after the annual harvest, finds a perfect pairing at every table, for any occasion.

The Appealing Aperitivo

Ah, the *aperitivo* - the alluring, beloved ritual of Sicilian society. Take a pre-prandial glass of DOC Etna and slivers of grilled tuna overlooking the Feudo di Mezzo vines *(www.planeta.it)*. Snaffle cocktails garnished with *arancia rossa* (blood orange) and garlicky bruschetta in the garden at Timoleone *(Via Timoleone 6)*. An *aperitivo* is never a substitute for supper, but a prelude of things to come.

On the Road

A network of twelve Wine Roads criss-cross the island. Sip refreshing muscat along the Val di Noto Wine Road. Swig high-altitude nero d'avola on the Etna route. Grab a bicycle and pedal the Erice DOC Wine Road through vine-corduroyed hills, medieval villages, even a salt works, with plenty of wine-tasting stops on the way. Lock up at Fazio Casa Vinicola *(www.casavinicola fazio.it)* to sample indigenous grapes blended with familiar favourites.

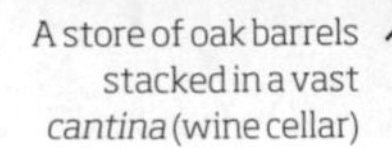

A store of oak barrels stacked in a vast *cantina* (wine cellar)

Set in Stone

For millennia, Sicily's citizens took shelter in caves - during storms, invasion, even in death - and left their mark on the rockface. Take the trail from Sortino to Pantalica *(p193)* to get to the Bronze Age necropolis honey-combed into the limestone cliff face. You'll find pieces excavated from the site exhibited at Museo Archeologico Regionale Paolo Orsi *(p173)* in Siracusia.Alternatively,treadpast10,000-year-old dancing figures in the caves of Favignana *(p124)* or the Byzantine frescoes in the Cava d'Ispica *(p197)* and feel time melt away.

→ The blink-and-you-miss-it entrance to the cave dwellings of Cava d'Ispica

SICILY FOR ANCIENT HISTORY

A visit to Sicily is a captivating voyage back in time. Turn any corner and come face to face with prehistoric tombs and early Christian settlements, archaeological relics of Greek and Roman origins and castles and fortresses left behind by the Normans, Aragonese and Bourbons.

MOUNT ETNA MYTHS

Mount Etna *(p210)* was seen as the home of Hephaestus, the god of fire, whom the Romans identified with Vulcan. Homer even chose the nearby island of Vulcano *(p220)*, in the Aeolians, as the workplace of this fiery god of blacksmiths. Other myths suggest that Typhon, the son of the goddess Gaia, was trapped under Mount Etna after he rebelled against Zeus, and that the flames that spit out from the volcano are his spouts of anger.

Visit Greek and Roman Ruins

Sicily is strewn with splendid ancient Greek and Roman sites. Wander the fascinating Valle dei Templi *(p150)*, home to the stunning Tempio della Concordia, dating to 430 BC, and the Telamons that supported the Temple of Olympian Zeus. Further inland continue the Olympian theme - at least as we understand it today - at Villa Romana del Casale *(p152)*. Amid the trove of mosaic floors is a rare depiction of ancient women athletes competing in different events.

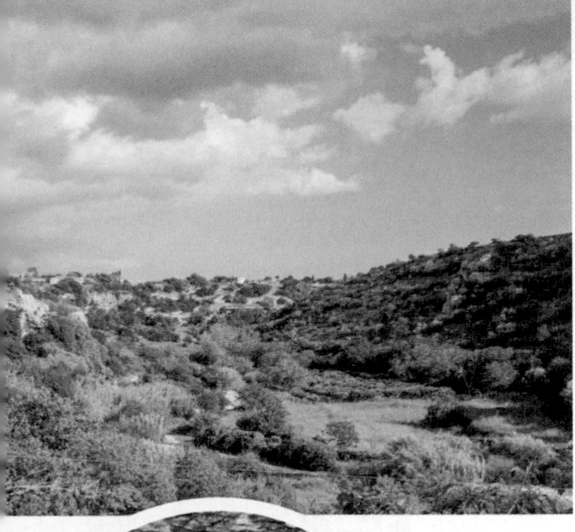

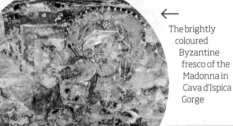

The brightly coloured Byzantine fresco of the Madonna in Cava d'Ispica Gorge

TOP 5 ANCIENT CIVILIZATIONS

Hellenic
The ancient Greeks left a legacy of awe-inspiring engineering from the 8th century BC.

Carthaginians
This formidable naval power settled in 580 BC.

Roman
The Romans took advantage of Sicily's sun-drenched hills to make wine.

Byzantine
Made cosmopolitan Siracusi its capital.

Arab-Norman
A mix of Christian and Muslim cultures forged across the island.

Towering columns of a crumbling Grecian temple at Selinunte

Storm the Castle!

Uncover Sicily's tumultuous history in the Norman Castello Ursino's *(p204)* fascinating museum. Then join ghost-hunters at Castello di Carini *(www.comune.carini.pa.it)*, where the spirit of a murdered baroness set spines tingling amid superb art exhibitions. Opt for more earthly sights at sumptuous Castello di Donnafugata *(www.comune.ragusa.gov.it)*, a key stop on any *Montalbano* tour.

The thick walls of bellicose Castello Ursino

INSIDER TIP
Getting Around the Islands

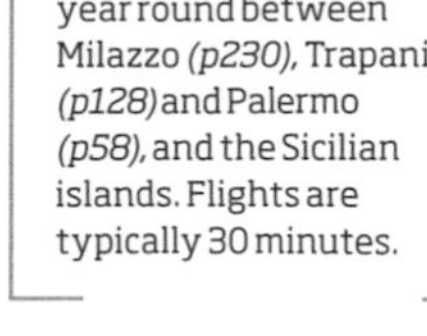

Traghetti (ferries) and high-speed *aliscafi* (hydrofoils) operate all year round between Milazzo *(p230)*, Trapani *(p128)* and Palermo *(p58)*, and the Sicilian islands. Flights are typically 30 minutes.

The View from Above

The best way to take in the Sicilian islands is from on high. Splash out on a helicopter tour with Sicily Spot *(www.sicilyspot.com)* for a bird's-eye view of steaming Stromboli *(p221)* and Panarea *(p220)*. A less expensive option is to climb up caper-lined paths to Salina's summit of Fossa delle Felci (961 m/ 3,156 ft) for epic views across the Aeolian islands.

SICILY FOR INCREDIBLE ISLANDS

Sicily's four clusters of picture-perfect archipelagos are marked by celestial seascapes. Escape to a serrated coastline, sputtering craters of steam and lava, and dazzling white-sand beaches that surround inland empires of inky volcanic rock.

ISLAND TRAGEDY

On 3 October 2013, tragedy stuck when a ship carrying migrants fleeing war and famine sank off the coast of Lampedusa, killing over 360 people. The island's quayside became a makeshift morgue during the search for survivors. Today the Giardino della Memoria, located in a nature reserve, remembers the tragedy with a tree planted for each victim.

Mineral Magic

Re-energize with a bath in the mineral-rich mud of pretty Pantelleria's *(p167)* heart-shaped volcanic lake – then rinse off its turquoise water. On Vulcano *(p220)*, jump from squelching mud into the sea.

↑ Swimming beneath the gentle, crystal-clear waves of secluded Salina

On Dry Land

Traversing an entire island in one day – by foot, cycle or scooter – is magical. Hire a bike to tour Favignana's *(p124)* epic scenery, then reward such virtuous behaviour with a wine tasting at Firriato *(www.firriato.it)*, the only vineyard in the Egadis. On far-flung Alicudi *(p219)* achieve zen on its peaceful footpaths.

↓ Abandoned bikes at the top of a path to the sea

↑ Solitude and sweeping vistas from a sandy stretch Vulcano's trails

East of Africa

Kissing the Tunisian coast, the Pelagian islands are more African than Italian from flora to architecture. Stroll around Linosa *(p167)*, camera at the ready – the North African-influenced pastel-coloured houses will brighten any photo album. Look out for fior di tigre cacti and nesting sea turtles on Lampedusa *(p166)*. More sobering is the "Porta di Lampedusa", which honours those who died at sea, trying to cross into Europe.

← Yachts bobbing in the still seas surrounding Lampedusa

Escape and Unplug

Leave the hustle and bustle behind for the tranquillity of island life. Sunbathe on the soft volcanic sands of distant Pantelleria, splash about in the translucent waters around pretty Salina or stroll around the rural hinterlands of Alicudi. Then recalibrate with an off-the-grid meditative retreat at Yoga Filicudi *(www.yogafilicudi.it)* on the Aeolian Island of Filicudi.

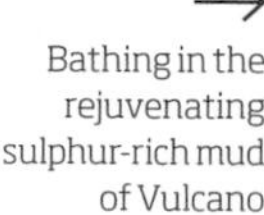

→ Bathing in the rejuvenating sulphur-rich mud of Vulcano

Save or Splurge

Whatever your budget, Sicily's beaches have everything you need for a day of sun and frolic. Public lidos (bathing beaches) are ideal for budget-conscious beach-goers. Head to Cala Modello, just outside Palermo *(p58)*, for powder-soft sands and nearby snack bars. Have funds to spare? Opt for a *stabilimento* (private beach club), such as uber-stylish Isola Bella in Taormina *(p206)* with convenient sunbed and umbrella rentals, plus toilets and showers - for a fee. Top tip: sunbeds often go by noon.

→

The gorgeous pebbly beach of Isola Bella Island *(inset)* at low tide and at sunrise

1,484

The total length of the Sicilian coastline in km (922 miles).

SICILY FOR BEACH LOVERS

A sun worshiper's Shangri-la, Sicily's jaw-dropping seascapes are peppered with powdery white and black volcanic beaches, pebbled coves and flinty promontories. With more than a dozen offshore islands and hundreds of miles of coastline, there's a beach for everyone.

Family Friendly Beaches

For easy days of fun in the sun, take your pick of beautiful beaches blanketed with soft, fine sand - perfect for building sandcastles. Resorts like San Leone near the city of Agrigento *(p146)* have wide expanses of golden sands for kids to romp, as well a wealth of services, such as good toilets and snack kiosks, ideal when you have youngsters in tow. At Sampieri near Scicli *(p197)* hire lounge chairs and shady umbrellas (a godsend when temperatures soar) and set up for a full day of fun.

Skipping into the blue flag surf at family-friendly Sampieri beach

Snorkelling in the clear waters of Ortigia Island, Syracuse

Snorkel in Splendour

All around Sicily, the beach slopes underwater to gorgeous coral reefs. Grab a mask and a pair of fins and learn the secrets of the Sicilian seabed from the expert guides at Dive Sicily *(www.divesicily.com)* as you drift across the surface of the sea at Taormina *(p206)*. Off Ustica's shore *(p141)*, spot vibrant sea stars and anemome clinging to the reef's famous red corals.

Blue skies above a secluded rocky beach biting into Bay of Panarea

LEGENDS OF THE SEA

The myths and legends of Sicily tie its inhabitants to the sea. One-eyed Cyclops, made famous in the *Odyssey*, is said to have tossed boulders from Mount Etna at Ulysses, forming the rock stacks off the Ionian Coast *(p206)*. Folklore also explains the rough seas in the Strait of Messina *(p214)* between Sicily and the mainland. It was here that Zeus turned beautiful Charybdis into a monster, condemned to swallow huge gulps of sea water, so causing treacherous whirlpools. It was also here that Scylla was transformed into a monster who still vents its rage on sailors passing through.

Escape the Crowds

Join Sicilians on hot, muggy days and abandon stifling cities in favour of *il mare* (the sea). Our favourite sun-and-sea spots are all solitude and pristine scenery. Dip into Vendicari nature reserve *(p196)* and choose between deserted dunes and isolated inlets biting the coastline. To really get away from it all, catch a Liberty Lines *(www.libertylines.it)* hyrdofoil to the untrammled Aeolian island of Salina and dive into the azure waters around the Perciato di Pollara.

Up Close and Personal

All over the island, many artisans open their *ateliers* (workshops) to visitors. Meet *tessitori* (weavers) at Antichi Intrecci and watch as they create intricate patterns. Alternatively, learn the secrets of papyrus-making at the workshop in the Museo del Papiro *(www.museodelpapiro.it)* in Ortigia, the only centre outside Egypt to make it.

A quintessential, pretty workshop brimming with ceramics in Caltagirone

MADE IN SICILY

Whimsical marionettes, delicately pieced jewellery, lustrously painted ceramics: Sicily is brimming with hand-made objects that delight and inspire. Visit an artisan's workshop, try your hand at pottery and immerse yourself in quintessentially Sicilian traditions.

SHOP

Opera dei Pupi Vaccaro

This traditional and magical workshop is where *burattinaio* (puppet makers) bring their creations to life.

G6 Via Giudecca 5, Syracuse 9am-1pm & 3pm-7pm Mon-Sat. pupari.com

Antichi Intrecci

Find hand-woven, colourfully zigzag-patterned Ericini rugs at this laboratory that continues the ancient art of artisan weaving.

A3 Via Pianoneve 31, Buseto Palizzolo, Trapani antichi intrecci.it

Art for the People

Walk through any Sicilian city and you'll discover it has been used as an unexpected canvas. Check out edgy murals by Ema Jons at Palermo's Mercato della Vucciria *(p76)*. In Catania, head straight to the port to see the largest piece of street art in the world adorning the silos, by graffiti great Vhils.

BURATTINI HERITAGE

Rooted in 13th-century *cantastorias* (singers of tales), Sicilian Opera dei Pupi brings Romantic poems to life with song and *burattini* (puppets and marionettes) moving through intricate scenery, and remains a key cultural tradition of Sicily. Once led by great families of marionnettists, today it is largely for tourists. It has been on the UNESCO Intangible Cultural Heritage list since 2008.

L'Opera Dei Pupi

Get ready to delight in Opera dei Pupi (puppet theatre), Sicily's most beloved tradition. Take in a live show at Marionettistica Fratelli Napoli *(www.fratelli napoli.it)* in Catania. In Palermo, discover the history at the marvellous Museo delle Marionette *(www.museodellemarionette.it)*.

→ A traditional puppet show put on at Teatro dell' Opera dei Pupi' in Palermo

The Ceramics of Caltagirone

Called "the city of a thousand faces" for the intricate *testa di moro* (Moor's head) vases produced here, Caltagirone *(p188)* is the indisputable centre of Sicilian ceramics. Stroll gold-tinged Baroque alleyways to the Giacomo Alessi workshop *(www.giacomoalessi.com)* and come away with one-of-a-kind souvenirs.

← A potter in Caltagirone hand-finishing a ceramic dish

Chocolate-mad Modica

The oldest chocolate maker in Modica *(p190)*, Antica Dolceria Bonajuto *(www.bonajuto.it)* has been creating confections since 1880. Uncover ancient Xocoàtl methods developed by the Aztecs on a tantalizing tour - and taste the difference in a yummy tasting session. Pop into Cioccolato Quetzel *(www.cioccolato-quetzal.it)* to master the sweet arts

→ Tempting samples on display at Antica Dolceria Bonajuto

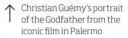

↑ Christian Guémy's portrait of the Godfather from the iconic film in Palermo

The tightly packed medieval core of Cefalù pressed against the water

SICILY FOR CHARMING VILLAGES

Sicily is bursting with impossibly picturesque fishing villages frozen in time, geranium-hung hamlets and towering clifftop fortresses straight out of a fairytale. Yet Sicily's villages also offer an authentic slice of life – they are the true heart and soul of the island.

Living the High Life

Dive into Sicily's medieval past with a jaunt into its best-preserved hill towns. Climb the graceful lanes of Erice *(p118)* to 12th-century Castello di Venere for staggering sea views, then reward yourself with an *ericine* pastry and a glass of local sparkling wine *(p120)*. Indulge in Modica's *(p190)* famous chocolate as you wend from sight to medieval sight. Celebrate it all, amid jesters and knights, each July at Randazzo's *(p226)* medieval festival.

An elaborate display outside an antiques shop in cliff-top Taormina's medieval core

By the Sea

Ancient fishing villages bite round the edges of Sicily's sun-baked shoreline. Inhabited before the Phoenicians, Marzamemi has been known for preserving tuna as far back as 1,000 AD. Stroll the waterfront, past drying fishing nets, to the Adelfio family's store *(www.adelfioonline.com)* and learn about traditional methods of smoking and salting fish, nibbling samples as you go. In the north, charming Cefalù *(p112)* spills onto the waterfront. Lined with cafés serving just-landed seafood, this is a favourite of Sicilian families. Mondello *(p101)* is squished between Monte Gallo and Monte Pellegrino. Bring your camera – a vision of rainbow-coloured boats bob in the harbour.

EAT

La Cialoma

Come for sea-fresh fish dishes and stay late for live music on the piazza in summer.

G6 Piazza Regina Margherita 23, Marzamemi Tue & Nov 0931841772

Monte San Giuliano

Sample delightful home cooking in a rough-hewn stone garden terrace – the *spaghetti nera* (squid ink pasta) and octopus is a must.

A3 Vicolo San Rocca 7, Erice Mon montesangiuliano.it

The Great Eight

To get a true sense of Sicily's Baroque past, check out the eight UNESCO-protected late-Baroque villages of Val di Noto, where Baroque architecture and art flourished here after a catastrophic 1693 earthquake. Wander the curving streets of Ragusa *(p184)*, to the glorious Duomo di San Giorgio. Enjoy the view with a wine-flavoured *gelato* from Gelati di Vini *(www.gelatidivini.it)*, opposite. Also not to be missed: the palaces along elegant via Penna in Scicli *(p197)* and ornate balconies lining Noto's *(p178)* Palazzo Nicolaci.

↑ Honey-stoned Santa Maria delle Scale *(inset)* overlooking old Ragusa

A Moveable Feast

Tantalize your tastebuds on a StrEaty *(www.streaty.com)* tour through Sicily's dynamic street food. Try stick-to-your-ribs local delicacies, such as *frittula* (Sicilian street meat) and *caponata* (briny aubergine). Sample more informal flavours at a *sagra* (food festival). Swanky Cibo Nostrum is the biggest, but the *gelato* makes Bronte's Sagre del Pistachio *(p52)* a favourite.

Foodies packed to meet chefs and sample treats at Cibo Nostrum in Catania

SICILY FOR FOODIES

The salty crunch of *panelle*, the oozing creamy centre of *cannoli*, the inky black of *spaghetti nera* coiled on the plate, inviting morsels of sea urchin and tender mussels - Sicily's food is a feast for the senses. Innovative street food and Michelin-starred dining make this the perfect foodie destination.

THE SLOW FOOD MOVEMENT

Formed in response to the island's growing reliance on processed fast food, Slow Food Sicilia *(www.slowfood sicilia.it)* seeks to bring seasonal ingredients grown locally back to the heart of Sicilian cooking. The cause also seeks to protect "at risk" produce, such as *pane nero* (black bread) from Castelvetrano *(p130)* and *cartucciaru* melon, that was falling out of favour. The idea has been picked up by KM0 *(www.km0slow food.com)*, which seeks to source food within 1 km (half a mile) of its kitchen.

Fine Dining

Indulge in out-of-this-world dishes cooked by Sicily's culinary new wave. Savour plates of purple potato gnocchi and black *cavatelli* with sea urchin at Michelin-starred Patrizia Di Benedetto's Bye Bye Blues *(www.byebyeblues.it)*. At Licata's chic La Madia *(www.ristorantela madia. it)*, sink your teeth into reinvented Sicilian classics served with a pinch of nostalgia.

Exquisite seafood dish at Michelin-star resturant Bye Bye Blues in Palermo

Learn to Cook, Sicilian Style

Take a slice of your holiday home with you. Zuleima cultural tours *(www.zuleima.org)* put you in *Nonna*'s kitchen so you can learn the secrets of making authentic homemade ravioli with herby ricotta or *pasta con le sarde* (pasta with sardines and saffron), using recipes passed through generations. Alternatively, join a workshop led by award-winning chef James Beard at Anna Tasca Lanza *(www.annatasca anza.com)*, and discover the joy of making *eratto* (tomato paste), *foccaccia* and other Sicilian food staples from scratch.

Heaped dollops of herby ricotta on a sheet of yet-to-be-folded ravioli

TOP 5 CLASSIC MUNCHIES

Pane Cunzatu
Each village claims that its version of this savoury, Arab-style herby bread is the best.

Arancina
Sicilian soul food, these deep-fried rice balls stuffed with ragu or *caciocavallo* cheese are best scoffed *portare via* (on the go).

Panelle
Delicate fritters made with chickpea flour. Try packed into a roll with *cazzilli* (potato croquets).

Granita con brioche
Subtly sweet toothsome rolls and a tumbler of shaved ice poured over with espresso -Sicily's breakfast of champions.

Pani ca' meusa
This moreish *panino* overflows with salty, chewy chopped veal spleen simmered in lard.

↑ Toothsome sugar-dusted, pistachio-speckled, crisp *cannoli*

La Dolce Vita

Oozing with thick, lemony-sweet ricotta, crispy *cannoli* is the quintessential Sicilian *dolce* (sweet). Crunch your way through every variety you can think of - and some you can't - at Palermo's annual Cannolo Festival *(p53)*. In contrast, *cassata Siciliana* is all melt-in-your-mouth, liqueur-drenched sponge wrapped in marzipan and a shell of pale green icing. Easier to grab on the go: *gelato* - pure joy in a cone.

The History of Cosa Nostra

For fans of *The Godfather*, the name Corleone is synonymous with the Mafia. The town *(p135)* of the same name gave birth to the criminal organization. Come to this pretty town to visit Il Laboratorio della Legalità *(www.laboratorio dellalegalita.it)*, located in a property confiscated from mob boss Bernardo Provenzano. Take the guided tour to discover more than 100 years of active resistance against the Mafia, including a collection of paintings by Gaetano Porcasi. Two blocks west, find CIDMA, a small antimafia museum that gives voice to those who have suffered under the Mafia-promoted culture of *omertà* (silence). Documents from the Maxi Trial and stories from the lives of the victims highlight the ongoing struggle for positive change.

→

Addiopizzo tourism *(inset)* striving to make constructive change in colourful Corleone

SICILY AND THE MAFIA

The brutal crime syndicate known as the Mafia has long cast a dark shadow over Sicily. Although its presence is still felt throughout the island, the "Black Hand" is slowly and steadily losing its grip, thanks to grassroots movements that are challenging its influence.

The Antimafia Movement

A grassroots network is afoot, helping Sicilians to say "*Addio pizzo*" (goodbye, Mafia protection money). Choose olive oil and wine bearing the *Libera Terra (www.liberaterra.it)* label. These products, grown on state-confiscated farmlands, help their producers stay free from Mafia control. Make a statement in more ways than one – La Coppola Storta *(091 324428)* has reclaimed the iconic Sicilian flat hat from a symbol of the Mafia to an emblem of a modern, free Sicily.

A bright array of flat caps, now symbolic of the move to free Sicily

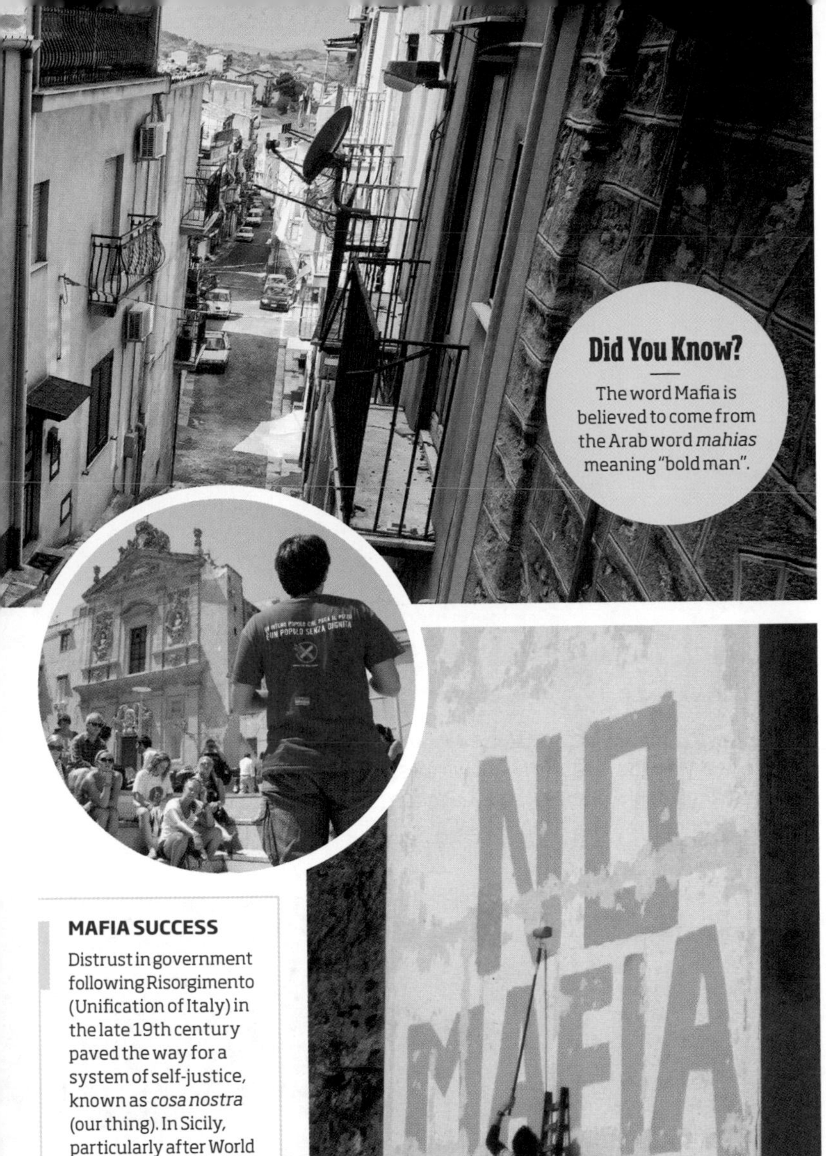

Did You Know?

The word Mafia is believed to come from the Arab word *mahias* meaning "bold man".

MAFIA SUCCESS

Distrust in government following Risorgimento (Unification of Italy) in the late 19th century paved the way for a system of self-justice, known as *cosa nostra* (our thing). In Sicily, particularly after World War II, systematic extortion of ordinary people b y criminal "families" grew into a vast underground criminal network. During the Maxi Trial in 1986–87, some 360 *mafiosi* were convic-ted, but it wasn't until 2006 that prosecutors were finally able to bring down the head of the Corleonesi family. Today, the Mafia is not yet fully extinguished.

On the Trail of the Mafia

It's possible to satiate Mafia curiosity and remain conscious of its victims. Retrace the history of the notorious *cosa nostra* by joining Addiopizzo Travel *(www.addio pizzotravel.it)* for a tour led by antimafia activists who examine the organization in a responsible and sensitive way.

↑ Repainting the words of murdered antimafia judge Giovanni Falcone

Theatre in the Round

Join the chorus at Syracuse's Greek Theatre *(p174)*, one of the most lauded summer performance venues in the world, to see millennia-old works of Aeschylus and Euripides come to life. Want even more? Book tickets all summer long to see opera, concerts and other cultural events at Taormina's *(p206)* impeccably preserved Greco-Roman amphitheatre.

Aristophanes' *Birds* captivating audiences at the Greek Theater

SICILY AL FRESCO

Blessed with 250 days of sunshine a year, Sicilian life is all about being out in the open. Join the locals in lively piazzas, on breezy terraces, at sidewalk cafés, taking leisurely Sunday *passeggiate* (strolls) around open-air art or sleeping under the stars – there's an outdoor space for everyone.

INSIDER TIP
Mozzies Galore

You're not the only one that enjoys al fresco dining. Mosquitos can be a nuisance. When enjoying an *aperitivo* at a pavement-side trattoria, be liberal with the mosquito repellent during the summer months.

Outdoor Festivities

Sicily's summer outdoor event season kicks off with the Taormina Film Fest (*www.taormina filmfest.it*). Snag a ticket and join film buffs and celeb-spotters at the ruins of the resort town's ancient Greek theatre *(p206)* to see premiers and old favourites under the stars. Continue the *festività* at Lipari's Un Mare di Cinema (*www.loveolie.com*), a joyful celebration of the arts, with food stalls and activities for all ages. Want something a little different? Check out the annual *Infiorata* (flower festival) in Noto when local and foreign artists blanket the streets with flowers in colourful mosaics.

Find Open-Air Art

The Sicilian islands are full of art in unexpected places. Venture to Gibellina *(p135)* and the outdoor Museo Civico d'Arte Contemporanea *(www.gibellina.siciliana.it)* to marvel at Italian sculptor Alberto Burri's *Cretto*, a striking monument that remembers those lost in the 1968 earthquake. Another modern must is Fiumara d'Arte *(www.ateliersulmare.com/it)*, a meandering natural park strewn with enormous, Instagram-ready installations. Here pieces by Hidetoshi Nagasawa and Tano Festa, among others, put man-made materials in juxtaposition against the wild north coast around Messina *(p214)*.

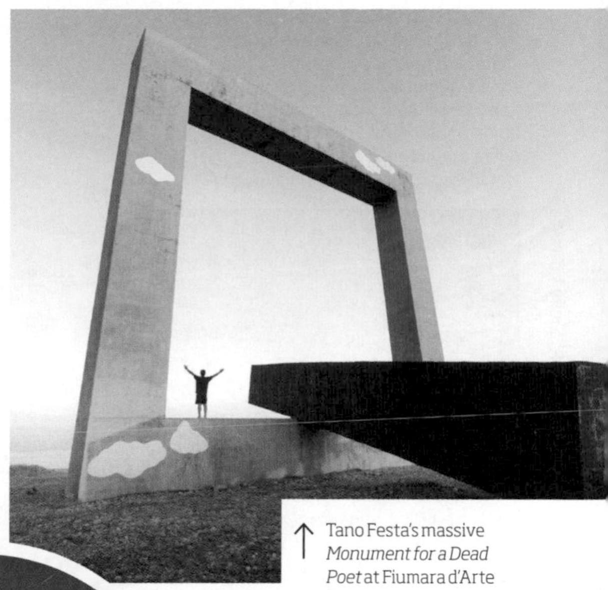

↑ Tano Festa's massive *Monument for a Dead Poet* at Fiumara d'Arte

Sleep Under the Stars

Experience Sicily's wild nightlife. Pitch a tent on the banks of a lake in Parco dei Nebrodi *(p231)*, slide a caravan under a grove of olive trees in a campsite next to the Riserva dello Zingaro *(p116)* or rough it in a rustic *rifugio* (hut) on the slopes of Mount Etna *(p210)*, and nod off under celestial skies.

← The welcoming glow of a tent as the sun sets over Mount Etna

↑ Night falls as the reel plays at Taormina's open-air theatre

↑ Views across Palermo from a restaurant terrace

Dine Al Fresco

When in Sicily, dine as the Sicilians do. Take a front-row seat for a panoramic *aperitivo* at Il Re di Girgenti *(p147)*, overlooking the Valle dei Templi. Alternatively, chow down on Palermitan staple *sfincione* (thick tomatoey, anchovy-laden slabs of pizza) at one of Francu U Vastiddaru's *(Corso Vittorio Emanuele 102)* pavement plastic tables.

Take to the Skies

For a truly white-knuckle experience - and some of the best views of Sicily - set your sights high with Etna Fly *(www.etnafly.com)* and soar off mountainsides and over the landscape by paraglider. Want more? Pitch out of a plane withSkydive Sicilia *(www.skydivesicilia.it)* on tandem jump.

→

The beautiful seascape of Cefalù stretching far below a paraglider floating on the air

SICILY FOR ADVENTURERS

A veritable playground for outdoor adventurers, Sicily's natural spaces offer endless opportunities for heart-pumping holidays. Dangle off petrified cliffs, paraglide over sun-baked hills, plunge into the shadowy deep. Whatever your kick, Sicily delivers what adrenaline junkies crave.

Into the Deep

The Sicilian archipelago is a watery playground for divers. Plunge beneath the waves to check out the bones of a WWII British cargo ship at Scopello - part of Riserva dello Zingaro *(p116)* - in a short course or day trip with Cetaria Diving Centre *(www.cetariasea.com)*. Cross to the transparent waters that surround Lampedusa *(p166)* to investigate underwater Roman ruins.

←

Exploring the crystal clear waters around Lampedusa island

INSIDER TIP
Wheel Fun

See Sicily by wheel, with a guided cycle tour. Choose a mountain, road, hybrid or even e-bike. On Sicily *(www.on-sicily.com/cycling-in-sicily)* has all the info.

A Natural High

The vertical challenges in Sicily send acrophiles' (lovers of heights) hearts soaring. For rope- and free-climbers, the craggy cliffs of San Vito Lo Capo *(p134)* are ideal. Cling to limestone and marble rock, crossing tufas with the sea at your back. Alternatively, opt for a multi-day trek to scale Filo Dell' Arpa, Filicudi's highest peak at 610 m (2,000 ft).

TOP 3 CYCLING ROUTES

Sicilia Dag 7
Starting in Cefalù, this 53-km (33-mile) loop passes through pristine medieval towns overlooking glittering sea to 868 m (2,850 ft) above sea level and back.

Ortigia-Syracuse Loop
Pass epic scenery over mostly paved surfaces, along this 85-km (53-mile) route. Reasonable fitness and intermediate skill level required.

Magna Via Francigena
This challenging route across the Sicani mountains, following the path of Frankish knights over 180 km (112 miles), is not for the faint of heart.

→ Scaling the rust-coloured craggy face of San Vito Lo Capo

Hoist the Sails

Sicily is the ideal place to test your mettle in water-based adventuring from sailing to kite surfing. Strong winds off the Aeolian *(p218)* and Egadi *(p124)* islands create ideal conditions for sailing. Sailing in? Mooring can be arranged at port. For everyone else, Sail Utopia *(www.sailutopia.com)* provides lessons and skippered excursions, with a keen eye on marine conservation and sustainability.

↑ Sailing the sun-beaten, wind-whipped seas around the Aeolian Islands

A YEAR IN SICILY

JANUARY

La Befana *(6 Jan).* Throughout Italy, children receive stockings containing sweets and gifts from La Befana, the friendly Epiphany witch.

△ **San Sebastiano** *(20 Jan).* Colourful religious processions take place across Sicily.

FEBRUARY

△ **Sant'Agata** *(3–5 Feb).* Processions, fireworks and food in Catania to honour the patron saint.

Carnival *(Shrove Tuesday and preceding days).* Carnival parades throughout Sicily.

MAY

Festival degli Aquiloni *(mid-May).* An impressive kite festival in San Vito Lo Capo.

△ **Infiorata di Noto** *(third May weekend).* Artfully arranged flowers create impressive decorations on the streets at this lively festival in Noto.

JUNE

△ **The Greek Theater Festival of Syracuse** *(May–Jul).* Greek tragedies under the stars in Syracuse's Greek amphitheatre.

Taormina Arte *(Jun–Sep).* An outdoor summer festival featuring music, dance, theatre and food in Taormina.

SEPTEMBER

△ **CousCous Festival** *(end of Sep).* San Vito Lo Capo celebrates this popular Mediterranean dish with competitions and stands.

La Vie dei Tesori *(Sep-Nov).* Explore Sicily's palaces and hidden treasures which are normally closed to the public.

OCTOBER

Sagra del Pistacchio *(late Sep/early Oct).* Head to Bronte to taste and celebrate the local pistachio.

△ **Ibla Buskers** *(first week of Oct).* Street artists perform in Ragusa.

MARCH

Feast of San Leoluca *(1 Mar).* Small bonfires light a religious procession in Corleone.

△ **Ballo dei Diavoli** *(Mar/Apr).* Prizzi hosts the "Dance of the Devils", symbolizing the struggle between good and evil.

APRIL

△ **Cannolo Festival** *(late Apr).* Sicily's *cannolo* bakers battle it out in Palermo.

Settimana Santa *(Easter week).* Processions and religious events take place all over Sicily to mark Holy Week.

JULY

△ **Santa Rosalia** *(4 Jul).* Relics of the saint who saved Palermo from the plague are paraded around the city's streets.

Ortigia Film Festival *(early-mid Jul).* Syracuse sets up an outdoor film arena to screen local and international films.

AUGUST

Palio dei Normanni *(12–14 Aug).* An impressive Medieval pageant in Piazza Armerina, reenacting the town's liberation from the Moors in 1087.

△ **I Giganti** *(13–14 Aug).* Messina commemorates the mythical founders of the city with floats and events.

NOVEMBER

△ **Festival di Morgana** *(early Nov).* Palermo's international puppet festival entertains audiences with traditional marionettes.

Festa di San Martino *(11 Nov).* Celebrations throughout Sicily combined with tastings of the year's new wine.

DECEMBER

△ **Festa dell'Immacolata** *(8 Dec).* Throughout Sicily expect processions, local food, and music to mark the beginning of the Christmas season.

I Presepi di Palermo *(Dec).* Palermo's most famous nativity scenes are showcased in the streets.

A BRIEF HISTORY

Due to its strategic position in the heart of the Mediterranean, Sicily has always been a meeting point of civilizations, and has seen periods of great splendour under the Greeks, the Arabs and the Normans. The island's art and culture bear witness to its eventful history.

Early Conquerors

Though traces of human presence in Sicily date back to the Stone Age, the first recorded inhabitants were the Elymians, the Sikanians, and the Sicels, who lived in Sicily around 1000 BC. When the Greeks arrived in the 8th century BC, the island was populated by the Sicels, who were quickly assimilated, and by the Pheonicians, finally ousted by the Greeks in 480 BC.

The Greek and Roman Eras

Under the Greeks, Sicily saw its first period of great prosperity. At the height of the Magna Graecia era, the main centres were

1 An old map of Catania. ↑

2 The Greeks triumphantly entering Syracuse in 480 BC.

3 A mosaic in Piazza Armerina, built during Sicily's rich period under the Roman Empire.

4 The Arab siege of Messina in 1040.

Timeline of events

7,000-650 BC

Rise and fall of the Siculan civilization.

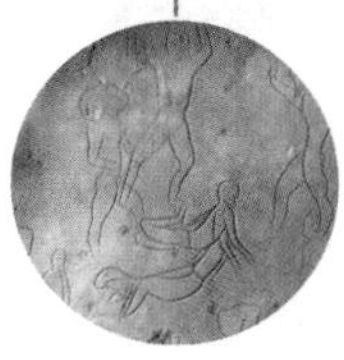

8th Century BC

Greeks colonize the east of the island. Palermo is founded.

212 BC

End of the Magna Graecia civilization, when Romans conquer Sicily.

300–400 AD

Under Roman rule, Sicily is Christianized.

476 AD

Fall of the Roman empire.

2

3

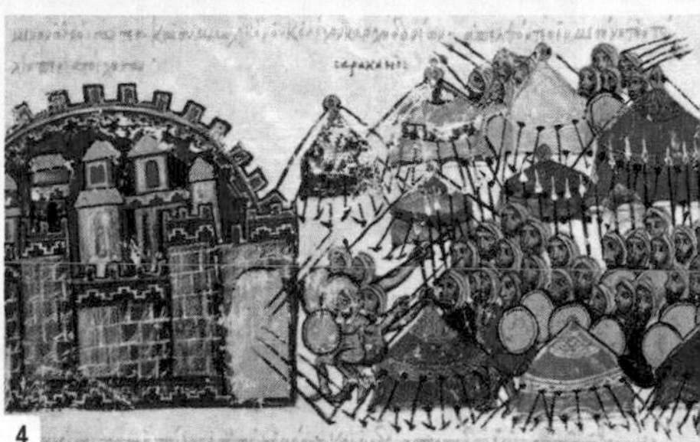

4

Catania, Syracuse, Gela, Agrigento, Messina, Taormina, and Selinunte, all of which still bear the remains of the Greek domination. Sicily was also a centre of scientific discoveries; the most prominent figure of the time was mathematician Archimedes, born in Syracuse in 287 BC. His ingenious war machines enabled the city to resist Roman siege for two years. The defeat of Syracuse in 212 BC, in which Archimedes was killed, brought the Greek era to an end.

For the following six centuries under the Roman Empire, Sicily became Rome's "bread basket", seeing the rise of large feudal estates and the imposition of taxes. Christianity also began to spread in the 3rd and 4th centuries.

Medieval Sicily

After the fall of the Roman Empire, Sicily suffered various waves of barbarian invasions until it fell under Byzantine rule (535-826). The Muslim conquest of Sicily, which began in 827, was successfully completed in 902. The Arab rule coincided with the economical, cultural and artistic rebirth of Sicily, which again became a focal point of trade in the Mediterranean region.

↑ An ancient Greek Kore bust found in Sicily, dating from the Greek empire

827 AD

Arabs begin invasion of Sicily and conquer the island in AD 902.

1091

Roger I, the Norman Lord, conquers Sicily after a war that lasts 30 years.

1216–25

Frederick II becomes emperor of the Holy Roman Empire first, and then King of Sicily. Court is moved to Palermo.

1355–77

Frederick III of Aragon dies, marking the end of the Kingdom of Sicily.

1

2

Norman Defeat and Frederick II

The Normans, warriors and seamen from Scandinavia defeated the Arabs in 1091, re-Christianizing the island and founding the Kingdom of Sicily. The Kingdom reached its zenith under Holy Roman Emperor Frederick II (1194–1250). A patron of culture, he played a major role promoting Sicilian poetry. In 1266, his son was defeated by the Angevin dynasty. The latter was replaced by the Aragonese in 1282, and a long period of decline began.

From Spanish Rule to a Unified Italy

In the early 15th century, Sicily became an Aragonese province ruled by a viceroy. The island's prosperity received the final blow with the expulsion of the Jews from Spanish territories in 1492. A slight recovery was triggered by the reconstruction following the earthquake of 1693. After brief periods of Savoyard and Austrian dominion, Sicily passed to the Bourbons in 1735. In 1816, the island became one of the two components of the Kingdom of The Two Sicilies, together with the Kingdom of Naples. Popular unrest led to Garibaldi's 1860 expedition and union with the burgeoning Kingdom of Italy.

THE 1693 EARTHQUAKE

On the night of 9 January 1693, Mount Etna *(p210)* burst into life. Two days later, "the Earth was rent from its bowels", as the historian Di Blasi put it. The earthquake hit parts of southern Italy and resulted in 60,000 deaths. It levelled 23 towns in Sicily including Catania, Noto and Lentini, which were later reconstructed in Baroque style.

Timeline of events

1693

A volcanic eruption followed by an earthquake devastates the eastern part of the island, and levels Noto, Catania, and Lentini.

1735

Charles III of Spain acquires Sicily from Austria.

1816

Ferdinand unifies the Kingdoms of Naples and Sicily.

1860

Garibaldi's Red Shirts invade Sicily; people vote for a unified Kingdom of Italy.

1861

Vittorio Emanuele II of Savoy becomes the first King of a unified Italy.

The 1900s

Following the banditry and poverty that marked Sicily's rural areas in the late 1800s, the 20th century also got off to a catastrophic start with the 1908 earthquake in Messina. Largely excluded from Italy's process of modernization in Italy, Sicily saw its cultural life juxtaposed against poverty, backwardness and the spread of the Mafia. In the 1980s, many courts began their mission to overthrow the organization, and in a 1987 trial in Palermo, hundreds of convicted Mafiosi were sentences to 2,600 years in prison. In 1992, judges Giovanni Falcone and Paolo Borsellino were assassinated a few months apart.

Sicily Today

The fight against the Mafia continues in Sicily today, but thanks to the growing public awareness of the problem, the organization is not as powerful as it used to be. In 2014, rescue operation Mare Nostrum brought 4,000 refugees from Africa and the Middle East to Sicily. This is an ongoing issue in Sicily, with daily arrivals of Northern African migrants causing political repercussions throughout the whole European Union.

1 Beautiful mosaic inside the Cathedral of Monreale, dating from the Norman era. ↑

2 Destruction caused by the 1693 earthquake.

3 Cycling through modern-day Palermo.

Did You Know?

Frederick II had a zoo in his own garden, and wrote the book *The Art of Falconry*.

1908

A massive earthquake and tsunami destroy Messina and kill 100,000 people.

1943

WWII allies land in Sicily and take it in 38 days; they then head north, defeat the Nazis and liberate Italy.

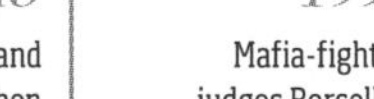

1992

Mafia-fighting judges Borsellino and Falcone are assassinated in a Mafia bombing.

2006

After 43 years on the run, Mafia boss Provenzano is arrested.

2014

Refugees from Africa and the Middle East brought to Sicily.

EXPERIENCE PALERMO

Praetorian Fountain on Piazza Pretoria

EXPLORE PALERMO

This guide divides Palermo into three sightseeing areas: the two shown on this map and a chapter for sights beyond the centre ***(p96)*****. Find out more about each area on the following pages.**

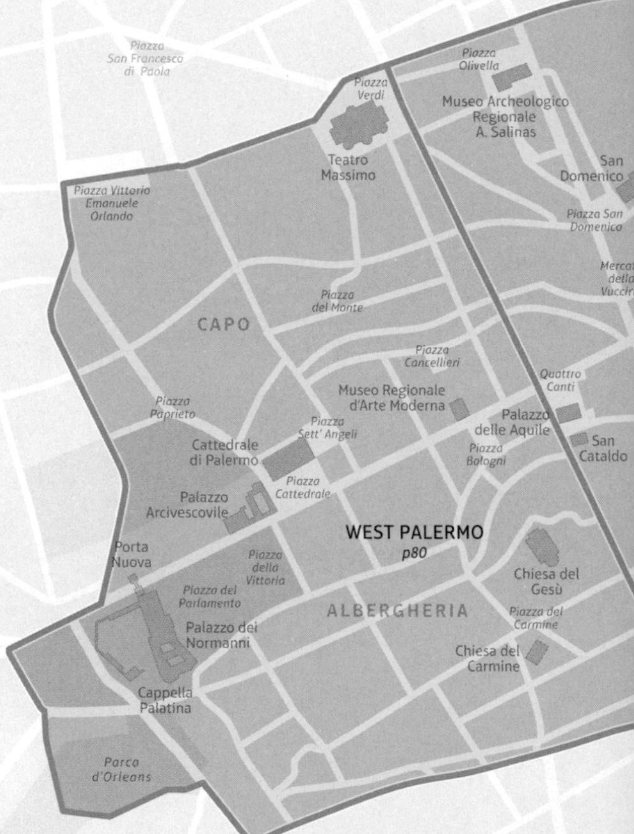

SICILY
PALERMO
Piazza San Giorgio
Porta Felice
Parco della Salute
Museo Internazionale delle Marionette
VUCCIRIA
Piazza Marina
Giardino Garibaldi
San Francesco d'Assisi
Villa a Mare
Palazzo Abatellis
EAST PALERMO
p64
Piazza S. Carlo
LA KALSA
Galleria d'Arte Moderna Sant'Anna
Piazza Magione
Santa Maria dello Spasimo
Villa Giulia
La Magione
Orto Botanico
Piazza Giulio Cesare
SANT' ERASMO
0 metres 500
0 yards 500
N

GETTING TO KNOW PALERMO

As audacious and flamboyant as it is courtly and formal, Sicily's capital is an exaggeration of riches and glimpses of its former aristocratic splendour. Built along the bay at the foot of Monte Pellegrino, Palermo is compact and easy to navigate, with its loveliest treasures fairly close to one another.

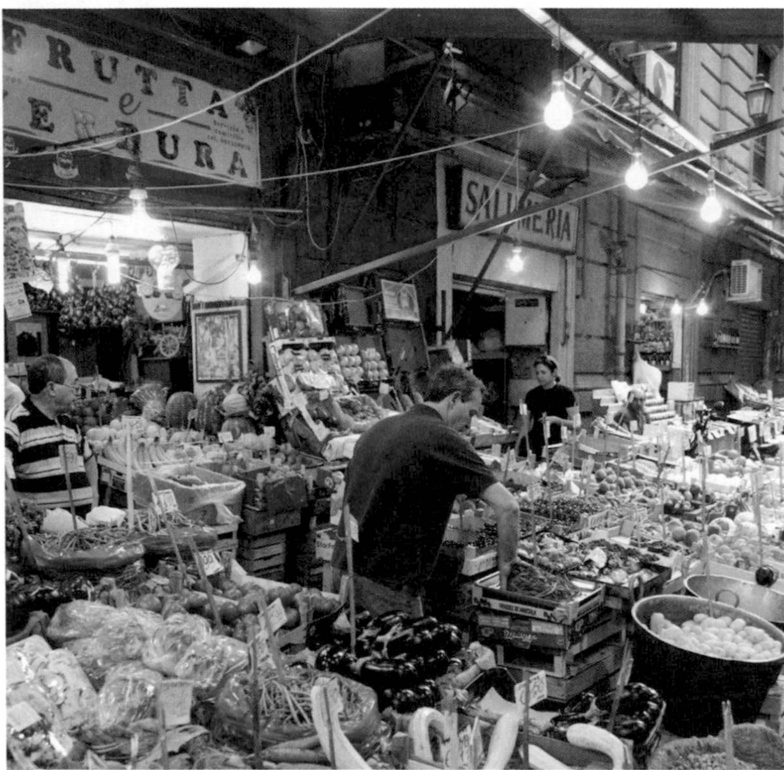

PAGE 64

EAST PALERMO

Palermo's international flavour becomes most apparent upon entering the hip La Kalsa district, the site of the old Arab citadel. Artisans tinker at their venerable trades, Vucciria market vendors sell their wares and true believers pray to the mysteries of the Rosary at Oratorio del Rosario di Santa Zita – a triumph in white plaster and gold. Take it all in at the centerpiece of this corner of the city and the largest square in the capital, the leafy Piazza Marina.

Best for
Art museums, markets and artisan workshops

Home to
Palazzo Abatellis

Experience
Marvelling at edgy street art as you wander the streets

PAGE 80

WEST PALERMO

The west side of Palermo is the oldest and busiest in the city. At Quattro Canti, streets intersect and point the way to Palazzo dei Normanni and the Cappella Palatina, a masterpiece of Byzantine mosaics. Look across the piazza to the domed Cathedral – a shining example of east-meets-west architecture. Once you've browsed the throbbing Ballarò open-air market in the Albergheria quarter, head to the Teatro Massimo to watch a world-class performance at the biggest opera house in Italy.

Best for
Arab-Norman architecture, opera and traditional puppet theatre

Home to
Cattedrale di Palermo, Cappella Palatina

Experience
Tucking into classic and delicious Sicilian street food

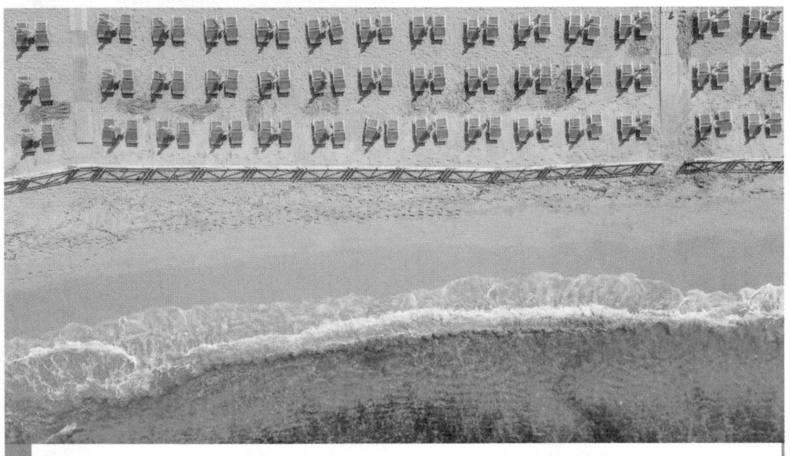

PAGE 96

BEYOND THE CENTRE

So compact is Palermo that few places require much effort to get to. On the periphery of the historic centre where city apartment blocks give way to summer-houses you'll find Mondello beach – a wide, sandy cove between two mountains, with rows of bathing and eating establishments. Further to the west you can delight in a show of royal wealth and divine power at the Duomo di Monreale, with a cloister of Arab archways and a million golden tiles glittering within.

Best for
Beaches and cathedrals

Home to
Duomo di Monreale

Experience
Creeping out at Catacombs of the Capuchins

FRUTTA
e
FRAGOLE DI MARSALA

Picking up fresh produce at Vucciria market

EAST PALERMO

Between Via Maqueda and the sea lie the old Arab quarters of Palermo, with their maze of narrow streets and blind alleys. This area includes the Kalsa quarter (from the Arabic al-Halisah, or the Chosen), which was built by the Arabs in the first half of the 10th century as the seat of the Emirate, the government and the army. During the Norman era it became the sailors' and fishermen's quarter. Most of the city's Aragonese monuments, dating from the late Middle Ages and the Renaissance, are in the Kalsa. It was badly damaged in World War II, and many parts are still being restored. The focal point is Piazza Marina, for centuries the heart of city life and seat of the Aragonese court and the Inquisition courtroom. Via Maqueda opens onto Piazza Pretoria, the civic heart of Palermo, with Palazzo delle Aquile, Santa Caterina and San Giuseppe dei Teatini. North of Corso Vittorio Emanuele is Castellammare, with the Vucciria market and the Loggia quarter near the port, where Catalan, Pisan and Genoese communities once lived.

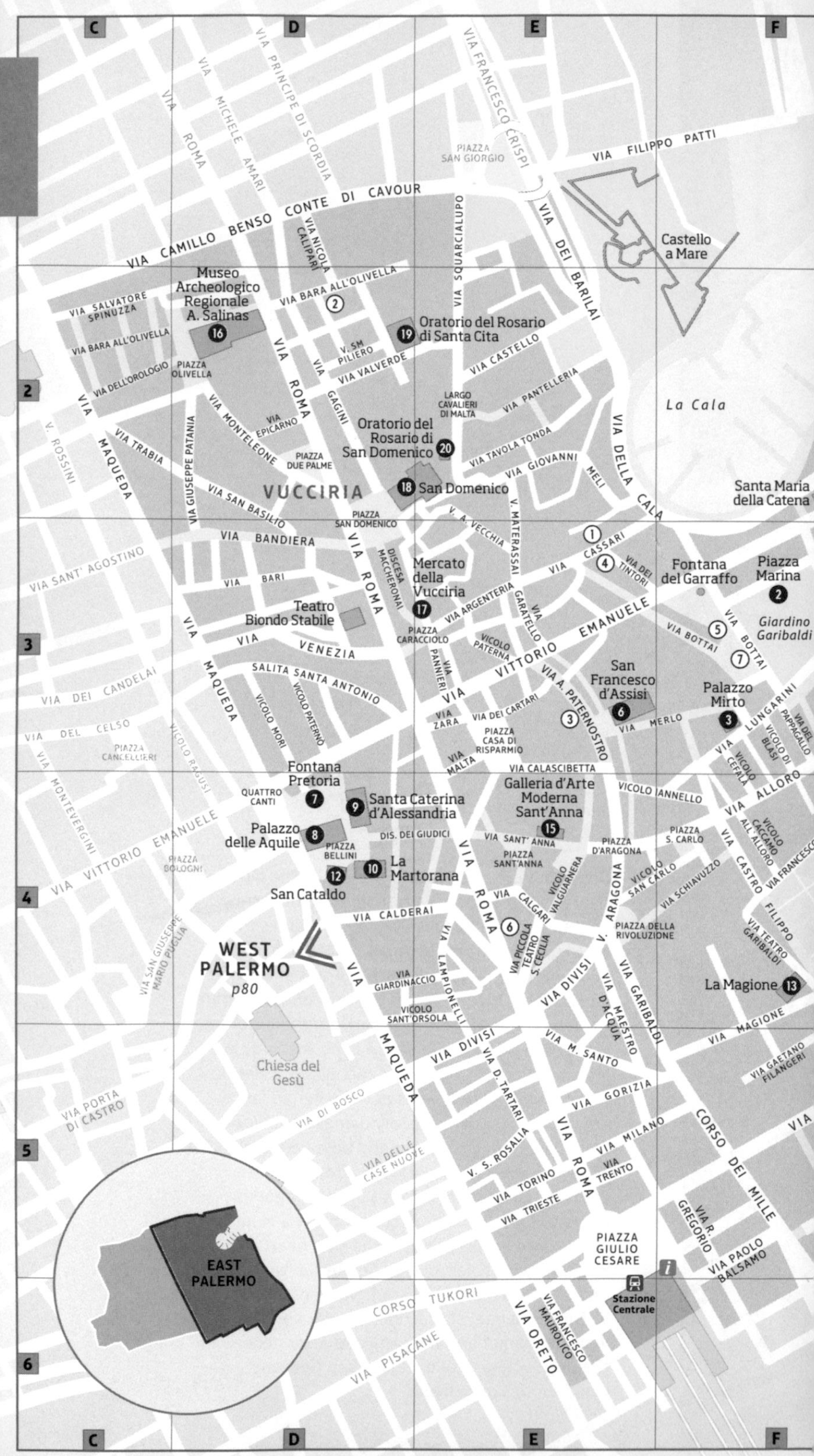
C
D
E
F
2
3
4
5
6
Via Camillo Benso Conte di Cavour
Via Roma
Via Michele Amari
Via Principe di Scordia
Via Francesco Crispi
Piazza San Giorgio
Via Filippo Patti
Via dei Barilai
Castello a Mare
Via Nicola Calipari
Via Squarcialupo
Museo Archeologico Regionale A. Salinas
16
Via Bara all'Olivella
2
Via Salvatore Spinuzza
Oratorio del Rosario di Santa Cita
19
V. SM Piliero
Via Valverde
Via Castello
Via dell'Orologio
Piazza Olivella
Via Gagini
Largo Cavalieri di Malta
Via Pantelleria
La Cala
Via Maqueda
V. Rossini
Via Trabia
Via Giuseppe Patania
Via Monteleone
Via Epicarno
Oratorio del Rosario di San Domenico
20
Via Tavola Tonda
Via Giovanni Meli
Via della Cala
Piazza Due Palme
Vucciria
18
San Domenico
Santa Maria della Catena
Via San Basilio
Piazza San Domenico
V. A. Vecchia
V. Materassai
1
Via Cassari
4
Via dei Tintori
Fontana del Garraffo
Piazza Marina
2
Via Bandiera
Via Sant' Agostino
Via Bari
Discesa Maccheronai
Mercato della Vucciria
17
Via Argenteria
Via Garaffello
Teatro Biondo Stabile
Giardino Garibaldi
Via Venezia
Piazza Caracciolo
Vicolo Paterna
Via Vittorio Emanuele
Via Bottai
5
7
Via Panniera
San Francesco d'Assisi
6
Palazzo Mirto
3
Via Dei Candelai
Salita Santa Antonio
Vicolo Paternò
Vicolo Mori
Via A. Paternostro
3
Via Merlo
Via Lungarini
Via Zara
Via dei Cartari
Piazza Casa di Risparmio
Via del Celso
Piazza Cancellieri
Vicolo Ragusi
Via Monteverqini
Via Pappagallo
Vicolo di Blasi
Vicolo Cefalà
Via Malta
Via Calascibetta
Vicolo Iannello
Via Alloro
Fontana Pretoria
7
Quattro Canti
Santa Caterina d'Alessandria
9
Galleria d'Arte Moderna Sant'Anna
15
Palazzo delle Aquile
8
Dis. dei Giudici
Via Sant' Anna
Piazza S. Carlo
Piazza d'Aragona
Vicolo Caccamo all'Alloro
Via Castro
Via Francesco
Piazza Bellini
Piazza Bologni
Piazza Sant'Anna
12
10
La Martorana
San Cataldo
Vicolo Valguarnera
Via Aragona
Vicolo San Carlo
Via Schiavuzzo
Via Calgari
6
Via Calderai
Via Filippo
Via Teatro Garibaldi
Piazza della Rivoluzione
Via San Giuseppe Mario Puglia
West Palermo p80
Via Lampionelli
Via Piccola Teatro S. Cecilia
Via Giardinaccio
Via Divisi
Via Maestro d'Acqua
Via Garibaldi
La Magione
13
Vicolo Sant'Orsola
Via Magione
Via M. Santo
Chiesa del Gesù
Via D. Tartari
Via Gaetano Filangeri
Via Gorizia
Via Porta di Castro
Via di Bosco
Corso dei Mille
Via Milano
Via delle Case Nuove
V. S. Rosalia
Via Trento
Via Torino
Via Trieste
Via R. Gregorio
Piazza Giulio Cesare
Via Paolo Balsamo
East Palermo
Corso Tukori
Stazione Centrale
Via Oreto
Via Francesco Maurolico
Via Pisacane

G
H
J
EAST PALERMO
Must See
1 Palazzo Abatellis
Experience More
2 Piazza Marina
3 Palazzo Mirto
4 La Gancia
5 Museo Internazionale delle Marionette
6 San Francesco d'Assisi
7 Fontana Pretoria
8 Palazzo delle Aquile
9 Santa Caterina d'Alessandria
10 La Martorana
11 Villa Giulia
12 San Cataldo
13 La Magione
14 Santa Maria dello Spasimo
15 Galleria d'arte Moderna Sant'Anna
16 Museo Archeologico Regionale A. Salinas
17 Mercato della Vucciria
18 San Domenico
19 Oratorio del Rosario di Santa Cita
20 Oratorio del Rosario di San Domenico
21 Orto Botanico
Eat
① Gagini Social Restaurant
② Ristorante Palazzo Branciforte
③ Antica Focacceria San Francesco
Drink
④ Bocum Mixology
⑤ Cheers Wine Bar
Stay
⑥ Hotel Ambasciatori
Shop
⑦ Antiques Market
PIAZZETTE ROSARIO LA DUCA
Parco della Salute
VIA DELLA CALA
Porta Felice
PIAZZA SANTO SPIRITO
FORO ITALICO UMBERTO I
Foro Italico
Museo Internazionale delle Marionette
VIC. NISCEMI
VIA BUTERA
Palazzo Chiaramonte Steri
Villa a Mare
VIA IV APRILE
VIA SCOPARI
Teatro Ditirammu
VIA ALLORO
VICOLO P. ALLORO
Palazzo Abatellis
VIA TORREMUZA
La Gancia
VIA N. GERVASI
PORTA DEI GRECI
VIA SAVONA
PIAZZA KALSA
LA KALSA
VIA SANTA TERESA
VIA DELLA VETRERIA
VIA DELLO SPASIMO
VIA DEL PALLONE
VIA CERVELLO
VICOLO DEL PALLONE
Piazza Magione
Santa Maria dello Spasimo
Villa Giulia
LINCOLN
ABRAMO
VIA CARLO RAO
Orto Botanico
VIA ANTONIO DI RUDINI
VIA ARCHIRAFI
VIA ANTONIO UGO
VIA MICHELE CIPOLLA
VIA PIETRO RANDEZZO
VIA GASPARE MIGNOS
VIA TIRO A SEGNO
CORSO DEI MILLE
VIA GIAN FILIPPO INGRASSIA
5
6
0 metres 200
0 yards 200
N

1

PALAZZO ABATELLIS

G3 Via Alloro 4 091-623 00 11
9am-6:30pm Tue-Fri, 9am-1pm Sat, Sun & hols

Palazzo Abatellis's muted facade offers little inkling of the cultural treasures that lie within. Its austere interior – last renovated by 20th-century architect Carlo Scarpa – creates the perfect backdrop to admire some of Sicily's finest medieval and Renaissance artwork.

This 15th-century Catalan Gothic palazzo now houses the 19 rooms of the Galleria Regionale della Sicilia. The elegant doorway leads to the large courtyard, which has a portico on the right side and a stairway to the upper floors. In the former chapel is one of the palazzo's most famous works, the 15th-century *Triumph of Death* fresco, as well as a fine collection of statues by Antonello Gagini and Francesco Laurana. The first floor features some noteworthy late medieval crucifixes, including one by Pietro Ruzzolone (16th century), and paintings by Antonello da Messina, including his masterpiece, the *Virgin Annunciate*. One of the most interesting works is the *Malvagna Triptych* by Jan Gossaert (also known as Jan Mabuse).

History of the Palazzo

Palazzo Abatellis was designed in 1490–95 by Matteo Carnalivari for Francesco Abatellis, the city's harbour-master and magistrate. He died without leaving an heir, and his mansion was taken over by the Benedictine order and then by the Region of Sicily. It was damaged in the 1943 bombings and reconstructed shortly after the war. It opened to the public in 1954.

↑ The towering *Triumph of Death* fresco in the ground floor gallery

HIDDEN GEM
Abatellis's Gargoyles

High atop the palace are a curious group of stone rain spouts carved in the form of grotesque or fantastic creatures. Gargoyles are a common sight in medieval Gothic architecture but rare in Sicily, only introduced in later Catalan Gothic buildings. These fanciful carvings are best seen from the Via Alloro side of the building.

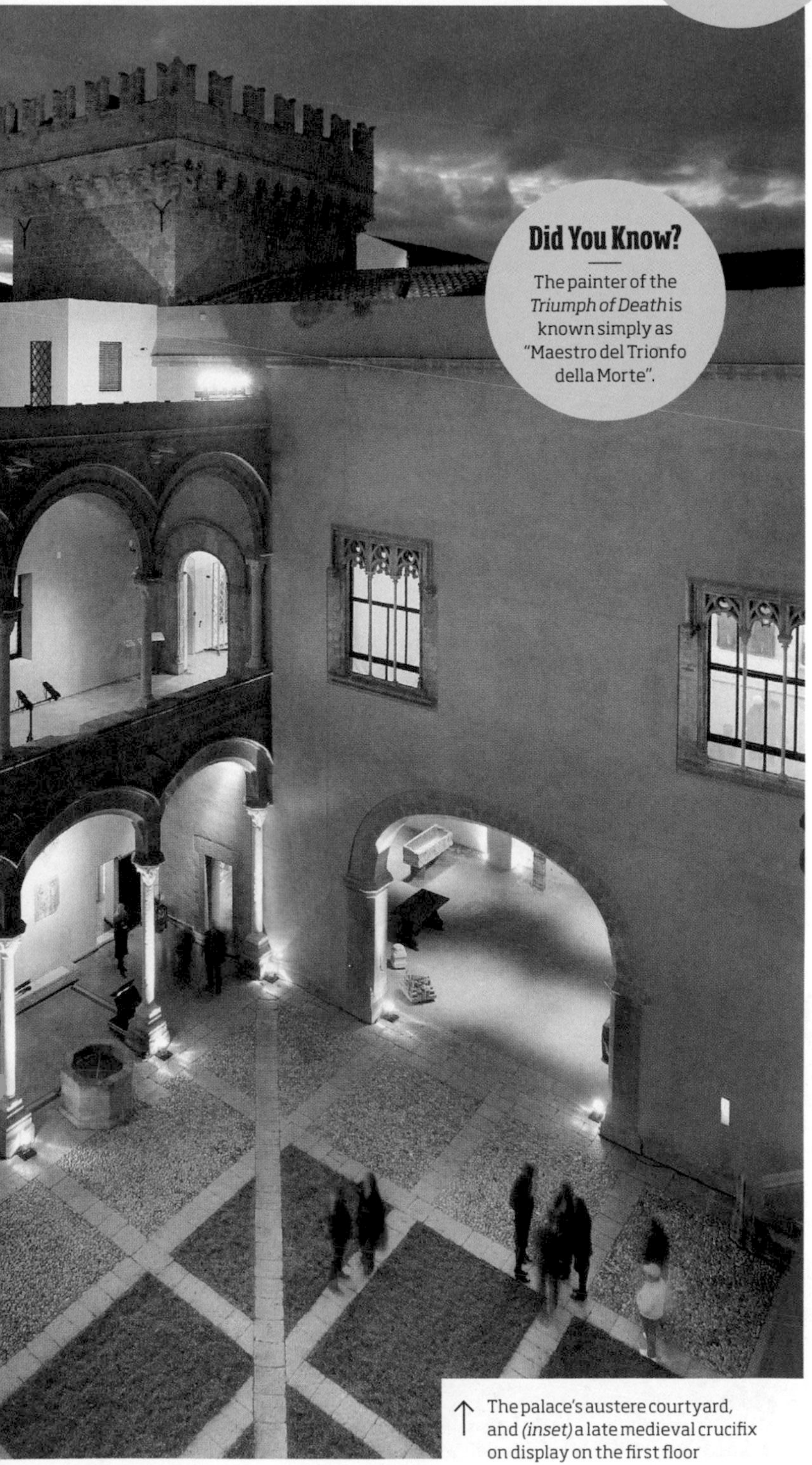

Did You Know?

The painter of the *Triumph of Death* is known simply as "Maestro del Trionfo della Morte".

↑ The palace's austere courtyard, and *(inset)* a late medieval crucifix on display on the first floor

EXPERIENCE MORE

Piazza Marina

F3

One of the largest squares in Palermo, Piazza Marina lies on what was once the southern side of the natural harbour. In the middle of Piazza Marina is the Giardino Garibaldi, designed in 1863 by G B Basile and planted with *Ficus magnolioides*, a large Ficus tree with very impressive aerial roots. The garden is surrounded by a cast-iron fence decorated with bows and arrows, rabbits and birds. Inside are a fountain and busts of Risorgimento figures, including sculptor Benedetto De Lisi's monument to the Italian leader Garibaldi.

Palazzo Chiaramonte Steri, also found in Piazza Marina, was built in 1307 by Manfredi III Chiaramonte, a member of one of Sicily's most powerful families. In the Middle Ages the Chiaramonte family controlled most of the island. The name "Steri" comes from *Hosterium*, or fortified building, as most patrician mansions were just that during the turbulent period of Hohenstaufen rule. Built in the Gothic style with Arab and Norman influences, the palazzo has an austere façade. The portal is decorated with a double arched lintel of ashlars and a series of double and triple Gothic lancet windows with multicoloured inlay.

When the new Aragonese rulers arrived in 1392, Andrea Chiaramonte was beheaded right in front of Palazzo Steri. It became the palace of the Aragonese kings and then of the viceroys. In the 17th century it housed the Inquisition courtroom, or Holy Office, where suspected heretics were interrogated and often tortured. Later, the palazzo became the city court of law and today it is the administrative headquarters of the University Rectorate. The courtyard is open to the public and tours of the palazzo are available.

On the corner of Via Vittorio Emanuele is the Baroque Fontana del Garraffo, a fountain with three shell-shaped basins supported by dolphins' heads.

SHOP

Antiques Market

Part antiques market, part rummage sale, each weekend the stalls on Palermo's Piazza Marina form a vast expanse of rusty trinkets, old books and one-of-a-kind vintage treasures.

F3 Piazza Marina Sat & Sun mornings

Palazzo Mirto

F3 Via Merlo 2 091-616 75 41 9am-6pm Tue-Sun (to 1pm Sun & hols)

This is a splendid example of a centuries-old nobleman's mansion that has miraculously

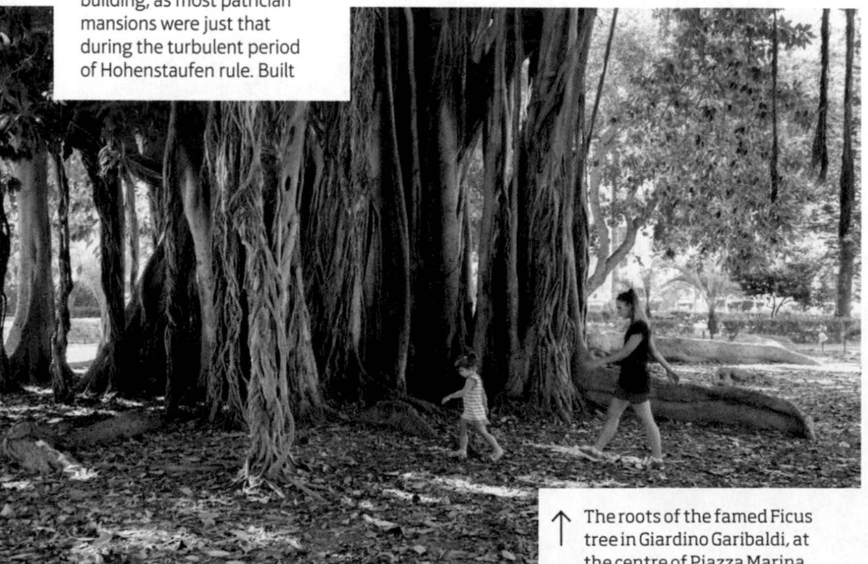

↑ The roots of the famed Ficus tree in Giardino Garibaldi, at the centre of Piazza Marina

The beautifully decorated Our Lady of Guadalupe Chapel inside La Gancia

preserved its lovely original furnishings. Built in the 18th century on top of pre-existing 15th- and 16th-century architectural structures, the palazzo passed from the aristocratic De Spuches family to the equally noble Filangeri, who lived here until 1980, when the last heir donated it to the Region of Sicily. An 18th-century portal with the coat of arms of the Filangeri family leads to the courtyard, where a majestic marble stairway takes you to the piano nobile. Here you will find an impressive series of elegantly furnished drawing rooms. The first of these is the Sala degli Arazzi (Tapestry Hall), with mythological scenes painted by the Italian artist Giuseppe Velasco in 1804, then there is the "Chinese" room, and lastly the so-called Baldachin Salon with late 18th-century allegorical frescoes. The furniture and other furnishings date from the 18th and 19th centuries. Some rooms overlook a courtyard garden dominated by a theatrical Rococo fountain flanked by two aviaries.

4 La Gancia

F3 Via Alloro 27 091-616 52 21 9:30am-1:30pm Mon-Sat, 10am-2:30pm Sun (call ahead to visit in the afternoon)

This fine church was built in 1485 and dedicated to Santa Maria degli Angeli. The façade is decorated with two Spanish-Gothic portals and the aisleless nave in the interior has 16 side chapels, a multicoloured marble floor and a wooden patterned ceiling. In the Baroque period, stucco decoration was added by the sculptor Giacomo Serpotta. The choir, in a separate room near the church's entrance, contains a late 16th-century organ. Panels dating from 1697 show Franciscan saints painted by the Italian artist and engraver Antonio Grano.

INSIDER TIP
Puppet Festival

Don't miss Festival di Morgana in autumn to see puppet theatre companies and artists from across the globe descend on Palermo for a jubilee of exhibitions and performances that bring wood, rod and string to life.

5 Museo Internazionale delle Marionette

F3 Piazzetta A Pasqualino 5 10am-6pm daily (to 2pm Sun & Mon) Public hols museomarionettepalermo.it

This museum houses one of the world's main collections of puppets, marionettes and shadow puppets. In the first room are the great schools of marionettes, from the Catania style to those of Liège, Naples and Brussels. The second room has a collection of figures belonging to puppeteers from Palermo, Castellammare del Golfo, Alcamo and Partinico. The international section includes Chinese shadow theatre puppets, Thai *hun krabok*, Vietnamese, Burmese and Rajasthan marionettes, and Javanese *wayang* figures, as well as animated figures from Oceania and Africa. Among the stage scenery in the museum is *Charlemagne's Council* and *Alcina's Garden*.

Intricate puppets at the Museo Internazionale delle Marionette

6

San Francesco d'Assisi

E3 Piazza San Francesco d'Assisi 091-582 370 7-11:30am & 4-6pm Mon-Sat, 7am-1pm & 4:30-6pm Sun

This church has retained its medieval aspect despite the numerous alterations it has undergone. Built in the early 13th century together with the Franciscan monastery, it was destroyed by Frederick II soon afterwards when he was excommunicated by the Pope. In 1255, work on the new church began, reaching completion only in 1277. The 15th and particularly the 16th centuries witnessed various additions and alterations; for example, the wooden roof was replaced and the presbytery was enlarged.

After the bombardments suffered in 1943, the church was restored to its original state. The austere façade has a large rose window and a fine Gothic portal, while the interior is home to many noteworthy works of art, including sculptures by Giacomo Serpotta and Antonello Gagini. The side chapels house funerary stelae and sarcophagi.

The fourth chapel in the left-hand aisle is the Cappella Mastrantonio, with one of the first Renaissance works in Sicily, the portal by Francesco Laurana. Behind the high altar is a wooden choir built in 1520, as well as 17th-century paintings of the *Resurrection*, *Ascension* and *Mission*.

Fontana Pretoria

D4 Piazza Pretoria

Located in the middle of Palermo, this fountain is on a slightly higher level than Via Maqueda. It was designed in 1552–5 by Tuscan sculptor Francesco Camilliani for the garden of a Florentine villa and was later installed in Piazza Pretoria. The concentric basins are arranged on three levels, with statues of mythological creatures, monsters, tritons, sirens and the four rivers of Palermo (Oreto, Papireto, Gabriele, Maredolce). Due to the nude statues it was once known as "the fountain of shame".

→ Baroque interior and Renaissance stairway *(inset)* of Santa Caterina d'Alessandria

Palazzo delle Aquile

D4 Piazza Pretoria 091-740 11 11 9am-5pm Mon-Sat

Palazzo Senatorio, or Palazzo del Municipio, is commonly called "delle Aquile" because of the four eagles *(aquile)* that decorate the exterior and the portal. Now the town hall, it is Palermo's major civic monument, although its original 16th-century structure was radically altered by 19th-century restoration. However, a statue of Santa Rosalia by Carlo Aprile (1661) still occupies a niche on the top of the façade. At the entrance, a grand staircase with a coffered ceiling takes you to the first floor and various public rooms: the Sala delle Lapidi, Sala dei Gonfaloni and Sala Rossa, which is also known as the Mayor's Hall.

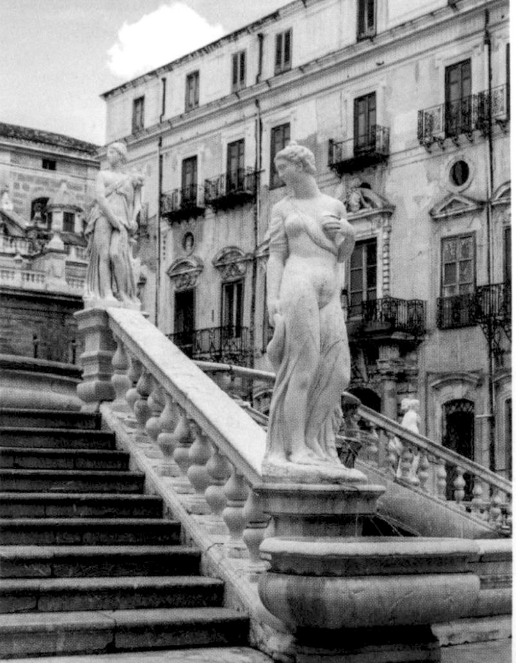

Nude statues flanking Fontana Pretoria on Piazza Pretoria

9

Santa Caterina d'Alessandria

D4 Piazza Bellini
9am-6pm daily

The church of the Dominican monastery of Santa Caterina is a splendid example of Sicilian Baroque art, despite the fact that both buildings originated in the 14th century.

The main features of the late Renaissance façade (the present church was built in 1580–96) are its double stairway and the statue of St Catherine (Caterina) in the middle of the portal. The large cupola was built in the mid-18th century. The interior has marble inlay, sculpture pieces, stuccoes and frescoes. In the chapel to the right of the transept is a fine statue of Santa Caterina, sculpted by Antonello Gagini in 1534.

Did You Know?

Palermo's oldest street, Via Vittorio Emanuele II, lies upon ancient Phoenician foundations.

La Martorana

D4 Piazza Bellini 3
091-616 16 92 9am-1pm & 3:30-5:30pm Mon-Sat, 9-10:30am Sun & hols

Santa Maria dell'Ammiraglio is called La Martorana in memory of Eloisa della Martorana, who founded the nearby Benedictine convent. Eloisa used to decorate the church with handmade marzipan fruit; as a result, Frutta di Martorana is now one of Palermo's most famed delicacies. Built in 1143 on a Greek cross plan, this church was partly altered and enlarged in the Baroque period, and combines Norman features and decor with later styles. You enter by the bell tower, whose dome was destroyed in the 1726 earthquake. The Baroque interior is decorated with stuccoes and enamel, and the bay vaulting has frescoes; the original church was decorated with 12th-century mosaics. The cupola shows *Christ Pantocrator Surrounded by Angels*; on the tambour are *The Prophets* and *The Four Evangelists*; and on the walls are an *Annunciation*, *The Nativity* and *The Presentation at the Temple*. Most intriguing of all, however, is the mosaic of Roger II being crowned; it is the only known portrait of the king.

DRINK

Bocum Mixology

This cosy, bohemian cocktail bar in the heart of the old town serves experimental drinks with a strong focus on mixology.

E3 Via dei Cassari 6
Tue good
companypalermo.it

Cheers Wine Bar

With tables spilling out onto Piazza Marina, this is the perfect spot to enjoy evening drinks.

F3 Piazza Marina 10
3:30pm-midnight Mon & Wed-Sat, 11:30am-midnight Sun cheers wineandfood.it

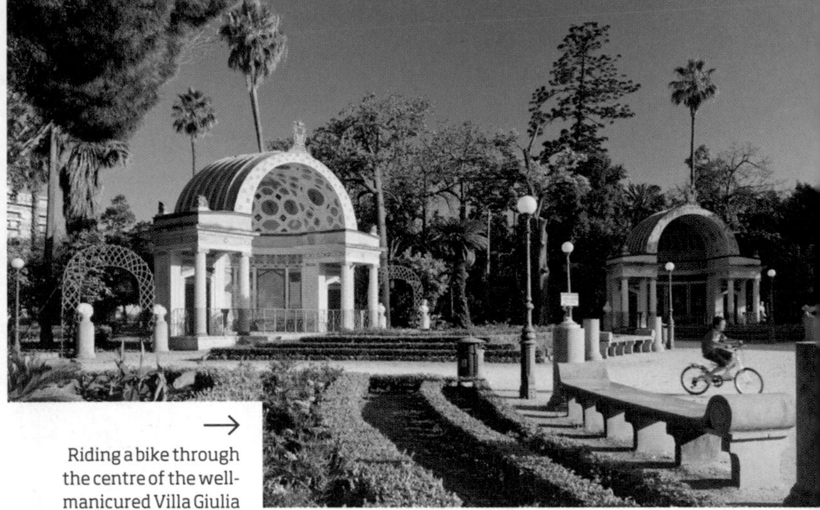

Riding a bike through the centre of the well-manicured Villa Giulia

Villa Giulia

H4 Via Abramo Lincoln

Despite its name, the Villa Giulia is not a house but an impressive Italianate garden. Designed in 1778 by Italian architect Nicolò Palma, it was then enlarged in 1866. It was named after Giulia Avalos Guevara, wife of the viceroy, and was the city's first public park. Its square plan is divided by roads that are decorated with statues, such as the marble image of the "Genius of Palermo", who is considered a symbol of the city, and the statues representing Glory vanquishing Envy and Abundance driving out Famine. The roads converge at the centre of the park in an area with four Pompeian-style niches, designed by Giuseppe Damiani Almeyda and decorated with frescoes in great need of restoration, surrounding a fountain that lies at the park's heart.

The Arab-Norman church of San Cataldo, alongside La Martorana

12  

San Cataldo

D4 Piazza Bellini 3 091-782 96 84 9am-6pm daily

San Cataldo was the chapel of a palazzo built by Maio of Bari, William I's admiral, in the 12th century. It has kept its linear Arab-Norman style, with three red domes raised above the wall, the windows with pointed arches and the battlement decoration. Inscriptions with quotations from the Koran can still be seen. Although the interior has no decoration, the mosaic-patterned floor is a beautiful adornment. In the middle of the nave is a series of Arab arches supported by ancient columns.

13 

La Magione

F4 Via Magione 44 091-617 05 96 3-6pm Mon, 8:45am-noon and 3-6:30pm Tue-Sat; Cloister & Chapels: 10am-1:30pm and 2:30-6pm Tue-Sat, 9:30am-1:30pm Sun

Founded by Matteo d'Aiello in the mid-1100s, this church was frequently rebuilt and was then damaged in the bombings of 1943. Careful restoration has revived its original Norman features. A Baroque portico, with marble columns and statues, affords access to a garden. The façade has three doorways with double arched lintels and convex rustication, a series of blind arches and windows. Pointed arches run along the length of the nave.

Santa Maria dello Spasimo

G4 Via dello Spasimo 091-616 64 80 8am-8pm daily

Santa Maria dello Spasimo lies in the heart of the Kalsa quarter. It was founded in 1506 by the monks of Santa Maria di Monte Oliveto and was dedicated to the Virgin Mary grieving before Christ on the Cross, the subject of a 1516 painting by Raphael that is now in the Prado Museum in Madrid. Santa Maria was the last example of Spanish-Gothic architecture in the city. The cells and courtyards of the monastery were built around the church and in 1536 the complex, at that time outside the city walls, was incorporated into a rampart, so that it now looks like a watchtower.

The church was bought by the city and became, in turn, a theatre, warehouse, hospice and hospital, while all the time falling into a state of neglect. In 1995, the Spasimo area was redeveloped and transformed into a cultural centre for exhibitions and concerts. Performances are now held inside the church, part of which no longer has a roof.

Galleria d'arte Moderna Sant'Anna

E4 Via Sant'Anna 21 9:30am-6:30pm Tue-Sun gampalermo.it

Housed in the restored 15th-century convent of Sant'Anna, this gallery features a range of works from the past 150 years. Many of the Italian and international artists on display have featured prominently in the Venice Biennale.

PICTURE PERFECT

Street Art and Murals

Palermo's various neighbourhoods are experiencing an urban renewal in illustration and colour. Keep your camera at the ready when exploring to snap close ups of unique art around every corner.

Museo Archeologico Regionale A. Salinas

D2 Piazza Olivella 24 091-611 68 05/6/7 9am-6pm Tue-Sun (to 1:30pm Sun & hols)

Housed in a 17th-century monastery, this museum holds treasures from excavations across the island. The former cells of a small cloister contain finds such as the large Phoenician sarcophagi in the shape of humans (6th–5th centuries BC) and the *Pietra di Palermo*, a slab with a hieroglyphic inscription from 2900 BC. Other displays include Punic inscriptions and objects, and mosaics and frescoes from digs at Palermo, Solunto and Marsala. The cloister houses Roman statues, slabs and tombstones. At the end of the cloister are three rooms with pieces taken from the temples at Selinunte; these include a leonine head from the Temple of Victory and metopes from other temples. Those from Temple C represent *Helios's Chariot*, *Perseus Helped by Athena while Killing the Gorgon* and *Heracles Punishing the Cercopes*; the metopes from Temple E are *Heracles Fighting the Amazons*, *Hera and Zeus on Mount Ida*, *Actaeon Attacked by Dogs in the Presence of Artemis* and *Athena Slaying the Giant Enceladus*. Currently, only the ground floor section is open to visitors.

STAY

Hotel Ambasciatori

This polished timepiece of Palermo's Liberty era has light-filled rooms with contemporary and classic decor. Head to the rooftop terrace for an afternoon *aperitivo*.

E4 Via Roma 111 ambasciatori hotelpalermo.com

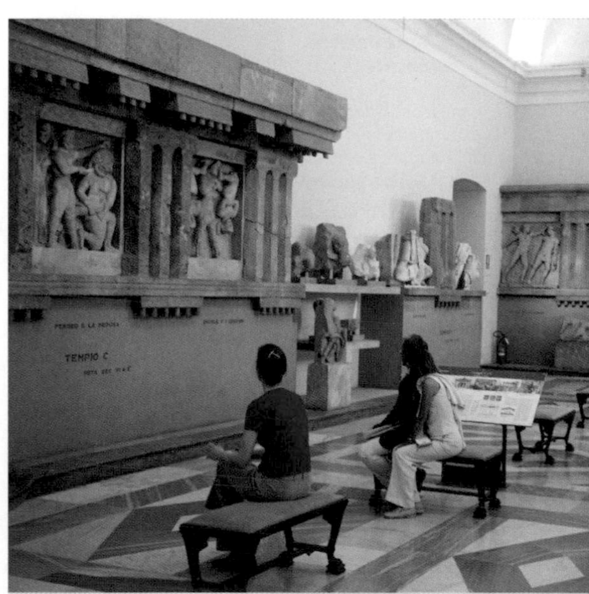

↑ Admiring amazing artifacts at Palermo's Museo Archeologico Regionale A. Salinas

↑ Colourful fruit and vegetables on display at Mercato della Vucciria

Mercato della Vucciria

E3 Piazza Caracciolo and adjacent streets

This is Palermo's most famous market, immortalized by Renato Guttuso in his painting *La Vucciria*. There are two theories as to the origin of the market's name: some say it is a corruption of the French *boucherie* (butcher), while others suggest the name means "the place of loud voices", from when vendors called out their wares. Today, this outdoor market trades in vegetables, dried fruit and preserves, as well as cheese, fish and meat, amid a tumult of colours, sounds and smells reminiscent of the souks in North Africa.
The Vucciria is especially impressive in the morning, when fishmongers set up shop. There are stalls that serve sea urchin or will skewer giblets for you on the spot. Another speciality is boiled spleen and liver fried in lard, also used for making the delicious *ca' meusa* bread, the locals' favourite snack.
In the evening, Vucciria Market transforms itself into one of Palermo's most lively locations for nightlife.

San Domenico

D2 Piazza San Domenico 091-589 172 8am-1:30pm Tue-Sun (Sat & Sun: also 5-7pm, Summer: also Mon)

This basilica, belonging to the Dominican monastery, has been rebuilt many times over the past six centuries. The most drastic alteration was in 1640, when the architect Andrea Cirincione tore down part of the cloister to enlarge the church. In 1724, when Piazza San Domenico was remodelled, the façade was rebuilt and is now animated by the fusion of curves on the one hand, and jutting columns and statues, niches and twin bell towers on the other.
The total lack of decoration heightens the elegance of the architecture. In contrast, the

EAT

Gagini Social Restaurant
This former workshop of a 16th-century sculptor is favoured by slow-food aficionados.
E3 Via Cassari 35
gaginirestaurant.com

Ristorante Palazzo Branciforte
Hidden in the Palazzo's museum, eclectic cuisine is served in a modern space alongside ancient Sicilian pottery.
D2 Via Bara All'Olivella 2
ristorantepalazzo branciforte.it

Antica Focacceria
A bustling, exuberant institution, this eatery has been serving the best in rustic Italian food since 1834.
E3 Via Alessandro Paternostro 58
anticafocacceria.it

The impressive façade of San Domenico at night and *(inset)* its interior

chapels are richly decorated. One of these, the tomb of the Oneto di Sperlinga family, has multicoloured marble funerary monuments, a statue of St Joseph by sculptor Antonello Gagini, and stucco- and putti-decorated walls. The altar in the transept is adorned with lateral volutes and bronze friezes, while the 18th-century high altar is made of marble and decorated with semi-precious stones.

19 

Oratorio del Rosario di Santa Cita

D2 Via Valverde 3 091-332 779 9am-6pm Mon-Sat (to 3pm Sat and in winter) Sun

Founded in 1590 by the Society of the Rosary, this was one of the city's richest oratories. A marble staircase opens onto a cloister and then goes up to an upper loggia decorated with marble busts, and to the vestibule, with portraits of the Superiors of the Society. The Oratory is an example of sculptor Giacomo Serpotta's best work, a lavish display of Baroque decoration, its fusion of putti volutes, statues, floral elements and festoons creating a theatrical atmosphere. The *Battle of Lepanto* sculpture group is spectacular. On the sides of the tribune are statues of Esther and Judith, while the altarpiece is Carlo Maratta's *Madonna of the Rosary* (1695). Along the walls are seats with mother-of-pearl inlay; the floor is made of red, white and black marble.

20 

Oratorio del Rosario di San Domenico

E2 Via dei Bambinai 091-332 779 9am-6pm Mon-Sat

The Oratory of San Domenico was founded at the end of the 16th century by the Society of the Holy Rosary. Two Society members were painter Pietro Novelli and sculptor Giacomo Serpotta, who left marks of their genius on this monument.

The black and white majolica floors fit in well with the tumult of figures of great ladies, knights and playful putti, which form a frame for the statues of Christian virtues by Giacomo Serpotta and paintings representing the mysteries of the Rosary. The latter were executed by Pietro Novelli and Flemish artists.

Did You Know?

Orto Botanico is home to a 150-year-old *Ficus magnolioides* fig tree with aerial roots.

21 

Orto Botanico

G5 Via Abramo Lincoln 2b Daily Mar & Oct: 9am-6pm; Apr & Sep: 9am-7pm; May-Aug: 9am-8pm; Nov-Feb: 9am-5pm ortobotanico.unipa.it

Laid out in 1785, this garden has attained international fame thanks to the wealth of its plant species.The Neo-Classical Gymnasium (now a museum), library and herbaria are by the entrance, a pond with waterlilies is in the centre, and glasshouses line both sides.

A SHORT WALK AROUND PIAZZA MARINA

Distance 1 km (0.6 miles) **Time** 15 minutes **Nearest bus stop** Vittorio Emanuele - Fontana Del Garraffo

The main square in Old Palermo lies at the edge of the historic Kalsa quarter. From the Middle Ages onwards it was used for knights' tournaments, theatre performances, markets and public executions. The irregular sides of the square are flanked by an array of incredible monuments, including the imposing 14th-century Palazzo Steri-Chiaramonte and striking Santa Maria della Catena, a 16th-century church. In the middle of the square is a verdant garden, the Giardino Garibaldi, which is home to enormous fig trees with strange, exposed roots.

Did You Know?

Built during Muslim rule, the Kalsa quarter takes its name from the Arabic word *khalis*, meaning "pure".

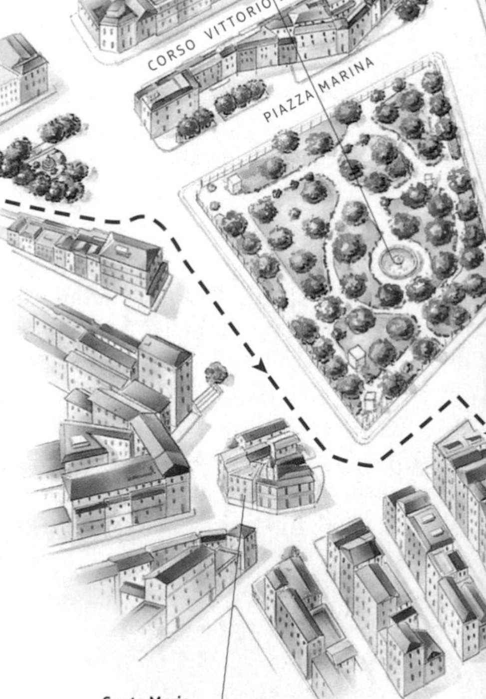
The **Santa Maria della Catena**, *a Catalan Gothic church, has a broad stairway leading to a beautiful three-arched porch.*
Piazza Marina (p70) *is one of the largest squares in Palermo. It lies on reclaimed land that was once part of the harbour.*
CORSO VITTORIO EMANUELE
PIAZZA MARINA
START
Santa Maria dei Miracoli

↑ Admiring one of the artworks in the Palazzo Abatellis

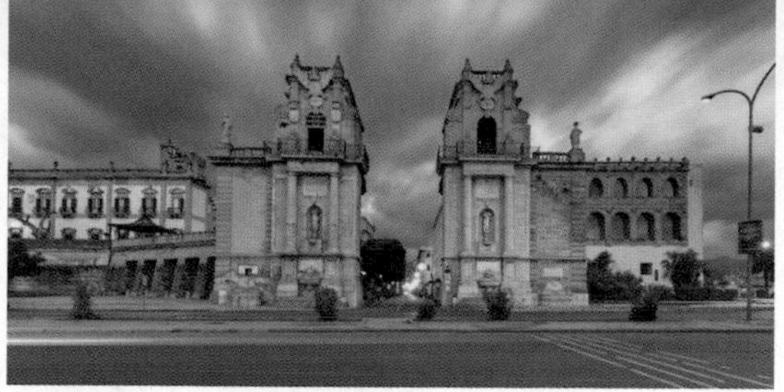

The monumental Porta Felice on the edge of the Kalsa quarter

Around Piazza Marina
EAST PALERMO

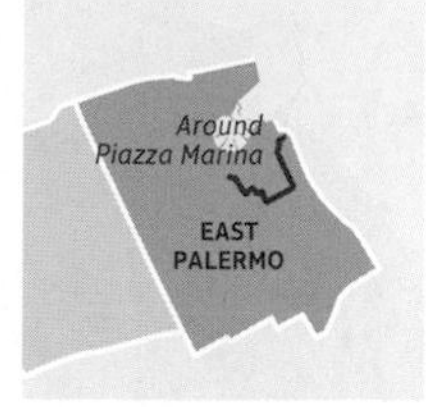

Locator Map

For more detail see p66

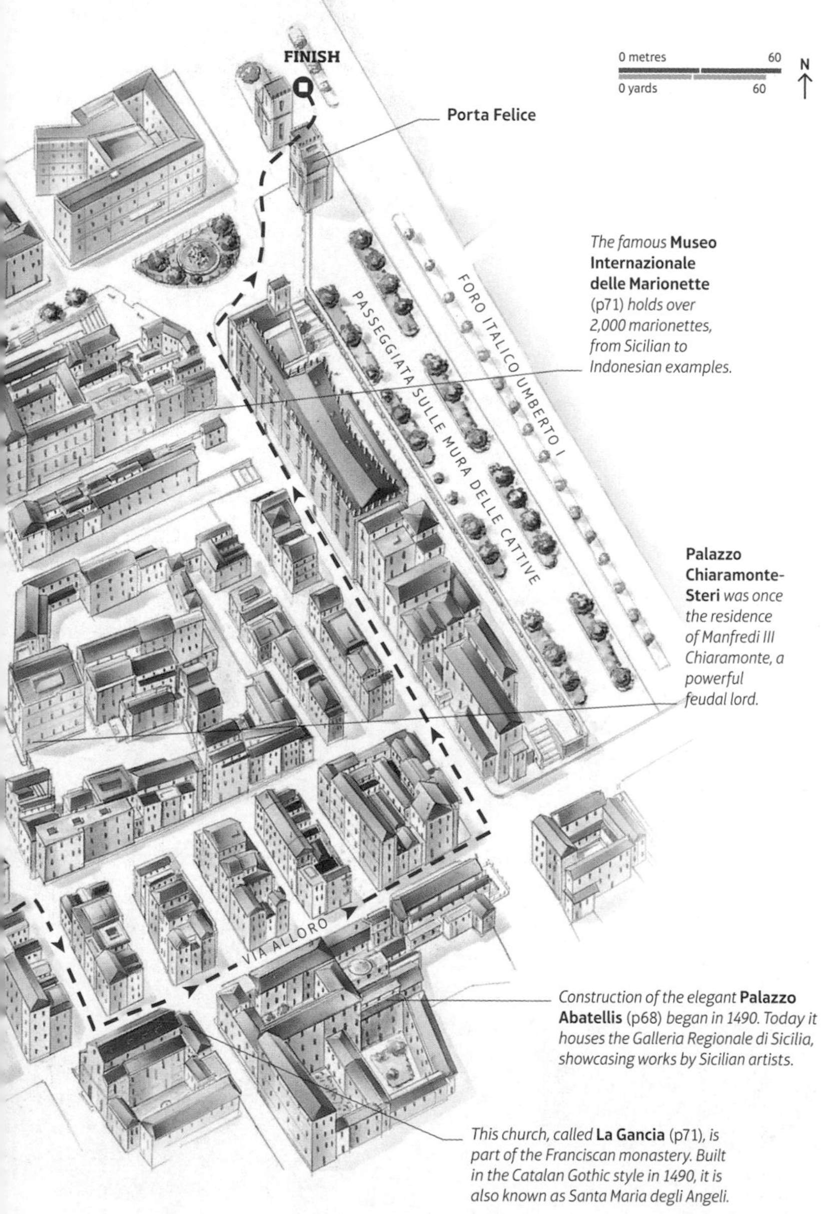

0 metres 60
0 yards 60
N
FINISH
Porta Felice
FORO ITALICO UMBERTO I
PASSEGGIATA SULLE MURA DELLE CATTIVE
VIA ALLORO
The famous **Museo Internazionale delle Marionette** (p71) *holds over 2,000 marionettes, from Sicilian to Indonesian examples.*
Palazzo Chiaramonte-Steri *was once the residence of Manfredi III Chiaramonte, a powerful feudal lord.*
Construction of the elegant **Palazzo Abatellis** (p68) *began in 1490. Today it houses the Galleria Regionale di Sicilia, showcasing works by Sicilian artists.*
This church, called **La Gancia** (p71), *is part of the Franciscan monastery. Built in the Catalan Gothic style in 1490, it is also known as Santa Maria degli Angeli.*

Astonishing mosaics in the Cappella Palatina

WEST PALERMO

The quarters south of Via Roma lie on the slopes occupied by the city's original Phoenician settlement, which was enlarged during the Roman era. In the 11th century the Arabs built a castle on the site where the Palazzo dei Normanni now stands. The Arabic Al Qasar (the castle) was used as the name of the quarter and the street that led to the castle, the present-day Corso Vittorio Emanuele, known as "Cassaro" to the people of Palermo. The area contains many impressive buildings and churches, including Palermo's centuries-old Cathedral and the Cappella Palatina. Between the Palazzo dei Normanni and Via Maqueda is the Albergheria quarter, the home of merchants and craftsmen in the Middle Ages. The many oratories of the medieval brotherhoods demonstrate the wealth and industry of the inhabitants. In the first half of the 20th century parts of the area were demolished, and the 1943 air raids dealt an additional blow. It is still enlivened by the daily market, the Mercato Ballarò, which is less famous but more authentic than the Vucciria market.

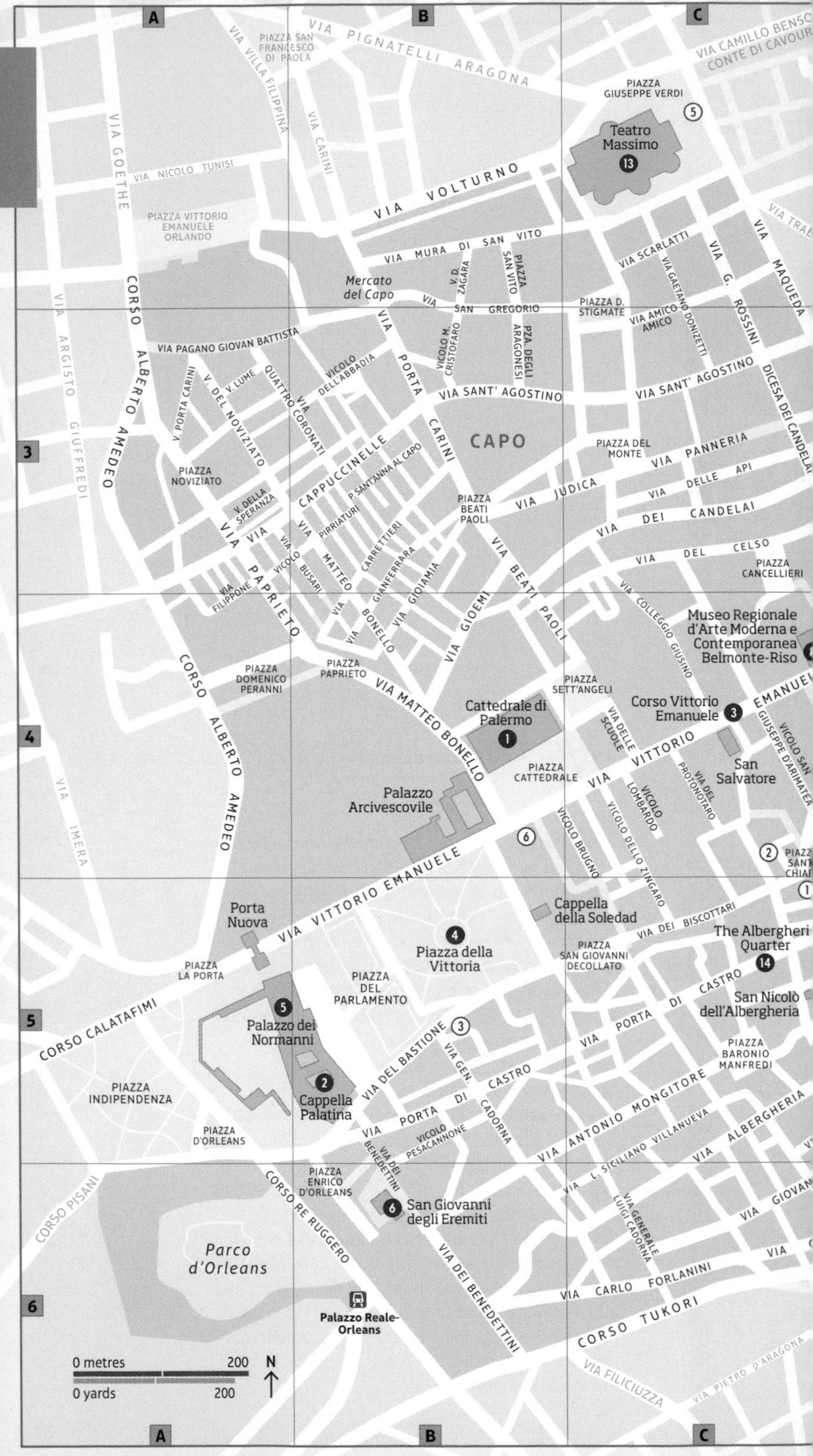

Teatro Massimo
Mercato del Capo
CAPO
Museo Regionale d'Arte Moderna e Contemporanea Belmonte-Riso
Corso Vittorio Emanuele
Cattedrale di Palermo
San Salvatore
Palazzo Arcivescovile
Porta Nuova
Cappella della Soledad
Piazza della Vittoria
The Albergheri Quarter
San Nicolò dell'Albergheria
Palazzo dei Normanni
Cappella Palatina
San Giovanni degli Eremiti
Parco d'Orleans
Palazzo Reale-Orleans
VIA VOLTURNO
VIA MAQUEDA
VIA VITTORIO EMANUELE
CORSO ALBERTO AMEDEO
CORSO CALATAFIMI
CORSO RE RUGGERO
CORSO TUKORI
VIA DEI BENEDETTINI
PIAZZA GIUSEPPE VERDI
PIAZZA INDIPENDENZA
PIAZZA DEL PARLAMENTO
PIAZZA CATTEDRALE
0 metres 200
0 yards 200

WEST PALERMO
Must Sees
1 Cattedrale di Palermo
2 Cappella Palatina
Experience More
3 Corso Vittorio Emanuele
4 Piazza della Vittoria
5 Palazzo dei Normanni
6 San Giovanni degli Eremiti
7 San Giuseppe dei Teatini
8 Museo Regionale d'Arte Moderna e Contemporanea Belmonte-Riso
9 Chiesa del Gesù and Casa Professa
10 Quattro Canti
11 Sant'Orsola
12 Chiesa del Carmine
13 Teatro Massimo
14 The Albergheria Quarter
Eat
① Moltivolti
② Ballarak Ballarò
③ Ai Normanni
Drink
④ Pasticceria Costa
⑤ Bistrò del Teatro
⑥ Bar Marocco
Shop
⑦ La Stanza di Carta
D
E
F
5
6
Museo Archeologico Regionale Antonio Salinas
Oratorio del Rosario di Santa Cita
Oratorio del Rosario di San Domenico
Piazza Due Palme
Piazza San Domenico
CASTELLAMMARE
EAST PALERMO p64
Quattro Canti
Hotel Centrale
San Giuseppe dei Teatini
Santa Caterina d'Alessandria
Piazza Bellini
San Cataldo
Piazza Casa di Risparmio
Piazza Sant'Anna
LA KALSA
Piazza Casa Professa
Chiesa del Gesù and Casa Professa
Sant'Orsola
Mercato di Ballarò
Piazza Ballarò
Piazza del Carmine
Chiesa del Carmine
Piazza Giulio Cesare
Piazza Porta Sant'Agata
Via Bara all'Olivella
Via Squarcialupo
Via Roma
Via Valverde
Via Monteleone
Via Gagini
Via San Basilio
Via Bandiera
Via Argenteria
Via Maqueda
Vicolo Marotta
Vicolo Ragusi
Via Vittorio Emanuele
Via Giuseppe d'Alessi
Via dell'Università
Via Calderai
Via Ponticello
Via N Basile
Rua Formaggi
Via Casa Professa
Via Divisi
Via D. Tartari
Via di Bosco
Via delle Case Nuove
V. S. Rosalia
Via Torino
Via Trieste
Corso dei Mille
Via Abramo Lincoln
Via Pietro Mignosi
Via Giovanni Naso
Via Carmine
Via delle Pergole
G. Verga
Via Cesare Battisti
Via Trapezzato
Via Rosselli
Corso Tukori
Via Pisacane
Via del Vespro
Via Francesco Paolo Perez
Via Oreto
Via Vito d'Ondes Reggio
WEST PALERMO

Did You Know?

A 22-m (72-ft) brass sundial is set into the floor of the cathedral's Chapel of Santa Rosalia.

Honey-stoned Cattedrale di Palermo, softly lit against the dawn sky ↑

1

CATTEDRALE DI PALERMO

B4 Via Vittorio Emanuele 7am-7pm Mon-Sat, 8am-1pm & 4-7pm Sun For Mass cattedrale.palermo.it

Palermo has been bequeathed a cathedral that remains one of the most astonishing in the world. Vaulting across a grand piazza, it is an Arab-Norman architectural wonder.

Dedicated to Our Lady of the Assumption, the cathedral stands on the site of an Early Christian basilica, later a mosque. Built in 1179–85, and despite frequent rebuildings and alterations, some of the original Norman structure remains; this can be seen under the small majolica-tiled cupolas, with the typical arched crenellation decoration on the wall tops. The exteriors of the apses have maintained much of their original character, with interlaced arches and small columns. In the late 1700s the nave was widened and the central cupola was added. As a result of the mixture of styles, the right-hand side forms a kind of "carved history" of the city. Opposite the façade, on the other side of the street, is the medieval campanile, where the tiara of Constance of Aragón is now kept.

THE INTERIOR OF THE CATHEDRAL

Alterations carried out in the 18th century gave the interior a Neo-Classical look. Of the many chapels, the most important are the first two on the right-hand side of the nave with the imperial tombs, and the Chapel of Santa Rosalia, where the saint's remains are kept in a silver coffer on the altar.

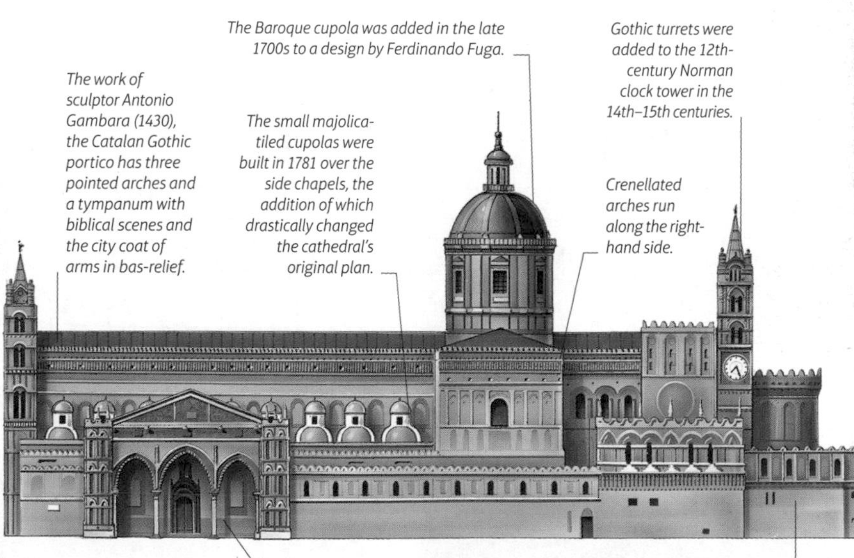

The Baroque cupola was added in the late 1700s to a design by Ferdinando Fuga.
Gothic turrets were added to the 12th-century Norman clock tower in the 14th–15th centuries.
The work of sculptor Antonio Gambara (1430), the Catalan Gothic portico has three pointed arches and a tympanum with biblical scenes and the city coat of arms in bas-relief.
The small majolica-tiled cupolas were built in 1781 over the side chapels, the addition of which drastically changed the cathedral's original plan.
Crenellated arches run along the right-hand side.
The portal was built in the 1400s and is decorated with a two-winged wooden door with a mosaic of the Virgin Mary above.
The exterior of the apses, decorated with interlaced arches, is the best-preserved part of the original design.

↑ Illustration of Palermo's oft-rebuilt Arab-Norman cathedral

CAPPELLA PALATINA

B5 Piazza del Parlamento 8:15am-5:40pm Mon-Sat, 8:15am-1pm Sun & hols federicosecondo.org

The dazzling jewel of the Palazzo dei Normanni *(p89)* **is the Cappella Palatina, a cocktail of Byzantine, Islamic and Norman influences built by Roger II (1132–40).**

Situated on the second of the Norman Palace's three floors, the Palatine Chapel is said to be rivalled only by the Vatican's Sistine Chapel in terms of its awe-inspiring decoration. Virtually every inch of the walls is covered with finely detailed Norman-Byzantine mosaics, most of which depict biblical scenes. On the cupola and the bowl of the central apse is the image of Christ Pantocrator surrounded by angels, while the niches house the Four Evangelists. Old Testament kings and prophets are on the arches, Christ blessing the faithful dominates the middle apse, and the transept walls bear scenes from the Gospel. The chapel's architectural features are themselves fascinating, particularly the wooden ceiling – a masterpiece of Islamic-style carving featuring *muqarnas*, a form of three-dimensional geometric decoration more commonly found in mosques – and the marble pulpit and candelabrum. The overall harmony of the design, and the perfection of the details, make the Capella Palatina a truly unique monument.

Did You Know?

The chapel once had 50 windows, so that the intricate biblical mosaics would always be illuminated.

The chapel's architectural features are themselves fascinating, particularly the wooden ceiling, a masterpiece of Islamic-style carving.

↑ Palm trees providing shade in the public gardens outside Palazzo dei Normanni

The ceiling over the central section of the nave consists of carved wooden coffers with paintings in tempera.

The royal throne opposite the central apse has a segmented back bearing the Aragonese coat of arms.

The entrance is a 19th-century portal with a two-winged wooden door.

The brightly lit interior of the Cappella Palatina, revealing its wonders

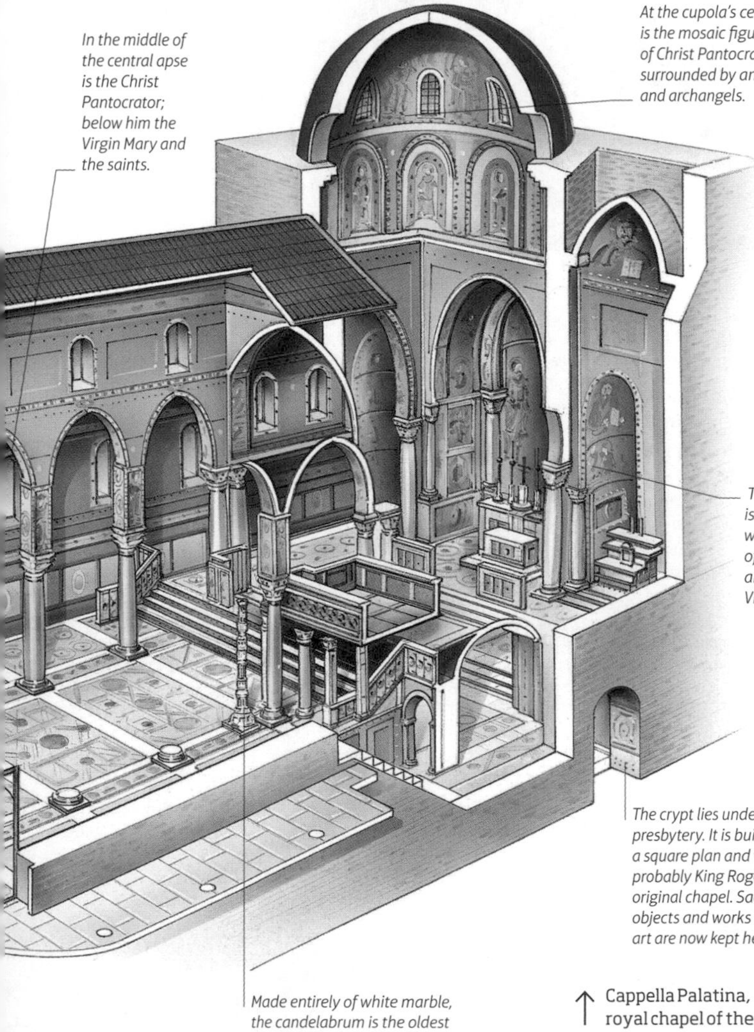

At the cupola's centre is the mosaic figure of Christ Pantocrator, surrounded by angels and archangels.

In the middle of the central apse is the Christ Pantocrator; below him the Virgin Mary and the saints.

The side apse is decorated with images of St Paul and the Virgin Mary.

The crypt lies under the presbytery. It is built on a square plan and was probably King Roger's original chapel. Sacred objects and works of art are now kept here.

Made entirely of white marble, the candelabrum is the oldest Romanesque work of art in Sicily.

Cappella Palatina, royal chapel of the Norman kings of Sicily

Strolling along Corso Vittorio Emanuele, with Italian flags blowing in the wind

EXPERIENCE MORE

Corso Vittorio Emanuele

C4

The main street in the heart of Palermo, Corso Vittorio Emanuele lies atop the Phoenician road that connected the ancient city with the seaside. The locals call this street "Cassaro", from the Arab *Al Qasar*, or castle, to which the road led. In the Middle Ages this road was the most important artery in the city, but in the 1500s it became an elegant street. In that period the street was extended to the sea and two city gates were built: Porta Felice to the north and Porta Nuova to the south, next to Palazzo dei Normanni. It was called Via Toledo during the Spanish period. The stretch between Porta Nuova and the Quattro Canti is home to several patrician mansions. On the western side is the former hospital of San Giacomo, now the Bonsignore barracks; the Baroque Collegio Massimo dei Gesuiti, the Regional Library; Palazzo Geraci, a Baroque residence rebuilt in the Rococo style; the Palazzo Belmonte-Riso, which houses the Contemporary Art Museum; and the 18th-century Palazzo Tarallo della Miraglia, restored as the Hotel Centrale. On the eastern side are San Salvatore, a lavishly decorated Baroque church, and San Giuseppe dei Teatini. Just beyond Vicolo Castelbuono is Piazza Bologni, which has several Baroque buildings, among them the Palazzo Alliata di Villafranca.

HIDDEN GEM
Room of Wonder

Unearthed during the renovation of a flat, Camera delle Meraviglie *(Via Porta di Castro 239)*, 5 minutes south of Piazza della Vittoria, is a secret room adorned with gold and silver Arabic inscriptions.

Piazza della Vittoria

B5

This square is completely occupied by the Villa Bonanno garden. In the middle is the Teatro Marmoreo fountain, built in honour of Philip V, with statues of the continents partly under this ruler's dominion (Europe, America, Asia and Africa). Archaeological digs have unearthed Roman villas and mosaics; the finds can be found in the Museo Archeologico Regionale *(p75)* and the Sala dell'Orfeo pavilion. Among the palazzi and churches facing the square are the Baroque Cappella della Soledad, with multicoloured marble and stucco decoration, and the former hospital of San Giacomo, with the lovely Norman Santa Maria Maddalena in the interior.

→
A figure from the Teatro Marmoreo fountain, Piazza della Vittoria

Palazzo dei Normanni

A5 Piazza Indipendenza 8:15am-5pm Mon, Fri-Sun (to 12:15pm Sun & hols) federicosecondo.org

The Arabs built this palace over the ruins of a Punic fortress in the 11th century. The following century it was enlarged and became the royal palace of the Norman king Roger II, with Arab architects and craftsmen building towers and pavilions for the king and his retinue. Not much is left from the Norman age, partly because the palace was abandoned when Frederick II left his Palermo court. The Spanish viceroys preferred to use the more modern Palazzo Steri.

The present-day appearance of the Palazzo dei Normanni, now the seat of the Sicilian Regional Assembly, dates back to alterations made in the 16th and 17th centuries. The entrance is in Piazza del Parlamento. A short walk uphill is the Maqueda courtyard, built in 1600 with three rows of arcades and a large staircase leading to the first floor and the Cappella Palatina *(p86)*, one of the few parts remaining from the Norman period.

The royal apartments, which now house the Sicilian Parliament, are on the second floor and can only be visited when accompanied by a guard. The most interesting room is the Sala di Re Ruggero, the walls and arches of which are covered with beautiful 12th-century mosaics with animal and plant motifs in a naturalistic vein that probably reveals a Persian influence: there are centaurs, leopards, lions, deer and even peacocks. The vault has geometric motifs and medallions with owls, deer, centaurs and lions. The tour ends with the Chinese Room, frescoed by Giovanni and Salvatore Patricolo, and the Sala Gialla, with tempera decoration on the vaults.

San Giovanni degli Eremiti

B6 Via dei Benedettini 18 091-651 50 19 9am-6:30pm Mon-Sun (to 1pm Sun & hols)

Built in 1132 for Roger II over the foundations of a Benedictine monastery that had been constructed in 581, San Giovanni degli Eremiti displays an Oriental influence. It was built by Arab-Norman craftsmen and labourers, and their work is most striking in the red domes and cubic forms. The delightful garden of citrus trees, pomegranate, roses and jasmine leads to the ruins of the monastery, a small cloister with twin columns and pointed arches.

The cross-plan interior has an aisle-less nave ending in the presbytery with three apses. The right-hand apse is covered by one of the red domes, while above the left-hand one is a fine bell tower with pointed windows and a smaller red dome on top.

DRINK

Reminiscent of a genteel time, Palermo's historic coffee bars remain a popular gathering place. Admire frescoes on the walls of Pasticceria Costa, sip coffee overlooking a palm-fringed garden at Teatro Massimo's literary-centric cafe, or visit the timeless Bar Marocco, where not much has changed since 1936.

Pasticceria Costa
D3 Via Maqueda 174 Mon pasticceria costa.com

Bistrò del Teatro
C2 Piazza G. Verdi Mon teatro massimo.it

Bar Marocco
B4 Via Vittorio Emanuele 494 barmarocco.it

↑ The Arab-Norman red domes of San Giovanni degli Eremiti casting a striking outline over the streets of Palermo

↑ The striking interior of San Giuseppe dei Teatini with its towering columns and frescoed ceiling

San Giuseppe dei Teatini

D4 Piazza Pretoria 091-331 239 7am-noon & 4:30-8pm daily

The Theatine congregation spared no expense in the construction of this church (1612–45). Despite the fact that the façade was finished in 1844 in Neo-Classical style, the church exudes a Baroque spirit, beginning with the cupola covered with majolica tiles. The two-aisle nave is flanked by huge columns, the ceiling is frescoed and the walls are covered with polychrome marble decoration. On either side of the entrance are two marble stoups held up by angels. The chapels are richly decorated with stucco and frescoes, and the high altar is made of semi-precious stones.

PICTURE PERFECT
Historic Centre

Take a self-guided tour through the historic centre to find the city's most photogenic spots. Look up and capture laundry strung across narrow alleys and elaborate gardens dangling from balconies.

8   

Museo Regionale d'Arte Moderna e Contemporanea Belmonte-Riso

C4 Corso Vittorio Emanuele 365 10am-7:30pm Tue, Wed & Sun, 10am-11:30pm Thu-Sat museoarte contemporanea.it

In a restored palazzo right in front of the Piazza Bologni, the Contemporary Art Gallery was conceived as a multi-functional centre, with a bookshop, café and multimedia room on the premises. The palazzo itself was built in 1784 by Venanzio Marvuglia, who was one of the most prolific architects of the time. The collection has been laid out so the whole building can be admired; works placed inside and outside take you through old courtyards and hidden corners. Works by great artists such as Pietro Consagra, Allesandro Bazan and Carla Accardi are part of the permanent collection.

Chiesa del Gesù and Casa Professa

D4 Piazza Casa Professa 091-33 22 13 9:30am-1:30pm & 4-7pm Mon-Sat, 9am-12:30pm & 5-6:30pm Sun & hols

This church perhaps represents the peak of Baroque art in Palermo. The late 16th-century façade was one of the sets for the film

→ One of the four concave façades that border the 17th-century Quattro Canti

The intersection of Corso Vittorio Emanuele and Via Maqueda is Palermo's most fashionable square: Quattro Canti. This Baroque piazza dates from 1600.

Il Gattopardo (The Leopard). Work on the decoration began in 1597 and was interrupted permanently when the Jesuits were expelled in 1860. The interior is covered with marble inlay – walls, columns and floor – in a profusion of forms and colours, blending in well with the fine stuccoes of Giacomo Serpotta, the imitation bas-relief columns and the various decorative motifs. The pulpit in the middle of the nave was the work of the Genoese School (1646).

To the right of the church is the western section of the Casa Professa, with an 18th-century cloister affording access to the City Library.

Quattro Canti

D4 Piazza Vigliena

The intersection of Corso Vittorio Emanuele and Via Maqueda is Palermo's most fashionable square: Quattro Canti. This Baroque piazza dates from 1600, when the new town plan was put into effect and the city was divided into four parts, called *Mandamenti*: Capo in the northwest, Castellammare or Loggia in the northeast, La Kalsa to the southeast and Albergheria in the southwest. The piazza is rounded, shaped by the concave façades of the four corner buildings (hence the name) with superimposed architectural orders – Doric, Corinthian and Ionic. Each façade is decorated with a delightful fountain that rises to the height of the second floor of the buildings and statues of the *Mandamenti* patron saints, of the seasons and of the Spanish kings.

SHOP

La Stanza di Carta

In this small, well-ordered bookstore, towering wooden shelves and secret, tucked-away nooks hold many new, used and rare volumes. The owner of La Stanza di Carta (which translates as "the paper room") is a passionate bookseller. He assures patrons that in his gorgeous shop "you can find what you didn't even think to look for".

D4 Via Giuseppe D'Alessi 1 10am-2pm & 4-7pm daily

Sant'Orsola

D5 Via Maqueda 091-616 23 21 8:30-11am daily (oratory visits by request only)

Sant'Orsola was built in the early 17th century by the Society of St Ursula, known as "Dei Negri" because of the dark habits the members wore during processions. The late Renaissance façade is decorated with figures of souls in Purgatory and angels. Three skulls lie on the architrave. Sant'Orsola's aisle-less interior is an example of a light-filled Baroque church, with deep semicircular chapels linked by galleries. The vault over the nave is decorated with the fresco *The Glory of St Ursula* and two medallions depicting Faith and Charity. The painting *The Martyrdom of St Ursula* by Pietro Novelli is in the second chapel on the right, while frescoes of scenes of the saint's life are on the vault. Another work by Novelli, *Madonna with the Salvator Mundi*, is in the sacristy. From the sacristy there is access to the Oratorio di Sant'Orsola, decorated with 17th-century paintings and stucco sculpture.

Chiesa del Carmine

D5 Via Giovanni Grasso 13a 091-651 2018 8:45-10:45am Mon-Sat

This church, seat of the Carmelite friars, dates from the 1600s. It lies on a much higher level than the nearby Mercato di Ballarò and is topped by a cupola covered with multicoloured majolica tiles supported by four Atlantes. The interior is dominated by an altar resting on pairs of spiral columns decorated with stuccoes by Giuseppe and Giacomo Serpotta (1683) of scenes from the life of Mary. The painting by Italian artist Pietro Novelli, *The Vision of Sant'Andrea Corsini*, is also worth a look.

Did You Know?

Most Italians don't understand Sicilian: it is recognised by UNESCO as an endangered language.

Teatro Massimo

C2 Piazza Giuseppe Verdi For tours: 9:30am-6pm Mon-Sun During rehearsals teatro massimo.it

The Teatro Massimo is one of the symbols of Palermo's rebirth, designed in 1864 by Italian architect Giovanni Battista Filippo Basile. To make room for it, the city walls of Porta Maqueda, the Aragonese quarter, San Giuliano convent and church, and the Chiesa delle Stimmate di San Francesco and its monastery were demolished. Dedicated to King Victor

Emanuel II, its 7,700 sq m (9,200 sq yd) size makes this the biggest opera house in Italy, and one of the largest in Europe. The theatre is now home to five rows of boxes, a lavishly decorated gallery and a ceiling frescoed by Ettore Maria Bergler and Rocco Lentini. The entrance, with its Corinthian columns, is also monumental in style.

Groups of ten or more can book in advance to attend the Cocktail Tour, which is a special guided tour of the theatre that includes having a cocktail in the Royal Box.

A sea of colour at the Mercato di Ballarò in Palermo's Albergheria quarter

14 The Albergheria Quarter

C5

The Albergheria is one of the poorest and most run-down quarters in the old town, but also one of the most intriguing. A highlight is the Mercato di Ballarò, a vivid combination of colours, smells and atmosphere. This noisy and gritty bazaar is a jumble of Sicilian fruit, vegetables, meat, fish and household items. A visit is not complete without tasting delicious *panelle* (pancakes made using chickpea flour), served in a bread roll with some excellent seasoning.

Within a stone's throw of the market is the unassuming Tower of San Nicolò dell'Alergheria. Erected in the 14th century to defend the walls of the Cassaro, you can get a rare, 360-degree view of Palermo's beautiful rooftops, impressive domes and countless spires from the soaring terrace.

An orchestra rehearsing in the opulent Teatro Massimo opera house, and *(inset)* its grand façade at dusk

EAT

Moltivolti

Intertwining a bar and restaurant with co-working and meeting space, Moltivolti is a fusion of industrial interiors, an ethnic menu and an inclusive, welcoming atmosphere.

C5 Via GM Puglia 21
moltivolti.org

Ballarak Ballarò

This hipster craft brewery offers more than an assortment of lagers, ales and pilsners; it also serves enticing pub grub.

C4 Via Saladino 7
ballarak.it

Ai Normanni

Dine on dishes such as spaghetti with truffles, prawns and sea urchins from Ai Normanni's seasonal seafood menu.

B5 Piazza della Vittoria 25
ainormanni.com

A SHORT WALK AROUND PIAZZA DELLA VITTORIA

Distance 1 km (0.6 miles) **Time** 15 minutes
Nearest bus stop Re Ruggero

Piazza della Vittoria, opposite the Palazzo dei Normanni, is one of the city's major squares. Since the time of the Roman *castrum superius* (military camp), this area has been the military, political and administrative heart of Sicily. Religious prestige was added in the 12th century when the magnificent Cattedrale di Palermo was built nearby. In the 17th and 18th centuries the square was the venue for public festivities. It became a public garden in the early 1900s, surrounded by important monuments such as Porta Nuova and Palazzo Sclafani.

The former hospital of **San Giacomo**

The imposing **Porta Nuova** *was built in 1569 to commemorate Charles V's arrival in Palermo in 1535.*

CORSO VITTORIO EMANUELE

Palazzo dei Normanni (p89) *has always been the palace of the city's rulers. The exterior still has traces of the original Arab-Norman architecture.*

PIAZZA DEL PARLAMENTO

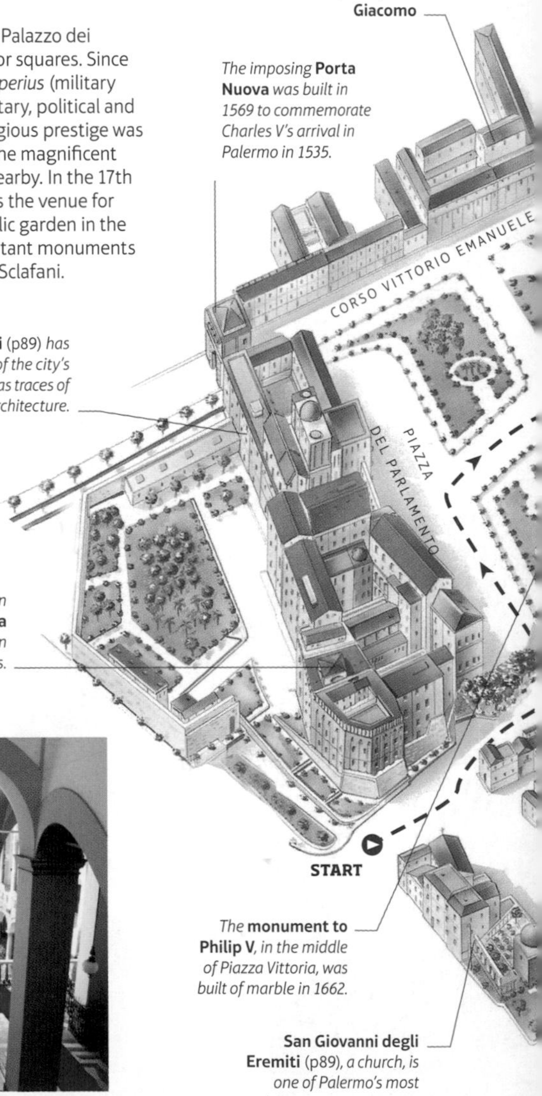

Founded in 1130 by the Norman king Roger II, the **Cappella Palatina** (p86) *chapel has an extraordinary cycle of mosaics.*

START

The **monument to Philip V**, *in the middle of Piazza Vittoria, was built of marble in 1662.*

San Giovanni degli Eremiti (p89), *a church, is one of Palermo's most important monuments,. partly because of its unique Arab-Norman architecture.*

↑ A stairway leading to the Palazzo dei Normanni's elegant cloister

PIAZZA SETT'ANGELI
FINISH
PIAZZA DELLA VITTORIA
PIAZZA SAN GIOVANNI DECOLLATO
VIA DEL BASTIONE
PALAZZO SCLAFANI
0 metres 100
0 yards 100
N

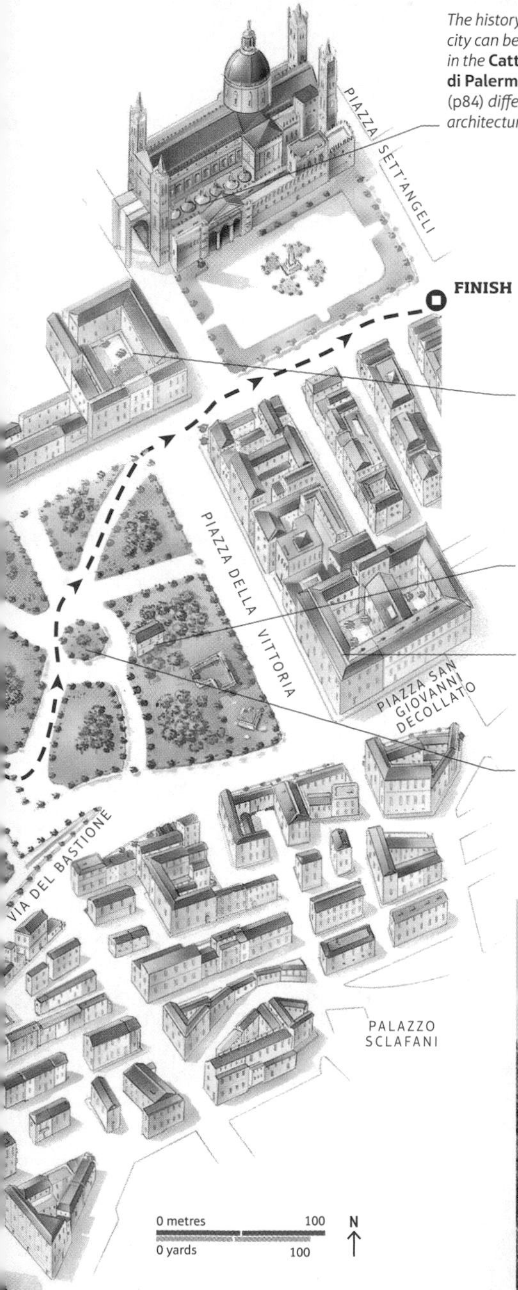

The history of the city can be traced in the **Cattedrale di Palermo's** (p84) *different architectural styles.*

WEST PALERMO
Around Piazza della Vittoria

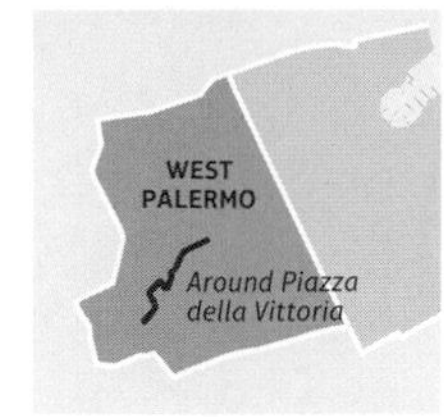

Locator Map
For more detail see p82

Palazzo Arcivescovile *and* **Museo Diocesano**

Villa Bonanno, *a leafy green park filled with plam trees, occupies the Piazza della Vittoria*

The 14th-century **Palazzo Sclafani** *is one of the oldest mansions in the city.*

Piazza della Vittoria (p88) *is a huge square that is entirely occupied by the palm trees and well-tended gardens around Villa Bonanno.*

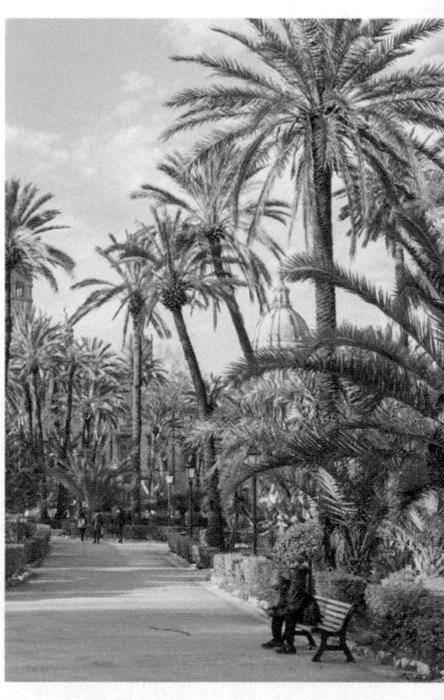

→ Palm-lined paths in the peaceful and verdant Villa Bonanno

Sun loungers on Mondello Beach

BEYOND THE CENTRE

The destruction of the 16th-century defensive ramparts took place in the late 1700s, but it was only after the Unification of Italy that Palermo expanded westwards past the city walls, which involved making new roads and demolishing old quarters. The heart of town shifted to Piazzas Verdi and Castelnuovo, where the Massimo and Politeama theatres were built. This expansion also meant the disappearance of many Arab-Norman gardens the rulers had used for hunting. At this time, "Greater Palermo" was created – an area that now includes Mondello and Monreale Cathedral.

Must See

1 Duomo di Monreale

Experience More

2 Casina Cinese
3 Parco della Favorita
4 Mondello
5 Museo Etnografico Pitré
6 Catacombe dei Cappuccini
7 Santo Spirito
8 La Cuba
9 Teatro Politeama Garibaldi
10 Castello della Zisa
11 San Giovanni dei Lebbrosi
12 Ponte dell'Ammiraglio

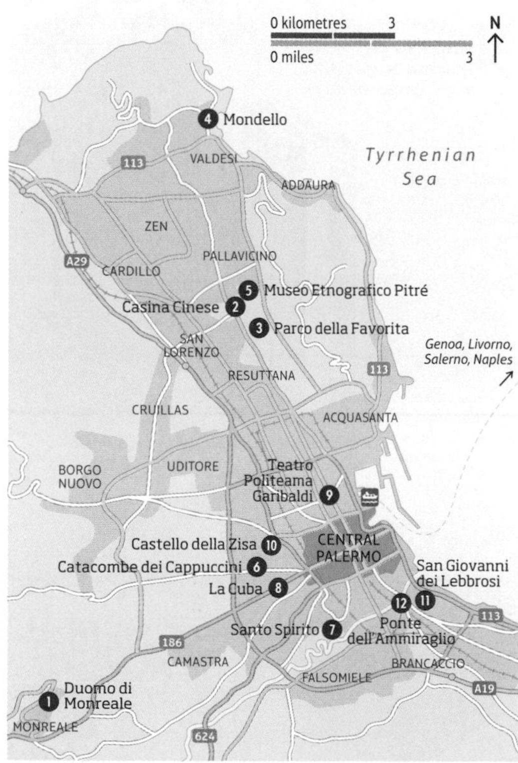

1

DUOMO DI MONREALE

Piazza Guglielmo II 1 389 from Piazza Indipendenza Times vary, check website monrealeduomo.it

The cathedral at Monreale sits high above the Conca d'Oro, a fertile plain overlooking Palermo. Despite its rather austere exterior, the cathedral's interior is embellished with the most extensive and significant mosaic cycle of its kind in Sicily.

Magnificently adorned, and with a splendid view of the Conca d'Oro, Duomo di Monreale is one of the greatest sights of Norman Sicily. Founded in 1172 by William II, it flanks a Benedictine monastery. The interior glitters with mosaics carried out by Sicilian and Byzantine artists – commissioned by a king who wanted to rival the power of the Archbishop of Palermo. Like Cefalù, and later Palermo, it was to serve as a royal sepulchre, housing the tombs of William I and William II.

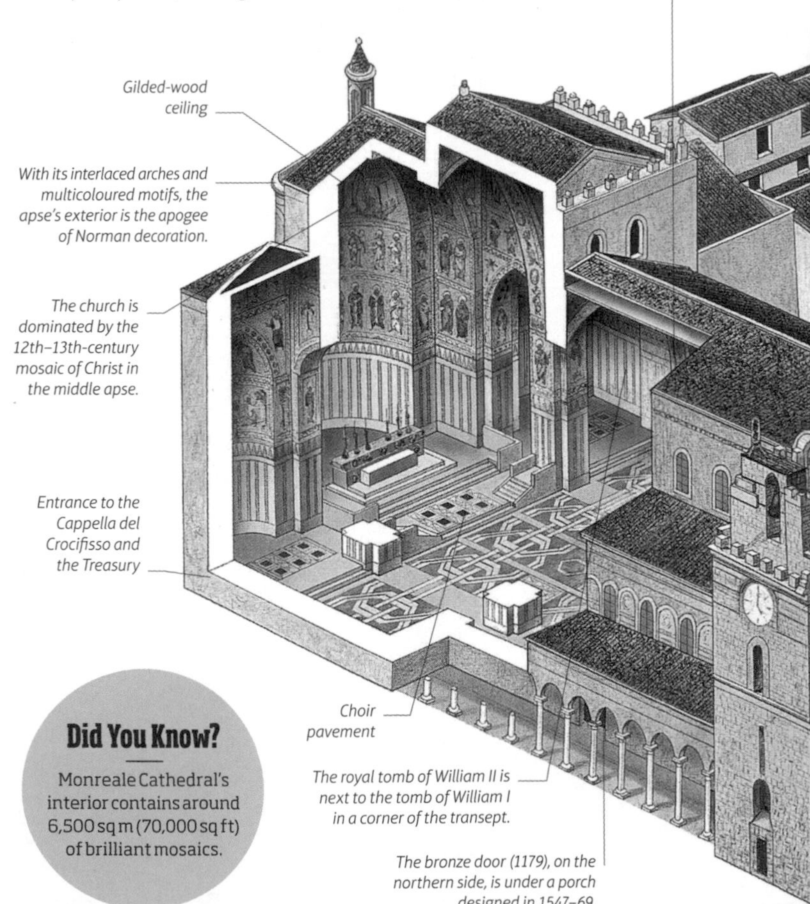
The stupendous 12th–13th-century mosaics illustrate scenes from the New and Old Testaments.
Gilded-wood ceiling
With its interlaced arches and multicoloured motifs, the apse's exterior is the apogee of Norman decoration.
The church is dominated by the 12th–13th-century mosaic of Christ in the middle apse.
Entrance to the Cappella del Crocifisso and the Treasury
Choir pavement
The royal tomb of William II is next to the tomb of William I in a corner of the transept.
The bronze door (1179), on the northern side, is under a porch designed in 1547–69.

Did You Know?

Monreale Cathedral's interior contains around 6,500 sq m (70,000 sq ft) of brilliant mosaics.

↑ Monreale Cathedral's fortress-like façade rising above Piazza Guglielmo at dusk

↑ The enormous mosaic of Christ Pantocrator (12th to 13th century)

The cloister, a masterpiece of Norman art

A wing of the original monastery lies over the southern portico.

Cloister columns made by skilled craftsmen from throughout southern Italy

The portal door has 42 elaborately framed images.

↑ The cathedral at Monreale, a triumph of Norman architecture

Casina Cinese, built in the 18th century for Ferdinand I and his wife

HIDDEN GEMS IN THE CITY

The English Garden
Via della Libertà
A wonderful place to seek refuge from the chaos of the city.

Foro Italico
Foro Italico Umberto I
A promenade along Palermo's breakwaters.

Monreale Cloisters
Piazza Guglielmo II 1
An Arab-Norman stylized garden encircled by columns.

EXPERIENCE MORE

Casina Cinese

Viale Duca degli Abruzzi, Parco della Favorita 091-707 14 08 9am-5pm Tue-Sun (to 1pm Sun & public hols)

At the edge of the Parco della Favorita, the former hunting grounds of the Bourbons, is the "little Chinese palace", the summer residence of Ferdinand I and his wife Maria Carolina during their period of exile in Sicily. The palace was designed by Venanzio Marvuglia in 1799 and, it seems, the king himself had a hand in the building's Oriental architecture, which was much in vogue at the time. Ferdinand I entertained such illustrious guests as Horatio Nelson and his wife, Lady Hamilton, here.

The Casina Cinese was the first example of eclectic architecture in Palermo, a combination of Chinese decorative motifs and Gothic, Egyptian and Arab elements. Overall it is an extravagant work, exemplified by details such as the repetition of bells in the shape of a pagoda on the fence, the cornices and the roof. The interior is equally flamboyant: Neo-Classical stuccoes and paintings are combined with 18th-century chinoiserie. The building is undergoing an extensive renovation to bring it back to its original splendour.

SANCTUARY OF SANTA ROSALIA ON MONTE PELLEGRINO

On Monte Pellegrino is the Sanctuary dedicated to Santa Rosalia *(right)*, the patron saint of Palermo. Daughter of the Duke of Sinibaldo, Rosalia decided to lead the life of a hermit in a cave. Five centuries after her death in 1166, the discovery of her remains coincided exactly with the end of the plague that had struck the city. The saint has been venerated twice a year since, with a procession through the city.

Parco della Favorita

Viale Ercole, Viale Diana

This public park, unfortunately in a state of neglect, extends for almost 3 km (2 miles) behind Monte Pellegrino. Originally a hunting reserve, King Ferdinand I turned it into a garden in 1799, when he fled to Palermo after being forced into exile from Naples by Napoleon's troops. At the end of Viale d'Ercole is a marble fountain with a statue of Hercules, a copy of the famous *Farnese Hercules* that the king had wanted for himself in his court at Naples.

Most of the park is occupied by sports facilities. On the edge of the park there are many villas built in the 18th century as summer residences for the Sicilian nobility. The most interesting are the Villa Sofia, now a hospital; Villa Castelnuovo, an agricultural institute; and Villa Niscemi, mentioned in di Lampedusa's novel *The Leopard* *(see p159)*, now the venue for cultural activities.

4

Mondello

10 km (6 miles) N of Palermo

A favourite with Palermitans, Mondello beach lies a short distance from the centre of the town, between the rocky promontories of Monte Pellegrino and Monte Gallo.

Mondello was once a small village of tuna fishermen, centred around a 15th-century square tower, but in the last 100 years it has become a residential area immersed in greenery. Mondello's golden age was at the turn of the 19th century, when a kind of garden-city was founded and well-to-do Palermitans had Art Nouveau villas built here. The Kursaal bathhouse, built on piles in the sea a few yards from the beach, also dates from this period. Designed by Rudolph Stualket in the Art Nouveau style, it is decorated with mythological figures and sea monsters. Mondello is a popular town, particularly on summer evenings when city dwellers come to escape the heat and dine in the many fish and seafood restaurants in the old fishing quarter.

5

Museo Etnografico Pitré

Viale Duca degli Abruzzi 091-616 01 24 9am-1pm Mon-Fri (except Wed), 9am-1pm & 3:30-5:30pm Wed Sat & Sun

The Ethnographic Museum has a collection of about 4,000 exhibits documenting Sicilian life, traditions and folk art. Rooms feature local embroidery and weaving, along with sections on traditional costumes and rugs. Cases contain ceramics and glassware, as well as a fine collection of oil lamps, traditional Sicilian carts, late 19th-century glass painting, and carts and floats dedicated to Santa Rosalia. The Sala del Teatrino dell' Opera dei Pupi has a number of rod puppets, traditional characters in Sicilian puppet opera, as well as playbills decorated with scenes taken from the puppeteers' works, while the Sala dei Presepi features more than 300 nativity scenes.

EAT

Bar Antico Chiosco

Grab a *brioscia con gelato e panna* (ice-cream in a brioche) from Bar Antico Chiosco near the water's edge.

Piazza Mondello 4, Mondello 7am-1am Thu-Tue

Bye Bye Blues

Splash out at this culinary standout, which houses an open-plan wine cellar and Sicily's first female Michelin-starred chef.

Via del Garofalo 23, Mondello 12:30-2:30pm & 7:30-11:30pm Tue-Sun byebyeblues.it

←

Palermitans and visitors enjoying the sunshine at the beach of Mondello

↑ Exploring the remains of some of Palermo's citizens at the Catacombe dei Cappuccini

6 Catacombe dei Cappuccini

Via Cappuccini 091-652 41 56 or 329-415 04 62 9am-1pm, 3-6pm daily Oct-Mar: Sun pm

The catacombs of the Capuchins contain the bodies – some mummified, others skeletons – of the prelates and well-to-do citizens of Palermo. They are divided according to sex, profession and social standing, wearing their best clothes, some of which are moth-eaten. You can even see the cells where the corpses were put to dry. At the end of the stairway is the body of the first friar "buried" here, Fra' Silvestro da Gubbio, who died in 1599. In 1881, internment in the catacombs ceased, but on display in the Cappella dell'Addolorata is the body of a little girl who died in 1920 and was so skilfully embalmed that she seems asleep. In the outdoor cemetery behind the catacombs is the tomb of writer Giuseppe di Lampedusa.

7 Santo Spirito

Via Santo Spirito, Cimitero di Sant'Orsola 091-422 691 8am-noon daily

Lying inside the Sant'Orsola Cemetery, this Norman church was founded by Archbishop Gualtiero Offamilio in 1178. It is also known as the "Chiesa dei Vespri" because, on 31 March 1282, at the hour of Vespers, a Sicilian uprising against the Angevin rulers began right in front of the church.

Simple and elegant, like all Norman churches, Santo Spirito has black volcanic stone inlay on its right side and on the apse. The two-aisle nave with three apses is bare but full of atmosphere. The wooden ceiling has floral ornamentation and there is a fine wooden crucifix over the high altar.

→ The grandiose Neo-Classical Teatro Politeama Garibaldi

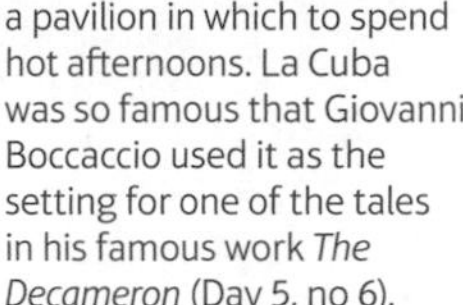

SHOP

Boutique Torregrossa

At this upmarket Palermo institution you'll find high-end Italian and international designer fashion.

Via della Libertà 5 9:45am-1pm & 4-5:45pm Tue-Sat, 4-7:45pm Sun & Mon torregrossa boutique.com

8

La Cuba

Corso Calatafimi 100 091-590 299 9am-6:30pm Mon-Sun (to 1pm Sun & hols)

William II ordered this Fatimite-style Norman palace to be built in 1180. It too stood in a large park, the Genoardo, surrounded by an artificial pond, and served as a pavilion in which to spend hot afternoons. La Cuba was so famous that Giovanni Boccaccio used it as the setting for one of the tales in his famous work *The Decameron* (Day 5, no 6).

The rectangular construction acquires rhythm and movement from the pointed blind arcading. The interior ran around an atrium that may have been open to the air, and recesses under the small towers originally would have housed fountains.

9 

Teatro Politeama Garibaldi

Piazza Ruggero Settimo 091-607 25 32 For guided tours at 11:30am Mon-Sat

This historic theatre is in the heart of modern-day Palermo, at the corner of Via Ruggero Settimo and tree-lined Viale della Libertà, the city's "outdoor living room". Giuseppe Damiani Almeyda designed the Neo-Classical building in 1867–74. The theatre's semicircular shape resembles a horseshoe, while the columns in the two tiers of colonnades are in the Doric and Ionian orders. The exterior is frescoed in Pompeii red and gold, in tune with the Neo-Classical movement at the time. The façade is a triumphal arch whose attic level is decorated with sculpture crowned by a chariot. While the Teatro Massimo was closed, the Politeama was the centre of the city's cultural life.

Home to the Orchestra Sinfonica Siciliana, the theatre still plays host to operatic and theatrical performances between October and June.

La Cuba was so famous that Giovanni Boccaccio used it as the setting for one of the tales in his famous work *The Decameron* (Day 5, no 6).

10

Castello della Zisa

Piazza Zisa 1 091-652 02 69 9am-6:30pm Mon-Sun (to 1pm Sun & hols)

This remarkable palace, built in 1165–7, once overlooked a pond and was surrounded by a large park with many streams and fish ponds. Sadly, the Zisa Castle now stands in the middle of an ugly fringe area of Palermo. After years of neglect, the castle has now been restored and once again merits the name given to it by the Arabs – *aziz*, or splendid. The handsome exterior gives the impression of a rectangular fortress; the blind arcades, which once enclosed small double lancet windows, lend it elegance. Two square towers stand on the short sides of the castle. On the ground floor is the Sala della Fontana (Fountain Hall), one of the rooms with a cross plan and exedrae (semicircular recesses) on three sides. The cross vault above is connected to the side recesses by means of a series of *muqarnas* (small stalactite vaults typical of Arab architecture). Along the walls is a fine mosaic frieze. Water gushing from the fountain runs along a gutter from the wall to the pavement and then pours into two square fish ponds. This water would have served as an air conditioning system, probably one of the first in history, cooling down the warm sea breeze entering the Sala della Fontana via an ingenious air circulation system that also featured air vents.

The second floor of the palace is home to the Museo d'Arte Islamica, which houses Islamic art and various gold and silver objects.

San Giovanni dei Lebbrosi

Via Cappello 38 091-475 024 9-11am, 4-7pm Mon-Sat (am only Tue), 7:30am-12:30pm Sun & hols

One of the oldest Norman churches in Sicily lies in the middle of a luxuriant garden of palms. San Giovanni dei Lebbrosi was founded in 1071 by Roger I and, in 1119, a lepers' hospital was built next to it, hence its name. It was most probably constructed by Arab craftsmen and workers, as can be seen in the pointed arches crowned by arched lintels (also visible in San Giovanni degli Eremiti, *p89;* and San Cataldo, *p74*). The façade has a small porch with a bell tower above. Inside the church there are three apses and a ceiling with trusses. Digs to the right of the church have unearthed remains of the Saracen Yahia fortress, which once defended south-eastern Palermo.

Ponte dell'Ammiraglio

Via dei Mille

A bridge without a river, Ponte dell'Ammiraglio, or the Admiral's Bridge, used to span the Oreto river until it was diverted in 1938. The oddly situated overpass is made of

large cambered blocks of limestone resting on 12 pointed arches, five of them no more than small openings in the imposts. This beautiful and amazingly well-preserved bridge was built in the second quarter of the 12th century by George of Antioch, Roger II's High Admiral (the *ammiraglio* of the name), but is now a rather incongruous sight, isolated without a river flowing beneath it.

The iconic bridge is an outstanding example of medieval engineering and a testament to the importance of civil architecture of the Norman age. Named a UNESCO World Heritage Site in 2015, the bridge was one of nine Arab-Norman Palermo civil and religious structures listed. Constructed entirely of stone, the large Ponte dell Ammiraglio stands as a remarkable engineering feat for its time.

↑ The magnificent Arabic fortress-like façade of Castello della Zisa

Constructed entirely of stone, the large Ponte dell Ammiraglio stands as a remarkable engineering feat for its time.

↑ The medieval Ponte dell'Ammiraglio, or Admiral's Bridge, no longer spanning a river

DRINK

White
Sip cocktails from your boat or come ashore for the buffet at this stylish bar on a gulf-side pier.

Scalo dell'Arenella 66, Aranella
9am-2am Tue-Sun
whiteclub.it

Plait Mare
On the Addaura seafront, the splendid terrace of Plait Mare provides a front-row seat to beautiful views.

Lungomare Cristoforo Colombo 2847, Addaura
093-20 570 5519

Charleston
Drink on the chic terrace at this Moorish-style palace of the Belle Époque era.

Viale Regina Elena 37/39, Mondello
1-2:30pm & 7:30-11:30pm Thu-Sat
ristorante charleston.com

EXPERIENCE SICILY

Exploring the lively market in Catania

The historic town and peaceful beach of Cefalù

THE EGADI ISLANDS AND THE NORTHWEST

Over the centuries, this area of Sicily has been particularly exposed to influences from different colonizing civilizations. The Phoenicians settled in Mozia and founded harbour towns at Palermo and Solunto. They were followed by the Greeks and then the Arabs, who began their conquest of the island at Marsala. These cultures are still very much alive in the names of the towns and sights, in the architecture, and in the layout of the towns from Marsala to Mazara del Vallo.

Unfortunately, northwestern Sicily is also one of the areas most affected by the scourges of uncontrolled property development and lack of care for the environment. Prime examples of this are the huge area of unattractive houses between Palermo and Castellammare and the poorly reconstructed towns in the Valle del Belice after the 1968 earthquake. However, there are other towns pursuing a policy of preserving and reassessing their history. Erice is one of these; its medieval architecture and town plan have been preserved, and many of the churches have been converted into art and culture centres. The same holds true for Cefalù, Nicosia, Sperlinga and the two Petralias.

USTICA 30

Tyrrhenian
Sea

Capo San Vito
13 SAN VITO LO CAPO
Golfo di Cófano
Castelluzzo
2 RISERVA DELLO ZINGARO
Aeroporto di Palermo
Isola delle Femmine
Terrasini
A29
Carini
Montelepre
Scopello di Sopra
Balestrate
Partinico
14
A29
113
Lago Poma
CASTELLAMMARE DEL GOLFO
15 ALCAMO
San Cipirello
624
Cagliari
ERICE
3
Valderice
TRAPANI
7
Isola di Levanzo
Isola Marettimo
Museo del Sale
Paceco
A29d
Fulgatore
5
EGADI ISLANDS
Favignana
Aeroporto di Trapani-Birgi
Isola Favignana
SEGESTA 4
Calatafimi
Camporeale
Rilievo
A29
MOZIA 10
115
Val di Mázara
Tabaccaro
SALEMI 12
GIBELLINA
17
Roccamena
Belice
MARSALA 8
188
Gibellina Vecchia
Santa Ninfa
Lago di Garcia
Salaparuta
Poggioreale
Strasatti
Pizzolato
115
Lago della Trinità
Partanna
Valle
CASTELVETRANO 9
Montevago
Santa Margherita di Belice
Belice
Capo Feto
11
MAZARA DEL VALLO
A29
Pantelleria
Campobello di Mazara
Sambuca di Sicilia
Menfi
SELINUNTE 6
Marinella di Selinunte
Caltabellotta
115
Sciacca
Seccagrande

0 kilometres 20
0 miles 20
N

THE EGADI ISLANDS AND THE NORTHWEST

Must Sees

1. Cefalù
2. Riserva dello Zingaro
3. Erice
4. Segesta
5. Egadi Islands
6. Selinunte

Experience More

7. Trapani
8. Marsala
9. Castelvetrano
10. Mozia
11. Mazara del Vallo
12. Salemi
13. San Vito lo Capo
14. Castellammare del Golfo
15. Alcamo
16. Corleone
17. Gibellina
18. Solunto
19. Piana degli Albanesi
20. Polizzi Generosa
21. Gangi
22. Caccamo
23. Petralia Sottana
24. Petralia Soprana
25. Castel di Tusa
26. Sperlinga
27. Bagheria
28. Nicosia
29. Santo Stefano di Camastra
30. Ustica

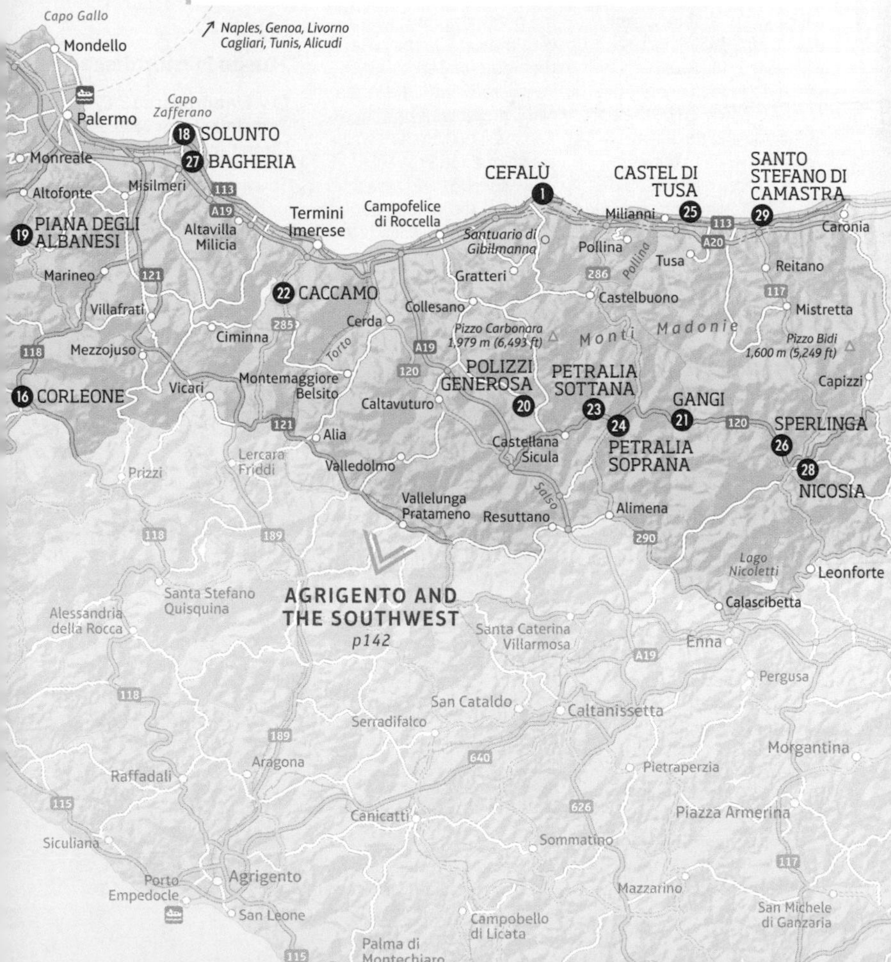

1

CEFALÙ

D3 Falcone e Borsellino Messina-Palermo
Corso Ruggero 77; www.comune.cefalu.pa.it

Cefalù was recorded for the first time in 396 BC, but it's more famous for its medieval monuments. Leave your car at Piazza Garibaldi to take a stroll around the town. Follow Corso Ruggero to reach the open space of Piazza Duomo.

Piazza Duomo

This lively square, dominated by the cathedral and the steep Rocca, is the heart of Cefalù. On the southern side are the Oratorio del Santissimo Sacramento; Palazzo Maria, which was probably Roger II's palace; and Palazzo Piraino, with its late 16th-century ashlar door. To the north, the square is bordered by the Seminario and the Palazzo Vescovile, while to the west is the Palazzo del Municipio (Town Hall), which incorporates the former Santa Caterina monastery.

Cathedral

Piazza Duomo Times vary, check website cattedraledicefalu.com

Cefalù Cathedral is one of Sicily's major Norman monuments; it is now a UNESCO World Heritage site. Building began in 1131 under Roger II and continued after his death. The façade is flanked by two bell towers. On the right-hand side you can see the interlaced arch motifs of the three side apses. The nave's wooden ceiling shows an Islamic influence, while the presbytery is covered with mosaics. In the apse is the figure of Christ Pantocrator with the Virgin Mary, archangels and the Apostles; on the choir walls are saints and prophets, while cherubs and seraphim decorate the vault. A door on the northern aisle leads to a delightful cloister.

INSIDER TIP
Cefalù Beach

Cefalù's long stretch of beach at the foot of a rocky promontory features crystalline waters, golden sands, and a gently sloping seabed. Visit in late spring and early autumn when the water is warm and the crowds are thinner.

Corso Ruggero

This avenue reaches across the old town, starting from Piazza Garibaldi. A few steps on your left is Palazzo Osterio Magno, built in the 13th and 14th centuries and said to have been the residence of Roger II. The palace is currently closed for renovation. The building almost opposite houses the remains of the ancient Roman road (open 9am–4:30pm). Continuing to the right, you will come to Piazzetta Spinola, with the Church of Santo Stefano (or Delle Anime Purganti), its Baroque façade complemented by an elegant double staircase.

Museo Mandralisca

V. Mandralisca 13 9am-7pm daily (Aug:to 11pm) fondazionemandralisca.it

This museum was founded by Enrico Piraino, Baron of Mandralisca, in the 19th century and includes fine

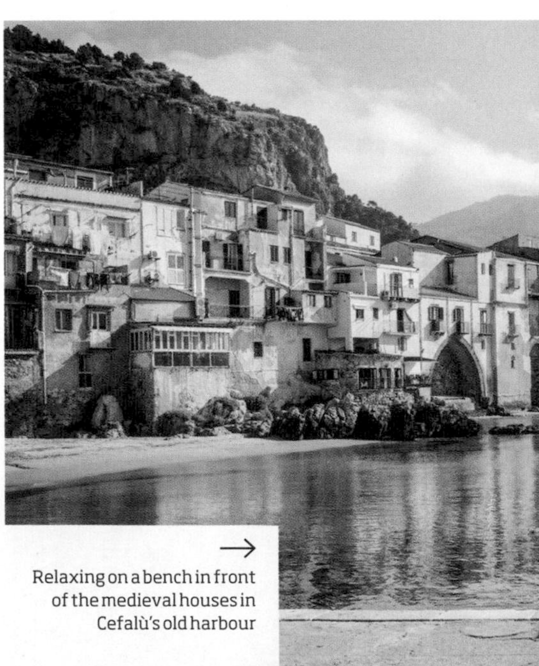

→ Relaxing on a bench in front of the medieval houses in Cefalù's old harbour

archaeological, shell and coin collections. It also houses an art gallery and a library with thousands of historic and scientific works, including incunabula (early printed books from around the 16th century) and nautical charts.

Among several important Renaissance paintings is the *Portrait of an Unknown Man* by Antonello da Messina. Archaeological exhibits include a late Hellenistic mosaic, a 4th-century BC vase and a collection of playing cards made out of precious materials.

PIAZZA CRISPI
V. PORPORA
VIA C. ORTOLANI DI BORDONARO
VIA VETERANI
PIAZZA MARINA
VIA GIUDECCA
Palazzo Vescovile
Piazza Duomo ①
Museo Mandralisca ④
② Cathedral
Lavatoio
VIA VITTORIO EMANUELE
VIA 25 NOVEMBRE
Municipio
Oratorio del Santissimo Sacramento
VIA GIOENI
CORSO RUGGERO
VIA COSTA
Via Vittorio Emanuele ⑤
VIA N. BOTTA
VIA VANNI
Palazzo Osterio Magno
③ Corso Ruggero
Tempio di Diana
VIA SPINUZZA
PIAZZA CRISTOFORO COLOMBO
VIA D. PARAMURO
PIAZZA GARIBALDI
Chiesa Santa Maria della Catena
⑥ La Rocca
LUNG. GIUSEPPE GIARDINA
VIA PRESTISIMONE
VIA CAVOUR
VIA G. MATTEOTTI
VIA UMBERTO I
VIA S. PASQUALE
VIA ROMA
VIA GIUSEPPE PITRÈ
VIA GIBILMANNA
VIA ALDO MORO
VIA PIETRAGROSSA
Cefalù Railway Station
Santuario di Gibilmanna 11 km (7 miles) ⑦
0 metres 200
0 yards 200
N

⑤

Via Vittorio Emanuele

This street runs along the seafront, separated by a row of medieval houses facing the bay. Under one of these is the famous Lavatoio, the stone fountain known as U'Ciumi, or river, which was mentioned by the medieval writer Boccaccio and was once used for washing clothes.

The lovely Porta Marina is the only remaining city gate of the original four that once afforded access to the town. It leads to the colourful fishermen's quarter, where scenes were shot for the film *Cinema Paradiso (p164)*.

La Rocca

From Piazza Garibaldi a path halfway up the hill offers a fine view of the old town and the sea and leads to the ruins of the Byzantine fortifications and the prehistoric sanctuary known as the Tempio di Diana. On the top are the ruins of a 12th–13th-century castle.

Santuario di Gibilmanna

Contrada Valle Grande, Frazione di Gibilmanna 0921-421 835 9am-7pm Mon-Fri, 8am-9pm Sat & Sun

On Pizzo Sant'Angelo is this sanctuary built in the 17th and 18th centuries and the most popular pilgrimage site in Sicily. The former convent stables house the Museo dell' Ordine, the museum of the Capuchin friars, with paintings, sculptures and vestments.

A SHORT WALK
CEFALÙ

Distance 1 km (0.5 miles) **Time** 15 minutes
Nearest station Cefalù

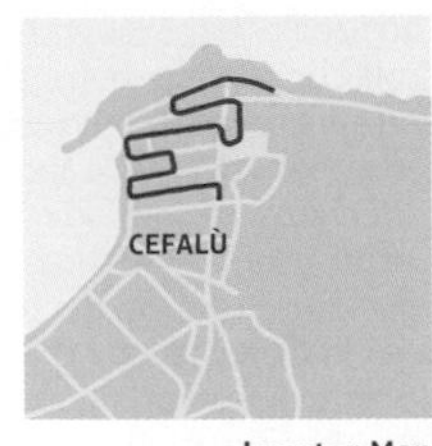

Locator Map
For more detail see p110

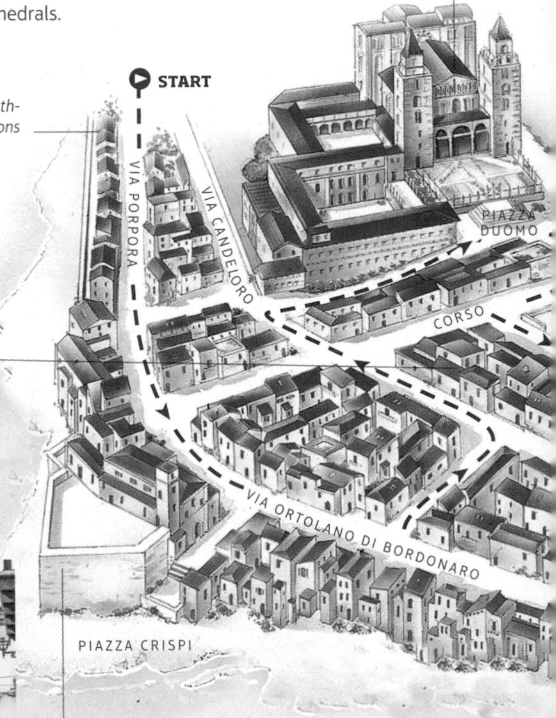

Founded on a steep promontory halfway between Palermo and Capo d'Orlando, Cefalù has retained its medieval appearance around the Norman cathedral, which was built by Roger II in the 12th century. The narrow streets of the town centre are lined with buildings featuring elaborate architectural decoration. There are also numerous churches, reflecting the town's status as a leading bishopric. The fishermen's quarter, with its old houses clustered along the seafront, is very appealing, as is the long beach with fine sand, considered to be one of the most beautiful stretches on the northern coast. The stunning open space of Piazza Duomo is home to one of Sicily's most splendid cathedrals.

Oversized compared with the rest of the town, the ***Cathedral*** *is a masterpiece of Norman art. Magnificent mosaics can be found in the presbytery.*

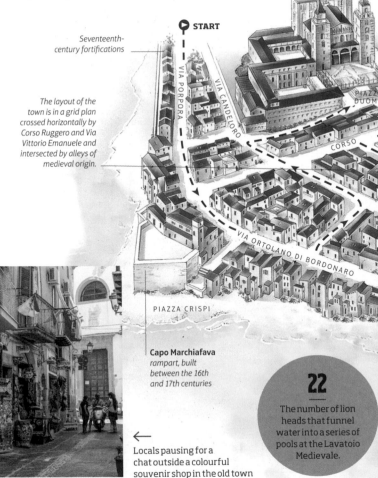

START

VIA PORPORA

VIA CANDELORO

PIAZZA DUOMO

CORSO

VIA ORTOLANO DI BORDONARO

PIAZZA CRISPI

Seventeenth-century fortifications

The layout of the town is in a grid plan crossed horizontally by Corso Ruggero and Via Vittorio Emanuele and intersected by alleys of medieval origin.

Capo Marchiafava *rampart, built between the 16th and 17th centuries*

← Locals pausing for a chat outside a colourful souvenir shop in the old town

22

The number of lion heads that funnel water into a series of pools at the Lavatoio Medievale.

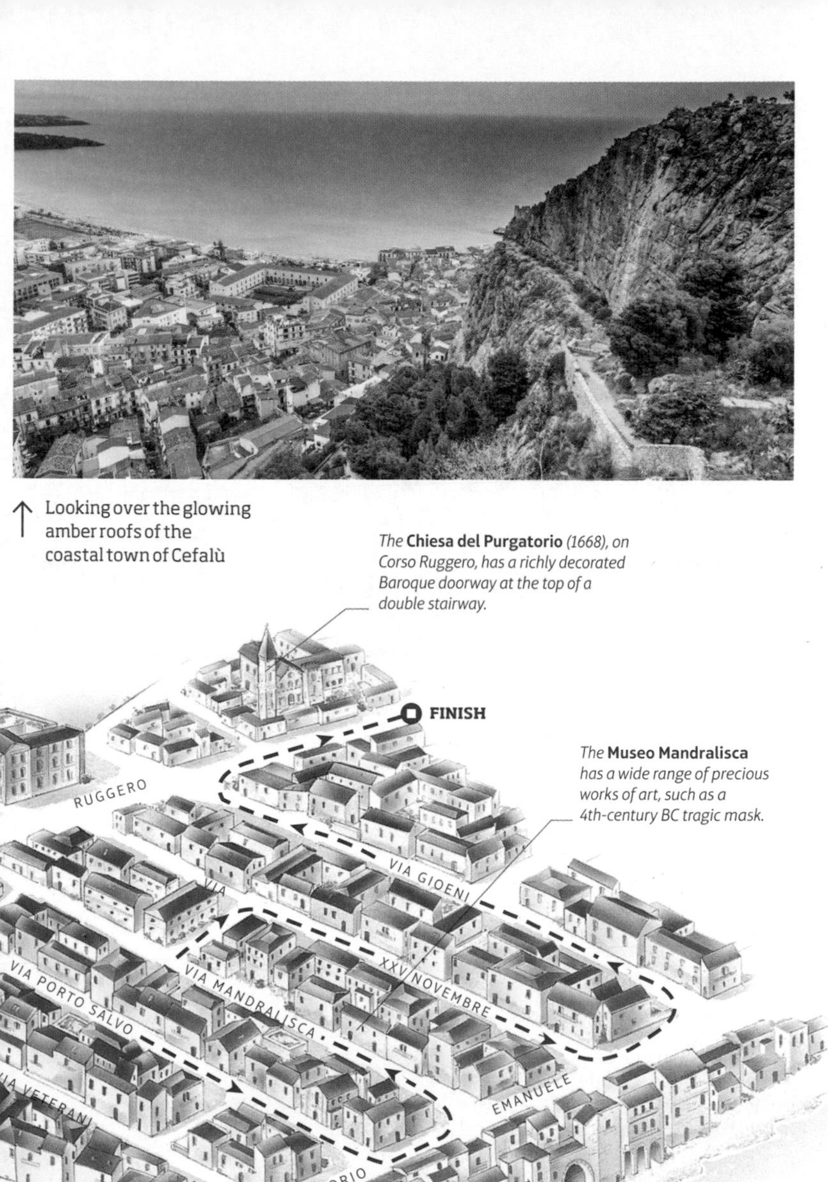

↑ Looking over the glowing amber roofs of the coastal town of Cefalù

The **Chiesa del Purgatorio** *(1668), on Corso Ruggero, has a richly decorated Baroque doorway at the top of a double stairway.*

The **Museo Mandralisca** *has a wide range of precious works of art, such as a 4th-century BC tragic mask.*

This restored **Lavatoio Medievale** *(medieval laundry) was once used for washing clothes.*

Porta Pescara *is a striking city gate overlooking the sea. It is the only Gothic arch remaining of the four that originally pierced the city wall.*

The setting sun bouncing off the blue waters on the rocky coast of Lo Zingaro

RISERVA DELLO ZINGARO

A3 San Vito Lo Capo From Castellammare del Golfo riservazingaro.it

Spoiled with nature's gifts, Lo Zingaro is an outdoor lover's oasis, where fields of brambly scrub give way to a profusion of springtime wild-flowers and salty beaches are kissed by crystal blue waters.

A hiker traversing the reserve on one of its well-marked paths

Situated some 20 km (12 miles) from Erice, along the coast going towards Palermo, Sicily's first nature reserve was instituted in 1980 to protect 7 km (4 miles) of pristine rocky coastline on the Tyrrhenian Sea between Scopello and San Vito Lo Capo.

Dotted with tiny white pebble bays and backed by steep mountains sloping down to the sea, the Lo Zingaro reserve is a fantastic place for a day's hiking. Make a pit stop at one of the many bars and cafés along San Vita Lo Capo's main street, Via Savoia, to pick up snacks and water before hitting the nature trails. The reserve doesn't have much in the way of facilities or services, and be sure to wear appropriate footwear at the very least.

Marked trails of varying levels of difficulty traverse the steep interior, or creep along the cliff above the sea, occasionally forking down to small coves with pebble beaches. The shortest trail

650

The variety of plant species on Lo Zingaro is thanks to its humid microclimate.

Lo Zingaro's lush green hills sloping down to an isolated beach

(6 km/4 miles) travels along the coast (heading north) from Scopello to Tonarella dell'Uzzo, taking around 2 hours. The longest and most challenging explores 19 km (12 miles) of the reserve's mountainous landscape, taking in the peaks of Mt Passo del Lupo, Mt Speziale and Mt Scardina, and takes about 9 hours. The reserve can also be explored on horseback.

Lo Zingaro protects some 650 species of flora such as wild orchids, limonium, wild carnations, dwarf palms, iris, once wide-spread ilex and cork oak forests, lichens and ferns. It is also a paradise for birds, especially raptors such as the rare Bonelli's eagles, peregrine falcons and kites, and even, on occasion, golden eagles. You may also spot porcupines and foxes.

TOP 3 ZINGARO RESERVE DIVES

Capua Wreck, Coast of Scopello

During WWII, a British cargo ship carrying arms for Italian troops sank. Mysteries still linger, making this 38-m (125-ft) dive all the more intriguing.

Grotta dell'Acqua Dolce, Uzzo Bay

One for experienced divers, this cave gradually decreases in depth, leading to a 60-m- (197-ft-) deep chamber of glassy water teeming with marine life.

Grotta del Camino, Park entrance

An awe-inspiring experience, this cave has two entrances: one at 18 m (59 ft) and the other at 35m (115 ft). A rock wall divides the cavity, where divers can discover troupes of red-and-white-striped shrimp.

3

ERICE

A3 Trapani Trapani (www.funiviaerice.it)
Via Castello di Venere; www.visitsicily.info/erice

The splendid town of Erice, perched on top of Monte San Giuliano, has ancient origins, as is shown by the cult of the goddess of fertility, Venus Erycina. Laid out on a triangular plan, the town has preserved its medieval character, with fine city walls, beautifully paved streets, stone houses with decorated doorways, small squares and open spaces with numerous churches, many of which have become venues for scientific and cultural activities.

Cyclopean Walls

These defensive walls extend for some 700 m (2,296 ft) on the northern side of the town, from Porta Spada to Porta Trapani.

The lower Cyclopean Walls, made up of megalithic blocks of stone, date back to around 800 BC and were likely built by the Elymians, an ancient Sicilian civilization. The Phoenician letters *beth* (house), *ain* (eye) and *phe* (mouth) are carved into some areas of the stone. This is thought to be a warning to invaders, roughly meaning "These walls are a safe house, with eyes to see attackers and a mouth to eat them." The upper parts of the walls and the gates were built by the Normans. The Porta Spada gate owes its name to the massacre of the local Angevin rulers during the 1282 Sicilian Vespers (*spada* means sword).

Nearby are Sant'Antonio Abate and Sant'Orsola. The latter houses the fine 18th-century *Misteri* or "Mysteries", sculptures representing the Passion of Christ, borne in procession on Good Friday.

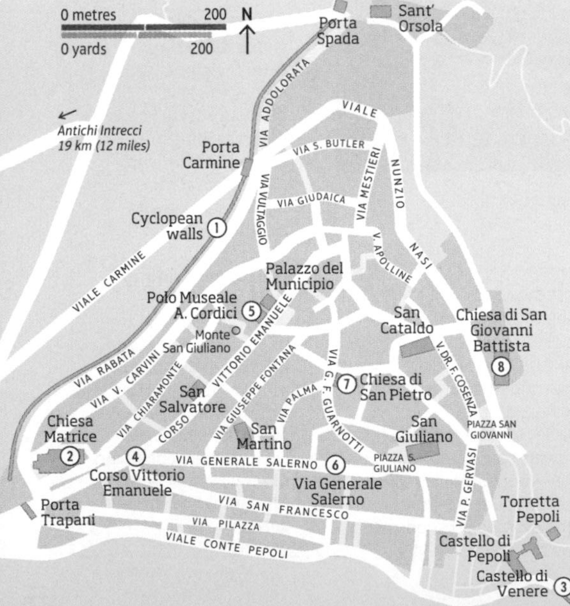

SHOP

Antichi Intrecci

Ericini carpets are still woven by women in their homes and sold from shops and boutiques along the main street of town. These artisans are one of the few still producing the vivid rugs.

Via Piano Neve, Buseto Palizzolo Sun antichintrecci.it

Chiesa Matrice

Piazza Matrice 0923-869123 Jul & Sep: 10am-7pm daily; Aug: 10am-8pm daily; Oct-Jun: 10am-6pm daily

The fortified Chiesa Matrice (Mother Church) was built in 1314 and is dedicated to Our Lady of the Assumption. The austere Romanesque façade has a portico with pointed arches surmounted by a beautiful rose window; this faces a detached bell tower with double lancet windows, which was originally built as a lookout tower during the War of the Vespers. The interior was dramatically restored in 1865, and little remains of its original look.

Castello di Venere

Via Conte Pepoli Apr-Oct: 10am-6pm daily (Summer: 8pm); Nov-Mar: 10am-4pm Sat & hols; weekdays by appt fondazione ericearte.org

This Norman castle was built on an isolated rock over the ruins of the Temple of Venus

Torretta Pepoli, perched on a cliffside beneath Castello di Venere

The lower Cyclopean Walls, made up of megalithic blocks of stone, date back to around 800 BC and were likely built by the Elymians, an ancient Sicilian civilization.

Erycina. Entrance is gained via a tower, the only remaining original part of the castle, which was used as a prison and watchtower. Above the entrance is a plaque with the coat of arms of the Spanish Habsburgs, crowned by a 14th-century double lancet window. Inside are a sacred well and the ruins of the Temple of Venus Erycina, a Phoenician house and a Roman bath.

The castle is the starting point of a system of fortifications including the Torri del Balio, formerly the headquarters of the Norman governor. Further down is the Torretta Pepoli, built as a hunting lodge in 1872–80 and one of the symbols of Erice.

Having been reinvented as a "political-cultural" destination, it now houses an interactive multimedia museum. In front of the castle are the 19th-century public gardens, Giardini del Balio, which link this zone with the eastern side of Erice.

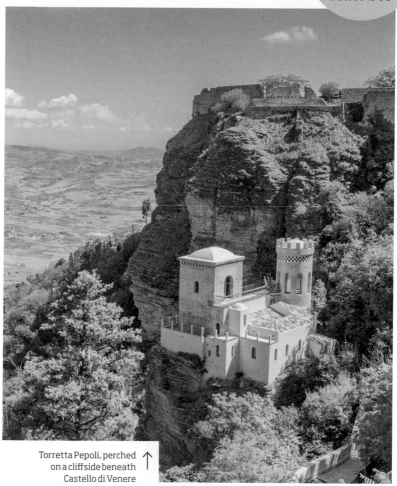

GREAT VIEW

Gaze Out to Sea

From Castello di Venere's perch on lofty Monte San Giuliano you'll experience sweeping vistas of the craggy Egadi Islands, the sprawling town of Trapani and, on a clear day, a glimpse of the Tunisian coast in North Africa.

↑ Porta Trapani opening onto the winding Corso Vittorio Emanuele

④

Corso Vittorio Emanuele

The *corso* (main street) in Erice begins at Porta Trapani, one of the three gates through the massive city walls, and goes uphill. The street is lined with Baroque patrician houses and tempting pastry shops selling local specialities.

To the left is San Salvatore, which once had a monastery annexe and boasts a 15th-century portal. At the end of the corso, formerly called Via Regia, is Piazza Umberto I, redesigned in the 19th century, and the Palazzo del Municipio (Town Hall), which houses the Polo Museale A. Cordici.

⑤ 

Polo Museale A. Cordici

Vico San Rocco 1 320-867 29 57 Apr-Oct: 10am-6pm daily (Aug: to 8pm); Nov-Mar: 10am-4pm Sat & hols; weekdays by appt fondazione ericearte.org

Housed in the former convent of the Third Order of Saint Francis, the Museo Antonino Cordici holds one of Renaissance sculptor Antonello Gagini's (1478–1536) most important works, the *Annunciation* completed in 1525. Along with the civic museum's vast display of classic paintings, statues, decorative arts, weapons and vases, you can admire its interesting collection of archeological artifacts, including stone inscriptions from the Punic, Greek and Roman periods, and a marble head of Aphrodite that dates back to the 4th century BC.

⑥

Via Generale Salerno

This street, with its noble palazzi, connects Corso Vittorio Emanuele with the castle area. Immediately to the left is San Martino, a Norman church with a Baroque portal and interior, as well as a fine 17th-century wooden choir. The sacristy takes you to the Oratorio dei Confrati del Purgatorio, built in the Rococo style, with a carved altar decorated with gilded stucco.

Further along the street is San Giuliano, which looks over a square made more spectacular by the pink façades of the buildings set around it. The church was begun in 1080 by Roger I but was radically altered in the 1600s. It was closed when the vault caved in on the central section of the nave; now

Did You Know?

Genovesi ericine, a dome-shaped pastry filled with ricotta, was inspired by hats worn by Genovese sailors.

restored, the church is used as a cultural and artistic centre.

Chiesa di San Pietro

Via Filippo Guarnotti

Founded in the 14th century in the middle of Erice, this church was rebuilt in 1745 and a fine Baroque portal added. The nearby convent is now one of the bases for the Polo Museale A. Cordici. This centre, founded in the early 1960s to honour the brilliant Sicilian scientist Ettore Majorana who disappeared in mysterious circumstances before World War II, runs courses and conferences on subjects ranging from medicine to mathematical logic. The centre makes use of abandoned buildings such as the former convents of San Domenico, San Francesco and San Rocco.

Chiesa di San Giovanni Battista

Piazzale San Giovanni
0923-869123 **Only for events**

This white-domed church is the largest and probably the oldest in Erice, despite the many alterations that have changed its appearance. The last refurbishing phase took place in the 1600s, when the nave was totally rebuilt.

The church is now used only as an auditorium, but several interesting works of art remain. These include the statue of St John the Baptist by Antonio Gagini, who came from a family of sculptors and whose work is generally accepted to be the first example of Renaissance art in Sicily. The 14th-century frescoes come from the Church of Santa Maria Maddalena.

Monte San Giuliano

Make your way up ancient steps and through a medieval arch to discover this scenic restaurant serving classic Sicilian dishes.

Vicolo San Rocco 7, Fulgatore/Erice
Mon **montesan giuliano.it**

↓ Chiesa di San Giovanni Battista, perched on a cliff overlooking the sea

Did You Know?

The Doric temple has 14 columns on each side to conform to Greek mathematical ratios.

The Doric temple standing in solemn isolation amid the rolling hills of Segesta ↑

4

SEGESTA

B3 32 km (20 miles) from Trapani 0924-952 356 Trapani From Trapani or Palermo 9am-7:30pm daily (Mar & Oct: to 6:30pm; Nov-Feb: to 5pm)

According to legend, ancient Segesta was founded by Trojan exiles. It presents one of the most spectacular sights on the island: a massive unfinished temple stranded on a remote hillside facing Monte Barbaro.

The ancient capital of the Elymians, founded on the rolling green hills of the Castellammare del Golfo, was constantly at war with Selinunte and was frequently attacked. Yet the majestic Doric temple, contructed some time around 420 BC but left incomplete, has miraculously survived sacking and the ravages of time.

The city of Segesta was built above the temple on the top of the mountain. Here lie the ruins of some buildings and the well-preserved 3rd-century BC theatre, where ancient Greek plays are performed every other summer.

↑ Segesta's 3rd-century BC amphitheatre, hewn out of the top of Monte Barbaro, looking out to the sea

EAT

Al Capolinea

Decent all-rounder with a playground and an outdoor dining area.

Stazione Ferroviaria, Calatafimi meditsegesta capolinea.it

Mirko's

Intimate family-owned restaurant with a stellar local reputation.

Via Discesa Annunziata 1, C'mare del Golfo Tue (winter) mirkosristorante.it

La Locanda di Nonna Ciccia

Generous portions and warm, friendly service.

Via Alcide De Gasperi 4, Calatafimi Mon 333-947 7085

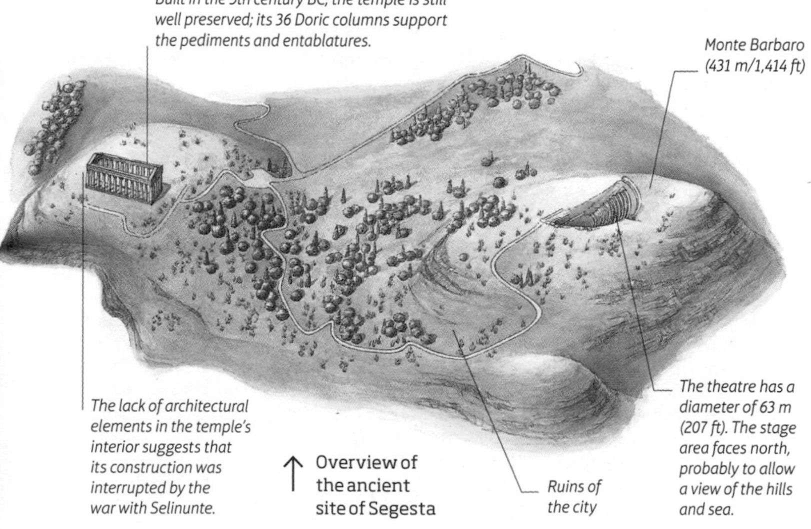
Built in the 5th century BC, the temple is still well preserved; its 36 Doric columns support the pediments and entablatures.
Monte Barbaro (431 m/1,414 ft)
The lack of architectural elements in the temple's interior suggests that its construction was interrupted by the war with Selinunte.
Ruins of the city
The theatre has a diameter of 63 m (207 ft). The stage area faces north, probably to allow a view of the hills and sea.

↑ Overview of the ancient site of Segesta

EGADI ISLANDS

A2 From Trapani (Siremar: www.carontetourist.it) Favignana town hall; Stazione Marittima Trapani; www.isoleegadi.it

The Egadi islands of Favignana (the largest of the three), Levanzo and Marettimo were connected to mainland Sicily 600,000 years ago. As the sea level gradually rose, the links were submerged, slowly changing the islands into an archipelago in the centre of the Mediterranean. These charming islands are now popular for holidays and swimming as they are easily reached from Trapani.

Favignana

This island is made up of two distinct parts. The eastern side is flat, with pastureland and farmland, while the other half is craggy and barren. In the middle is the small town of Favignana, which was rebuilt in the 1600s over its original medieval layout. Sights worth visiting are the Chiesa Matrice (dedicated to the Immaculate Conception), the buildings constructed during the height of the tuna fishing industry and the 19th-century Palazzo Florio, which is now the Town Hall.

There are different coves to visit, from the beautiful Cala Stornello to the Previto Islet, from Cala Rotonda to Cala Grande, and from Punta Ferro to Punta Faraglione, where you will find prehistoric caves with Paleolithic rock art. The perimeter of the eastern part starts from Punta San Nicola and arrives at Cala Rossa, where there are heaps of tufa from the island quarries. From Cala Rossa to Bue Marino and from Cala Azzurra to Punta Lunga, the coast is characterized by fine sandy beaches and crystalline waters.

Levanzo

The smallest of the Egadi Islands has a wilder aspect than Favignana: the tall, rocky coastline is dominated by a cultivated plateau. There is only one small village, Cala Dogana, and the landscape is largely barren and desolate,

INSIDER TIP
Island Escape

For those looking to practise the fine art of doing nothing (*dolce far niente*), spend some time on the peaceful island of Levanzo or remote, car-free Marettimo – unspoilt sanctums for strolling and lazing on the beach, and less than an hour by hydrofoil from Trapani.

Strolling along the promenade beside the clear blue waters of Levanzo's small harbour

interrupted here and there by the thick scrubby underbrush common in this part of the Mediterranean. A series of footpaths crosses the island and provides some spectacular walks to the beautiful Cala Tramontana bay.

Northwest of Cala Dogana is the Grotta del Genovese, which can be reached on foot in about two hours or by boat. The grotto is decorated with a series of carved Palaeolithic and Neolithic drawings of human figures, animals and idols, some in a rather naturalistic style, others rendered more schematically.

---

③

Marettimo

The rugged, mountainous and varied landscape of Marettimo, the first island in the group to break off from the mainland, is rather striking. The paths crossing the island – there are no roads or hotels here – will introduce you to a world of limestone pinnacles and caves leading up to Monte Falcone (686 m/ 2,250 ft). Marettimo has many rare plant species that are found only on the island – the result of its long isolation from the mainland – as well as moufflon (long-horned mountain sheep) and wild boar. The Punta Troia fort housed a Bourbon penal colony where the Risorgimento hero Guglielmo Pepe was held for three years. Not far from the tiny village of Marettimo there are some ancient Roman buildings and, in the vicinity, a small Byzantine church.

EAT

La Bettola

Sit on the pavement-side patio of this pleasant, informal restaurant and eat local dishes such as fish couscous, busiati pasta with a pesto of tuna, anchovies, tomato and basil, or fish grilled on lava stone.

Via Nicotera 47, Favignana Winter: Mon
0923-921 988

Il Giardino delle Aloe

Fresh fish from the island's fleet is served in a garden of aloes near the tremendous bay of Cala Rossa. The menu depends on the catch, but try a slice of the famous tuna.

Contrada Grotta Perciata, Favignana Nov-Mar: Mon
ilgiardinodellealoe.it

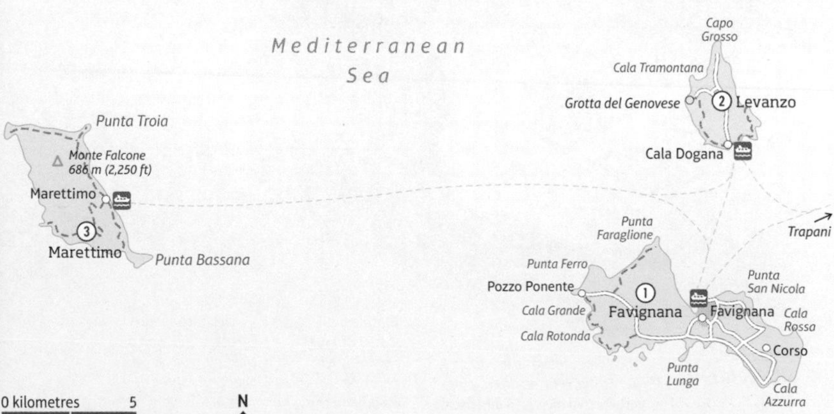

6

SELINUNTE

A4 80 km (50 miles) SW of Trapani Palermo and Trapani Castelvetrano From Castelvetrano 9am-6pm daily (to 4pm in winter) 0924-46277/46251

The ruins of Selinunte, overlooking the sea, are among the most striking archaeological sites in the Mediterranean and a supreme example of the fusion of Phoenician and Greek culture.

Founded in 651 BC, Selinunte was one of the great cities of Magna Graecia. Its ancient name, Selinus, derives from the wild celery that still grows here. It was an important port, and its defences can still be seen around the Acropolis. The Carthaginians, under Hannibal, completely destroyed the city in 409 BC. While the city itself has virtually disappeared, eight of its temples are distinguishable, particularly the so-called Eastern Temples (Temples E, F and G). Higher on the Acropolis lie the remains of Temples A, B, C, D and O. Metope sculptures from Temple C (6th century), originally located on the frieze between the triglyphs, can be seen in the Museo Archeologico Regionale in Palermo *(p149)*. A small museum on site houses other finds, as does another in Castelvetrano, 14 km (9 miles) north of Selinunte. The ancient city is still being excavated; its North Gate entrance is well preserved, and further north you'll find a necropolis.

EAT

Ristorante Pizzeria Pierrot

This unpretentious restaurant on a seaside promenade not far from the ruins offers an excellent seafood menu. Order the swordfish or a simple pizza margherita cooked in a wood-burning oven.

Via Polo 108, Marinella Selinunte, Castelvetrano
ristorante pierrotselinunte.com

€€€

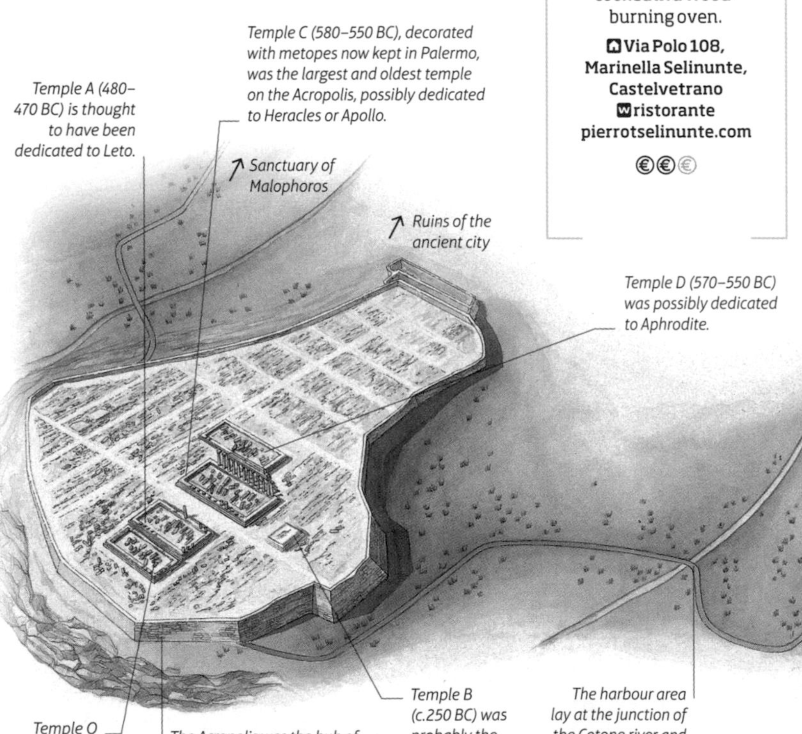

Temple A (480–470 BC) is thought to have been dedicated to Leto.

Temple C (580–550 BC), decorated with metopes now kept in Palermo, was the largest and oldest temple on the Acropolis, possibly dedicated to Heracles or Apollo.

Temple D (570–550 BC) was possibly dedicated to Aphrodite.

Temple O (480–470 BC)

The Acropolis was the hub of public life, centred around two streets that divided it into four quarters protected by a wall.

Temple B (c.250 BC) was probably the only one to be built in the Hellenistic age.

The harbour area lay at the junction of the Cotone river and the road connecting the Acropolis to the Eastern Hill.

↑ Temple C rising above the scrub at sunset, and (*inset*) visitors strolling through the Doric columns of Temple E

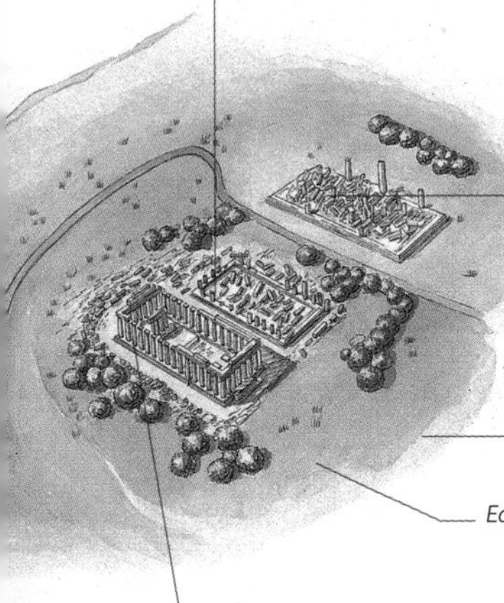

Temple F (560–530 BC) may have been dedicated to Athena and is the most ancient temple on the Eastern Hill. Sadly, it is totally in ruins.

Temple G (540–480 BC) is in ruins but was once one of the largest temples in antiquity, reaching a height of 30 m (98 ft) when complete.

Entrance and car park

Eastern Hill

Temple E (490–480 BC), located at the top of an eight-stepped base (crepidoma), was partly rebuilt in the 1960s. It was probably sacred to Hera and is considered one of the finest examples of Doric architecture in Sicily.

← Ruins of the Acropolis and the Eastern Hill at Selinunte

100

The number of hectares (240 acres) that make up Selinunte, the largest archaeological park in Europe.

EXPERIENCE MORE

STAY

For slow travel at its best, *agriturismi* (working farms and vineyards) offer lodgings that range from informal to rustic chic.

Fontana Salsa
A2 Via Cusenza 78, Trapani
fontanasalsa.it

Baglio Spano
A4 Contrada Triglia Scaletta, Marsala
bagliospano.com

Resort Baglio Soria
A2 Contrada, Via Soria, Trapani firriato-baglio-soria-trapani.it

Trapani

A2 Vincenzo Florio a Birgi Tourist Information Point, Via Torrearsa, 0923-544 533

The pretty, coastal town of Trapani was built on a narrow, curved promontory (hence the name, which derives from the Greek word *drepanon*, or sickle) that juts out into the sea opposite the Egadi Islands. In ancient times Trapani was the port town for Erice *(p118)*. It flourished under the Carthaginians and languished under the Vandals, Byzantines and Saracens. The economy has always been linked to the sea and reached its peak in the 1600s and 1700s with shipyards and tuna fishing. The town now extends beyond the promontory to the foot of Monte San Giuliano and the edge of the salt marshes.

One of the first places to start in Trapani is at the **Museo Pepoli**. The museum opened in 1906 in the former Carmelite monastery, thanks to Count Agostino Pepoli, who donated his private collection. A broad polychrome marble staircase leads to the first floor, which has archaeological finds, 12th–18th century Sicilian painting, jewellery and ceramics on display. The art produced in Trapani itself is interesting and worth viewing: wooden 16th-century angels, an 18th-century coral and alabaster nativity scene, jewellery, clocks with painted dials, tapestries with coral and majolica from Santa Maria delle Grazie.

Via Garibaldi leads to the old town area of Trapani. It begins in Piazza Vittorio Veneto, the heart of the town, with Palazzo d'Ali, now the Town Hall. The street is lined with 18th-century patrician residences such as Palazzo Riccio di Morana and Palazzo Fardella Fontana. Almost directly opposite the 1621 Baroque façade of Santa Maria d'Itria are the steps

↑ Pretty buildings line the wide streets of Trapani's old town

20

life-sized wooden effigies are taken through Trapani on Good Friday.

leading to San Domenico, built in the 14th century and restructured in the 18th century. Inside the church is the sarcophagus of Manfred, natural son of Frederick II.

The main street in the old town, Corso Vittorio Emanuele, is lined with late Baroque buildings and San Lorenzo Cathedral, which has a fine portico. The main features of the interior are the painted ceiling, stucco decoration and, in the right-hand altar, a *Crucifixion* attributed to Van Dyck.

Santuario di Maria Santissima Annunziata, also known as the Madonna di Trapani, is a church built by the Carmelite fathers in 1224. The portal and part of the rose window are the only original elements remaining, as the rest of the church is Baroque, thanks to restoration effected in 1714. Inside you will find the Cappella dei Pescatori, the Cappella dei Marinai, and the Cappella della Madonna di Trapani with the *Madonna and Child* by Nino Pisano, one of the most important Gothic sculptures in Sicily.

The **Chiesa del Purgatorio** is a well known church of Trapani because it houses unusual 18th-century wooden statues with precious silver decoration representing the Stations of the Cross (called *Misteri*). At 2pm on Good Friday, they are carried through the streets in a 24-hour procession, a ritual dating from the 1700s.

At the tip of the peninsula, the Torre di Ligny (1671) affords a fine view of the city and its port. The tower is now used as an archaeological museum, the **Museo di Preistoria**, with objects from the Punic Wars and from the shipwrecks that occurred on the ancient trade routes. On display are amphoras that were used to carry wine, dates and garum – a prized fish sauce.

From Trapani to Marsala the coast is lined with salt marshes. The area is now a WWF nature reserve, a unique habitat for migratory birds. The landscape, with its salt marshes and wind-mills (three of which can be visited), is striking. A museum, the **Museo del Sale**, illustrates the practice of salt extraction.

Museo Pepoli
Via Conte Agostino Pepoli 200 0923-553 269 9am-1:30pm Mon-Sun (to 12:30pm Sun & hols; free first week of the month)

Santuario di Maria Santissima Annunziata
Via Conte Agostino Pepoli 0923-539 184 7am-noon & 4-7pm daily (summer: to 8pm) madonnaditrapani.it

Chiesa del Purgatorio
Via San Francesco d'Assisi 329-707 88 96 (Curia Vescovile) 7:30am-noon & 4-7pm Mon-Sat, 10am-noon & 4-7pm Sun

Museo di Preistoria
Torre di Ligny 0923-547 275 Summer: 10am-12:30pm & 5-7:30pm In winter

Museo del Sale
Via delle Saline, Contrada Nubia, Paceco WWF Reserve: 320-663 58 18/ 320-657 54 55 9:30am-7pm daily museodel sale.it

THE SALT MARSHES

The Stagno and Trapani salt marshes extend along the Sicilian coastline from Trapani to Marsala, and those who visit will be rewarded with an impressive sight. The salt marshes were exploited in antiquity and reached the height of their importance in the 19th century, when salt was exported as far away as Norway. The long periods of sunshine (five or six months a year) and the impermeable nature of the land made these marshes very productive, although activity has declined in the last 20 years. At one time, windmills supplied energy for the Archimedes screws that were used to take water from basin to basin; some of them have now been restored. At Nubia the Museo del Sale (Salt Marsh Museum) is now open, and the Stagnone area is a fully fledged nature reserve. The museum is a great, informative introduction to the practice of salt extraction. The seawater will be protected from pollution, and the age-old tradition of salt extraction will survive.

8

Marsala

A4 31 km (19 miles) from Trapani and 124 km (77 miles) from Palermo 0923-714 097

Sicily's largest wine-producing centre was founded by the colonists from Mozia who survived the destruction of the island by Dionysius of Syracuse in 397 BC. It then became a major Carthaginian city, but in the first Punic War it was conquered by the Romans, who made it their main Mediterranean naval base. The city plan is basically Roman, with other quarters being added by the Arabs who conquered the city in 830 AD and made it a flourishing trade centre.

Piazza della Repubblica, bounded by Palazzo Senatorio and the Cathedral, dedicated to St Thomas of Canterbury, is the heart of the town. The cathedral was founded by the Normans and completed in the 1950s and houses sculptures by the Gaginis and their school. Behind the apse is the **Museo degli Arazzi Fiamminghi**, which displays eight 16th-century Flemish tapestries depicting Titus's war against the Hebrews. They were donated by Philip II of Spain to the Archbishop of Messina and later taken to Marsala Cathedral.

Museo degli Arazzi Fiamminghi

Chiesa Madre, Via G Garaffa 57 0923-711 327 9am-1pm, 4-6pm Tue-Sun

9

Castelvetrano

A4 73 km (45 miles) from Trapani; 110 km (68 miles) from Palermo Town hall, Piazza Aragona E Tagliavial; 0924-902 004

The town centre here consists of three linked squares. The main one is Piazza Garibaldi, where you'll find the mostly 16th-century Chiesa Madre and its interesting medieval portal. Inside are stuccoes by Ferraro and Serpotta, and a *Madonna* by the Gagini School. By the church are the Municipio (Town Hall), the Campanile and the Mannerist Fontana della Ninfa. Nearby is the Chiesa del Purgatorio, its façade filled with statues, and a Neo-Doric theatre, the Teatro Selinus (1873).

At Delia, a short 3.5 km (2 miles) from town, is Santa Trinità, a church built in the Norman period.

SHOP

Marsala DOC

The story goes that Garibaldi landed at Marsala, visited the winery and then conquered the island. Don't miss a tour of the prestigious Cantine Florio cellars before stopping by the wine shop.

A4 Via Vincenzo Florio 1, Marsala, 10am-4pm Mon-Sat duca.it/florio

Marsala Cathedral, lit up as evening falls upon the town

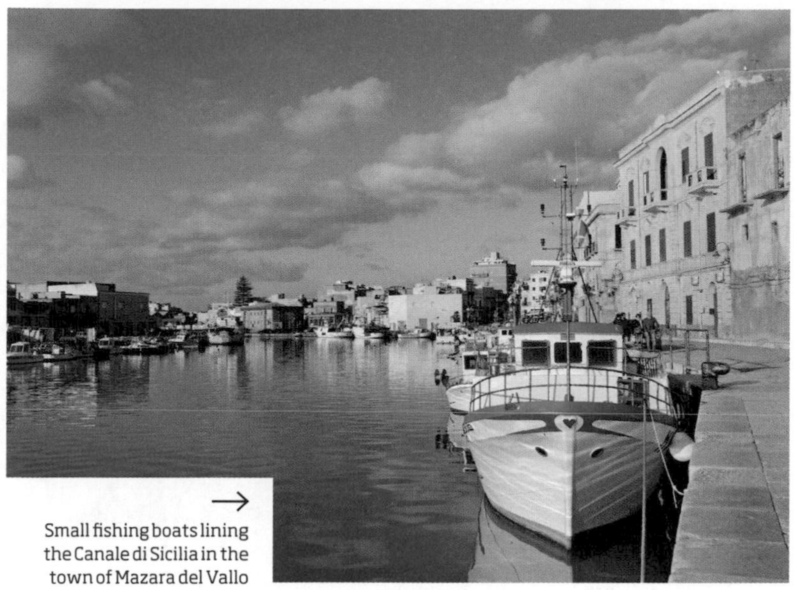

Small fishing boats lining the Canale di Sicilia in the town of Mazara del Vallo

The Phoenician city of Mozia was built on the island of San Pantaleo, just off Sicily. The site is linked with Joseph Whitaker, the son of an English wine merchant.

Mozia

A3 From Trapani and Marsala (sunrise to sunset) STR Trapani; 0923-565 412/872 652

The Phoenician city of Mozia was built on the island of San Pantaleo, just off Sicily. The site is linked with Joseph Whitaker, the son of an English wine merchant who made his fortune from Marsala wine. He became owner of the island in the early 1900s, began archaeological digs in 1913, and founded the **Museo Whitaker** that houses the "young man from Mozia" statues. Along with those in Carthage, the dry docks here are the most ancient in the Mediterranean.

Museo Whitaker

Apr-Oct: 9:30am-6:30pm; Nov-Mar: 9am-3pm fondazionewhitaker.it

Mazara del Vallo

A4 50 km (31 miles) from Trapani; 124 km (77 miles) from Palermo Via XX Settembre; 0923-671 670

Facing the Canale di Sicilia, at the mouth of the Mazarò river, this town – a colony of Selinunte – was destroyed in 409 BC by the Carthaginians. It was passed to the Romans and then became a prosperous city under the Arabs, who made it the capital of one of the three "valleys" into which they split Sicily. In 1073 Mazara was conquered by Roger I; he convened the first Norman Parliament of Sicily here.

In Piazza Mokarta remains of the castle can be seen. Behind this is the Cathedral, of medieval origin but rebuilt in 1694. It houses the *Transfiguration*, a sculpture group by the iconic Italian sculptor Antonello Gagini. The left side of the Cathedral closes off Piazza della Repubblica, with the façade of the Seminario dei Chierici and the Palazzo Vescovile. On Lungomare Mazzini you will see the Collegio dei Gesuiti, seat of the Museo Civico, and can enter the old Arab town.

THE DANCING SATYR

The fishing port of Mazara del Vallo gained worldwide attention in 1998, when a Hellenic bronze of the *Satiro Danzante* ("dancing satyr") was discovered nearby on the fine Mediterranean seabed by a local fisherman. After restoration, the rare bronze statue, believed to be from the 4th century BC, now sits in its own museum on the town's Piazza Plebiscito in the former Sant'Egidio Church.

A windmill and salt marshes lining Trapani's serene coast

DRINK

Pollara Principe di Corleone

After touring the Pollara Principe di Corleone Estates sample their award-winning, territorial white wine, Biano d'Alcamo.

Contrada Malvello, Monreale
principedicorleone.it

12 Salemi

A3 95 km (59 miles) from Palermo Town hall, Piazza Dittatura 1; 0924-991111

This agricultural town in the Valle del Delia dates from ancient times (it was probably the Halicyae mentioned by Diodorus Siculus). Despite the 1968 earthquake, the Arab town plan has remained, with a jumble of narrow streets at the foot of the three towers of the castle. Here, on 14 May 1860, Garibaldi proclaimed himself ruler of Sicily in the name of King Vittorio Emanuele II.

In the old town, interesting sights are Sant'Agostino with its large cloister and the 17th-century Collegio dei Gesuiti, which houses the Chiesa dei Gesuiti, the Oratorio del Ritiro and the town's museums, in particular the Museo Civico d'Arte Sacra.

13 San Vito Lo Capo

A2 38 km (24 miles) from Trapani comune.sanvitolocapo.tp.it

A popular holiday resort set on the magnificent Golfo di Castellammare, San Vito Lo Capo is a lively place with one of the finest sandy beaches in Sicily. The focus of life is pedestrianized Via Savoia, lined with shops and restaurants. Another highlight is the promenade backing the sweeping crescent of white sand that stretches east of town. A short walk beyond the harbour is a lighthouse perched on a windswept cape. Beyond there are great views across the entire gulf from the cliffs, although in hot weather you may prefer to take in the coast from one of the many boat trips operating from the harbour. Just 12 km (7 miles) south of San Vito, the Zingaro Nature Reserve is a pristine 7-km (4-mile) stretch of coastline with tiny white pebble bays backed by steep mountains. Home to the rare Bonelli's eagle and some 600 species of plant, it is a fantastic place for a day's hiking. There are two main paths, the upper Sentiero Alto and the lower Sentiero Basso, which keeps close to the shore, with access to little coves. There are no shops or facilities here, so bring food and plenty of water.

14 Castellammare del Golfo

B3 Palermo-Trapani Pro Loco, Corso B Mattarella 24; www.prolococastellammare.it

This town was the Greek port for Segesta and Erice, and then an Arab fortress. It became an important trading and tuna-fishing centre in the Middle Ages. In the heart of the town, on an isthmus, is the Norman-Swabian castle, and the old picturesque streets of the medieval quarter

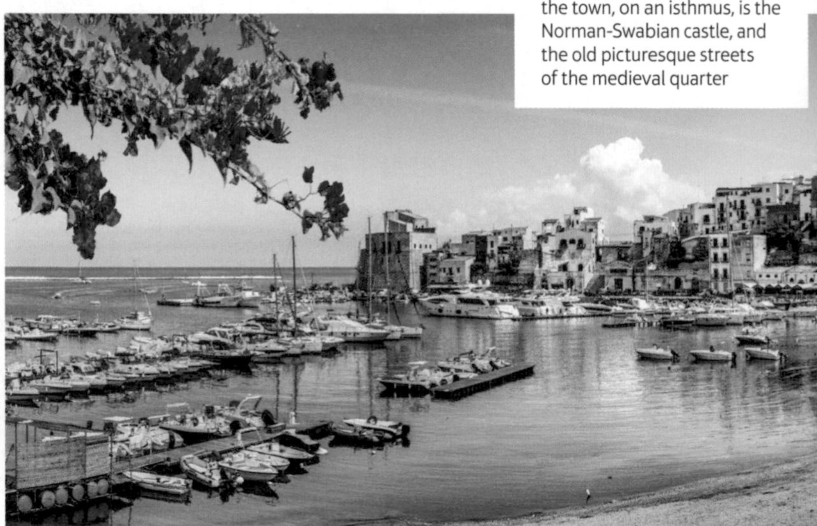

known as *castri di la terra*. On Via Garibaldi is the Chiesa Madre, frequently rebuilt in the 1700s and 1800s.

Alcamo

B3 Palermo-Trapani line Town hall, Piazza Ciullo; 0924-590 219

During the Arab period the fortress of Manzil Alqamah was built as part of this area's defensive network. The town of Alcamo developed later, and between the 13th and 14th centuries centred around the Chiesa Madre and the castle, which has been restored. In Piazza Ciullo is Sant'Oliva, built in 1724 over an earlier church, while the nearby Chiesa del Rosario houses late 15th-century frescoes. Facing Piazza della Repubblica is Santa Maria del Gesù. But the most important church here is the Chiesa Madre, founded in 1332. Its Baroque façade has a 14th-century bell tower with double lancet windows, and many paintings and sculptures can be seen in the chapels.

INSIDER TIP
Couscous Festival

San Vito Lo Capo's Couscous Festival is held in September, with a preview event in June. Sample dozens of kinds of couscous, and see concerts and a fireworks display on the last night.

The stunningly colourful Sicilian coastal port of Castellammare del Golfo

Corleone

B3 60 km (37 miles) from Palermo

The central zone around the village of Corleone is referred to as il Corleonese. Remote villages sprinkled throughout are worth a visit to witness a way of life that is slow to change, including Bisacquino, Palazzo Adriano *(p164)* and Prizzi *(p159)*. Corleone itself is a mountain community with an active historic centre and a church on nearly every corner. The Il Laboratorio della Legalità (AntiMafia Museum) within the confiscated home of mafioso boss Bernardo Provenzano offers a stunning visual history of the crime organization, while at the C.I.D.M.A. a vast collection of documents takes you on a journey from the beginnings of the mafia to present day.

Gibellina

B4 89 km (55 miles) from Trapani Town hall, Piazza XV Gennaio; www.fondazioneorestiadi.it

In 1968 a terrible earthquake destroyed all the towns in the Valle del Belice and the vicinity, including Gibellina.

↑ Driving through Pietro Consagra's iconic *Stella* sculpture in Gibellina

The new town was rebuilt, after years of bureaucratic delay, in the Salinella zone about 20 km (12 miles) from the original village. Over 40 years after the event, the new Gibellina already seems old and rather sad. However, it is worth visiting because, thanks to contemporary architects and artists, the area has been enriched with many works of art, including a huge sculpture, *Stella* (Star) – the city gate and symbol of Gibellina Nuova – by sculptor Pietro Consagra. Other attractions are the Torre Civica Carillon, a tower in Piazza del Municipio, and the Centro Culturale, the cultural centre built over the remains of the 17th-century Palazzo Di Lorenzo. Lastly, be sure to visit the Museo Antropologico-Etnologico, with everyday objects and tools illustrating local folk customs, and, above all, the **Museo Civico d'Arte Contemporanea**. This museum contains works by artists such as Fausto Pirandello, Renato Guttuso, Antonio Sanfilippo and Mario Schifano.

Museo Civico d'Arte Contemporanea

Via Segesta 0924-67428 9am-1pm, 4-7pm Mon-Sat

Gymnasium ruins from the city of Solunto on the slopes of Monte Catalfano

18 

Solunto

C3 Museum: 338-784 51 40 Santa Flavia-Solunto-Porticello 9am-7am Tue-Fri (last adm: 6:30pm), 9:30am-1:30pm Sat, Sun & hols (last adm: 1pm)

The ruins of the city of Solunto lie on the slopes of Monte Catalfano with a beautiful panoramic view of the sea. Solunto was one of the first Phoenician colonies in Sicily and was mentioned by the Greek historian Thucydides, along with Palermo and Mozia. In 254 BC it was conquered by the Romans. By the 2nd century AD the city had been largely abandoned, and was later almost destroyed by the Saracens. At the entrance there is a museum displaying a site plan and finds from various digs, which began in 1826 and are still ongoing. Solunto follows a traditional layout. The path leading to the site takes you to Via dell'Agorà, with a fired-brick pavement and gutters for drainage. This street makes a right angle with the side stairs, which mark off the blocks of buildings *(insulae)*. Six Doric columns and part of the roof of one of these, the Gymnasium, are still standing. Other *insulae* have mosaic floors and plastered or even painted walls. At the eastern end is the Agora, with workshops, cisterns to collect rainwater and a theatre with the stage area facing the sea.

19 

Piana degli Albanesi

B3 Pro Loco, Via Kastrota 207; www.prolocopianadegli albanesi.com

During the expansion of the Ottoman Empire in the Balkans, many groups of Albanians *(Albanesi)* fled to Italy. At the end of the 15th century, John II allowed an Albanian community to settle in this area, which originally took the name of Piana dei Greci because the inhabitants belonged to the Greek Orthodox Church. The place was renamed Piana degli Albanesi in 1941. The town is famous for its colourful religious festivities, such as those during Epiphany and Easter, which are still celebrated according to the Orthodox calendar.

Did You Know?

Many locals of Piana degli Albanesi speak an Albanian dialect, and street signs are bilingual.

The celebrations in honour of the patron saint Santa Maria Odigitria are followed by traditional folk festivities. Piazza Vittorio Emanuele, in the heart of town, is home to the Byzantine church of Santa Maria Odigitria, which has a beautiful iconostasis in the interior. Opposite the parish church is the town's oldest church, San Giorgio, which was altered in the mid-1700s. Along the avenue named after Giorgio Kastriota Skanderbeg, an Albanian national hero, is the cathedral, San Demetrio. As is customary in Orthodox churches, the apses are closed off by the iconostasis.

The area is well known for Italo-Albanian dishes, such as *strangujët* (similar to *gnocchi*), *kanojët* (a waffle made of flour, wine and lard filled with sweetened goat ricotta and sprinkled with chocolate), and *të plotit* (little pastries stuffed with sweet fig jam and topped with candied sprinkles).

Polizzi Generosa

D3 93 km (58 miles) from Palermo Pro Loco, Via Garibaldi 13; 329-337 75 66

On the western slopes of the Madonie mountains, this village grew up around an ancient fortress rebuilt by the Normans. Among its many churches is the Chiesa Madre, with a fine 16th-century *Madonna and Child* altarpiece by an unknown Flemish artist and a relief by Domenico Gagini (1482). A small museum shows the natural history of the area.

From Polizzi, ascend to Piano Battaglia, part of the nature reserve, which has footpaths in summer and ski runs in winter.

Gangi

D4 51 km (32 miles) from Cefalù Piazzetta Zoppo di Gangi; 0921-644 076

This town lies on the south western slope of Monte Marone, facing the Nebrodi and Madonie mountains. The birthplace of painters Gaspare Vazano and Giuseppe Salerno has retained its medieval character, with winding streets and steps connecting the different levels. The towering Chiesa Madre has a 14th-century bell tower and a lovely *Last Judgment* by Salerno, inspired by Michelangelo's painting in the Sistine Chapel.

POLIZZI HAZELNUTS

At Polizzi Generosa, a medieval village on the slopes of the Madonie mountains, they grow a variety of *nocciole* (hazelnuts) called *racinante* – a major source of the town's economy up until the 1960s. Although the Nebrodi mountains *(p231)* are the leading producers of hazelnuts on the island, the crunchy fruit still plays an important role in Polizzi. These sweet and buttery nuts are celebrated with the Sagra delle Nocciole, an annual food festival that takes place for two days every August.

Caccamo

C3 48 km (30 miles) from Palermo Town hall, Piazza Duomo; 091-810 32 07

Beautiful Caccamo lies under the castellated walls of its Norman castle, in a lovely setting of softly rolling hills only 10 km (6 miles) from the Palermo-Catania motorway. The town is laid out on different levels, with well-maintained roads that open onto pretty squares. The most appealing of these is Piazza Duomo, with the Chiesa Matrice dedicated to San Giorgio, flanked by statues and two symmetrically arranged Baroque buildings: the Oratorio della Compagnia del Sacramento and the Chiesa delle Anime Sante del Purgatorio. The former was built by the Normans but was enlarged in the 17th century. Its richly decorated interior has a font by Gagini and his workshop. The latter includes catacombs where a large number of townspeople were buried until the mid-19th century. Not far away are the Annunziata, with twin bell towers, San Marco and San Benedetto alla Badia. The last is perhaps the loveliest of the three, with its Baroque stucco and majolica decoration and a colourful floor depicting a ship sailing on the high seas, guarded by angels.

→ The medieval town of Caccamo set upon the rolling hills of Sicily

Petralia Soprana sits high above the landscape, offering stunning views ↑

23

Petralia Sottana

D3 98 km (61 miles) from Palermo Town hall, Corso Agliata; 0921-684 311/ 641 811

Perched on a rock 1,000 m (3,300 ft) up, and nestled at the foot of the tallest peaks in the Madonie mountains, is the picturesque town of Petralia Sottana. It is laid out around its main street, Via Agliata, which ends in Piazza Umberto I, opposite the Chiesa Madre. The late Gothic church, which was partially rebuilt in the 17th century, contains a fine wooden triptych, *The Virgin Mary and Child between Saints Peter and Paul*. An arch connects the bell tower with the Santissima Trinità, which has a marble altarpiece by sculptor Domenico Gagini.

Perched on a rock 1,000 m (3,300 ft) up, and nestled at the foot of the tallest peaks in the Madonie mountains, is the picturesque town of Petralia Sottana.

24

Petralia Soprana

D4 104 km (65 miles) from Palermo 0921-684 111

Situated on a plateau 1,147 m (3,760 ft) above sea level, where the panoramic view ranges from the Nebrodi mountains to the volcanic cone of Mount Etna, Petralia Soprana is the highest village in the Madonie mountains. This village was an extremely important Greek and Phoenician city. Under Roman dominion ancient "Petra" was one of the largest wheat-producing *civitates* in the Empire. The city became Batraliah after the Arab conquest and a powerful defensive stronghold under the Normans. Later, the two Petralias (Soprana and Sottana) were taken over by noble families.

Did You Know?

Petralia was the first centre in Sicily to fall under the control of the Romans.

The village has preserved its medieval layout, with narrow paved streets, patrician residences and churches. The old Chiesa Madre, dedicated to saints Peter and Paul and rebuilt in the 14th century, stands in an attractive square with a 17th-century double-column colonnade designed by the Serpotta brothers. In the interior is the first crucifix by sculptor Fra' Umile Pintorno (1580– 1639), who also painted many other crucifixes throughout the island. Santa Maria di Loreto was built in the 18th century over the remains of a castle; it has a cross plan and the façade is flanked by two decorated bell towers.

Castel di Tusa

D3 0921-330 405

This beautiful swimming resort is dominated by the ruins of a 14th-century castle. The characteristic alleys with old stone houses and villas converge in a stone-paved central square. The banks of the nearby Tusa river have become an outdoor gallery with works by contemporary artists. Only a few miles away are the **Ruins of Halaesa Arconidea**, a Greek colony founded in 403 BC, which prospered until it was sacked by the Roman praetor Verres. Excavations have revealed the Agora, remains of cyclopean walls and a Hellenistic temple. Near the archaeological site is the Monastery of Santa Maria della Balate.

Ruins of Halaesa Arconidea

3 km (2 miles) on the road to Tusa 0921-334 531 Summer: 9am-6:30pm Tue-Sun (winter: to 4:30pm)

26

Sperlinga

E4 47 km (29 miles) from Enna 0935-643 025

Sperlinga seems to have been pushed against a spectacular rock face, its parallel streets on different levels connected by steps. In the eastern section, up against the sandstone cliff, many troglodytic cave dwellings have been carved out. Until the mid-1960s many of them were inhabited, but some of them are now an ethnographic museum. During Norman rule, inhabitants from Northern Italy and the south of France settled here, and for this reason residents today speak a strange dialect called Galloitalico.

↑ Many of the caves carved into the cliffs of Sperlinga were inhabited until the 1960s

DRINK

Alla Vucciria Risto Pub

Tables are piled high with inventive finger foods in this buzzy gastropub that serves artisanal beer, excellent cocktails and local wine until late.

D3 Via Vittorio Emanuele 45, Geraci Siculo 10am-3am Tue-Sun

Bar Lombardo

On the main square in Petralia Soprana, Bar Lombardo is an offbeat, local haunt with a tiny patio in front for people-watching.

D4 Piazza del Popolo 11, Petralia Soprana 12:30-3pm & 7:30-10pm Thu-Tue

---

Al Punto

A few scenic steps from the gulf of Castel di Tusa, this is a great drinking spot. Each evening there is a generous *apericena* - a hybrid of *aperitivo* and *cena* (dinner).

D3 Viale Europa Unita 50, Castel di Tusa 10am-11:30pm daily

SHOP

Enoteca Lo Balbo

Located in the heart of the village of Gangi, this intimate wine shop carries a large selection of wines, spirits and authentic Sicilian products.

D4 Via Nazionale 178, Gangi 9am-1pm & 4-8pm Mon-Sat enotecalobalbo.it

Bagheria

C3 Palermo-Cefalú

In the 18th century, the town of Bagheria was the summer residence of Palermo's nobility, who built luxurious villas surrounded by orange groves as retreats from the heat of the capital. Prince Ettore Branciforti built the first, Villa Barbera, in 1657. The most famous is the Villa Palagonia on Piazza Garibaldi, decorated with hundreds of statues of monsters and mythological figures. Built in 1736 by Prince Francesco Bonnano, Villa Cattolica on Via Ramacca has a style similar to a castle. Today it houses the Museo Renato Guttuso – named after the Neo-Realist painter born in Bagheria in 1912. Step back in time with a visit to Museo del Giocattolo e delle Cere Pietro Piraino on Via Dietro la Certosa, containing a delightful collection of porcelain dolls, old mechanical toys and children's vintage games.

Nicosia

E4 129 km (80 miles) from Catania; 44 km (27 miles) from Enna
Town hall, Piazza Garibaldi; 0935-672 111

Sprawled over four hills, Nicosia is dominated by the ruins of an Arab-Norman castle. Originally a Byzantine settlement, the town was repopulated in the Norman era by Lombard and Piedmontese colonists, who have left traces of their local dialects. The many churches and patrician mansions are a sign of the town's former splendour. Narrow streets and alleys run up the hills, often providing spectacular views. Piazza Garibaldi is the heart of Nicosia, with the Gothic San Nicolò Cathedral and old buildings, including the

STAY

Stella Marina Residence

This hotel offers stylish, self-catering apartments in a small complex above the port.

B1 Via Cristoforo Colombo 35, Ustica
stellamarinaustica.it

Statues decorate the elaborate walls of Villa Palagonia in Bagheria ↓

current Town Hall. The Salita Salomone steps lead to Romanesque San Salvatore. There is a fine view of the old town from the porch. The church has a series of sundials which, according to tradition, were once used as the town's "clocks". Via Salomone, lined with aristocratic palazzi, leads up to Santa Maria Maggiore, just under the castle rock. In the interior is Charles V's throne, in memory of the emperor's visit here in 1535, a gilded marble altarpiece by Antonello Gagini and a crucifix known as *Father of Mercy*. From here you can go up to the castle, with its Norman drawbridge and the remains of the keep. At the foot of the castle is the Norman Basilica of San Michele, with its austere apses and majestic 15th-century bell towers.

Santo Stefano di Camastra

A E3 FS Messina-Palermo i Town hall; 0921-331 127/110

This town facing the Tyrrhenian Sea is one of the leading Sicilian centres for the production of ceramics. Local craftsmen display their wares, from vases, jugs and cornices, to tiles with period designs, and there is a ceramics museum in the Palazzo Trabia. In the centre of town stands the Chiesa Madre, or San Nicolò, with a Renaissance doorway and late 18th-century stucco decoration in the interior.

Did You Know?

Locals refer to Ustica as "black pearl" because of the unique volcanic rocks here.

↑ Fish swim among colourful coral in the waters around Ustica

Ustica

A B1 Palermo Punta Raisi From Palermo i Town hall and Guardia Costiera; www.ampustica.it

Ustica is the result of ancient volcanic eruptions: its name derives from the word *ustum* (burned) and the land is made up of sharp black volcanic rock. The emerged part of the gigantic submerged volcano, about 49 km (30 miles) from the Sicilian coast, is only 8.6 sq km (3.32 sq miles), but its extremely fertile lava terrain is ideal for the cultivation of capers and lentils. The steep and rocky coasts and the seascape that surrounds the island make it an ideal spot for underwater sports. Because of the importance of the sea beds, the first Marine Reserve in Italy was established here on 12 November 1986; it is run by the local authorities. Guided tours are organized by the Marine Reserve itself, and in July the island plays host to a series of international skin- and scuba-diving programmes. A particularly interesting underwater excursion is the one that starts off at Punta Gavazzi, with what could be described as an archaeological diving tour of the ancient Roman amphorae, old anchors and traces of the passage of sailors since the beginning of human history in this part of the sea.

The village of Ustica is dominated by the Capo Falconara promontory, where the Bourbon rulers built a little fort offering a splendid view as far as the Sicilian coast. Local life revolves around Piazza Umberto I, where there is a whitewashed parish church.

The main feature of a boat tour of the island is the great number of underwater caves in the rocky coastline: the Grotta Azzurra, whose large caverns are preceded by an imposing natural arch, the Grotta delle Colonne, with a cliff of the same name, and the Grotta Blasi, Grotta dell'Oro and Grotta delle Barche (where fishermen used to moor their boats during storms) are only a few of the many caves to be seen.

TOP 3 USTICA DIVE CENTRES

Alta Marea

Lungomare Cristoforo Colombo altamarea ustica.it

Alta Marea offers courses for all abilities, from single dives to deep-sea immersion.

Orca Diving Ustica

Via Cristoforo Colombo orcadivingustica.com

Scuba-certified or snorkel-ready, equipment can be hired to experienced divers.

Ustica Diving Centre

Piazza Umberto I usticadiving.it

There's no need to go deep to enjoy Ustica's waters - opt for a snorkelling course followed by a swim.

Snorkeling in the clear waters of Lampedusa island

AGRIGENTO AND THE SOUTHWEST

This corner of Sicily is only about 150 km (95 miles) from North Africa. Along the coast, steep craggy cliffs alternate with flatter stretches of sand. This southern shore was a favourite landing place for travellers plying the Mediterranean, with their ships putting in at places like Agrigento, Eraclea and Sciacca. Agrigento became an important Greek centre, and an entire valley of temples remains as evidence of their skills. Some are still in good condition 2,000 years later. Meanwhile, the Romans left an extensive villa at Piazza Armerina, saved for posterity by being buried under mud.

Around the towns of Enna and Caltanissetta lies the stony heart of the island, exploited for its sulphur mines and quarries for centuries. Inland, Southwestern Sicily is a totally different world from the coast. Many of the people of these rather isolated places have retained a deep-seated religious faith, which is expressed in the colourful processions held during Easter Week. The flatter land and slopes nearer to the sea were once the domain of ancient feudal estates with their olive and orange groves, vividly described in Giuseppe di Lampedusa's novel *The Leopard*. This, perhaps the most truly "Sicilian" part of Sicily, was also the birthplace of the great Italian writer Pirandello.

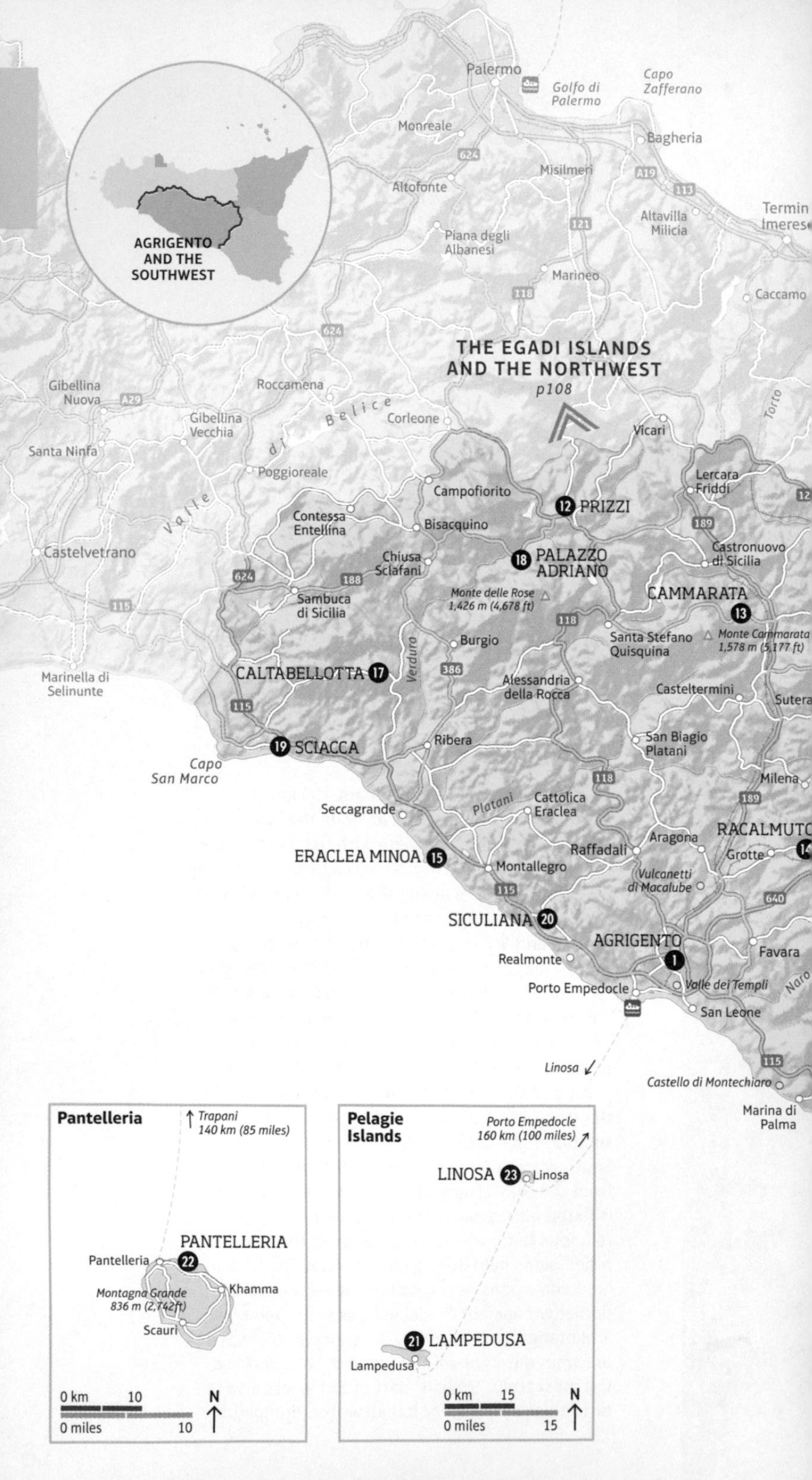

AGRIGENTO AND THE SOUTHWEST
THE EGADI ISLANDS AND THE NORTHWEST
p108
Palermo
Golfo di Palermo
Capo Zafferano
Monreale
Bagheria
Misilmeri
Altofonte
Termini Imerese
Altavilla Milicia
Piana degli Albanesi
Marineo
Caccamo
Gibellina Nuova
Roccamena
Gibellina Vecchia
Corleone
Santa Ninfa
Poggioreale
Valle del Belice
Vicari
Lercara Friddi
Campofiorito
12 PRIZZI
Contessa Entellina
Bisacquino
Castelvetrano
Chiusa Sclafani
18 PALAZZO ADRIANO
Castronuovo di Sicilia
Sambuca di Sicilia
Monte delle Rose 1,426 m (4,678 ft)
CAMMARATA 13
Burgio
Santa Stefano Quisquina
Monte Cammarata 1,578 m (5,177 ft)
Verdura
Marinella di Selinunte
CALTABELLOTTA 17
Alessandria della Rocca
Casteltermini
Sutera
Ribera
San Biagio Platani
19 SCIACCA
Capo San Marco
Milena
Seccagrande
Platani
Cattolica Eraclea
Aragona
RACALMUTO 14
ERACLEA MINOA 15
Raffadali
Grotte
Montallegro
Vulcanetti di Macalube
SICULIANA 20
AGRIGENTO 1
Favara
Realmonte
Porto Empedocle
Valle dei Templi
Naro
San Leone
Linosa
Castello di Montechiaro
Marina di Palma
Pantelleria
Trapani 140 km (85 miles)
PANTELLERIA 22
Pantelleria
Khamma
Montagna Grande 836 m (2,742 ft)
Scauri
0 km 10
0 miles 10
N
Pelagie Islands
Porto Empedocle 160 km (100 miles)
LINOSA 23
Linosa
21 LAMPEDUSA
Lampedusa
0 km 15
0 miles 15
N

AGRIGENTO AND THE SOUTHWEST

Must Sees

1. Agrigento
2. Villa Romana del Casale

Experience More

3. Piazza Armerina
4. Castello di Falconara
5. Enna
6. Morgantina
7. Caltanissetta
8. Licata
9. Palma di Montechiaro
10. Canicattì
11. Naro
12. Prizzi
13. Cammarata
14. Racalmuto
15. Eraclea Minoa
16. Mussomeli
17. Caltabellotta
18. Palazzo Adriano
19. Sciacca
20. Siculiana
21. Lampedusa
22. Pantelleria
23. Linosa

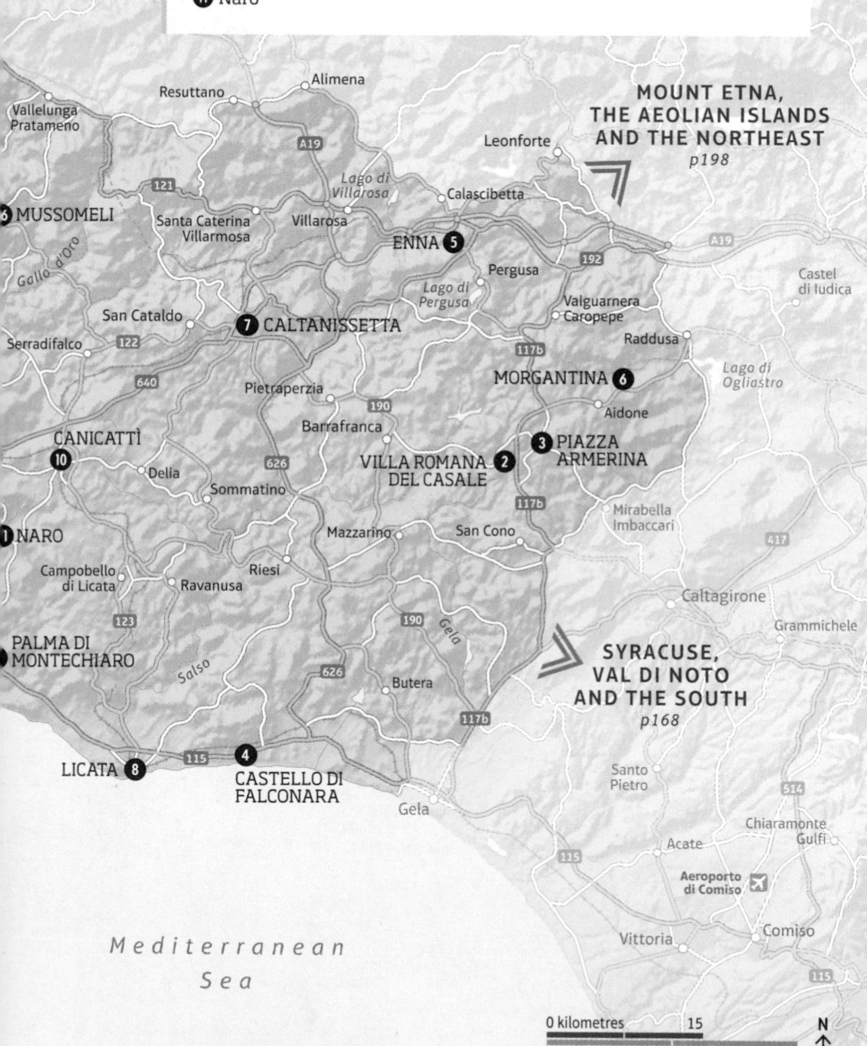

1

AGRIGENTO

C5 Palermo From Palermo (892 021) Via Empedocle 73; www.visitsicily.info/agrigento

There are two main sights in Agrigento: the magnificent remains of the Greek colony in the Valle dei Templi *(p150)* and the rocky hill where the medieval town was built. The town of Akragas was founded by the Greeks, then conquered by the Romans. During a period of barbarian invasions the town moved from the valley to the rock. It was subsequently ruled in turn by the Byzantines, the Arabs, and the Normans.

Cathedral and Museo Diocesano

Piazza Don Minzoni

Agrigento's Cathedral was founded in the 12th century and subsequently enlarged and altered. The bell tower has a series of Catalan-Gothic single lancet windows, while others are in the original style. Inside is the Cappella di San Gerlando, which boasts an impressive Gothic portal. The ceiling features painted sections dating from the 16th and 17th centuries. An acoustic phenomenon known as *portavoce* takes place in the chapel: stand under the apse and you will clearly hear people at the other end of the nave, 80 m (262 ft) away. The **Museum Diocesano** features Roman sarcophagi and frescoes taken from the Cathedral in 1951.

Museo Diocesano

10am-7pm Tue-Sat, 10am-1:30pm & 3-7pm Sun
museodiocesanoag.it

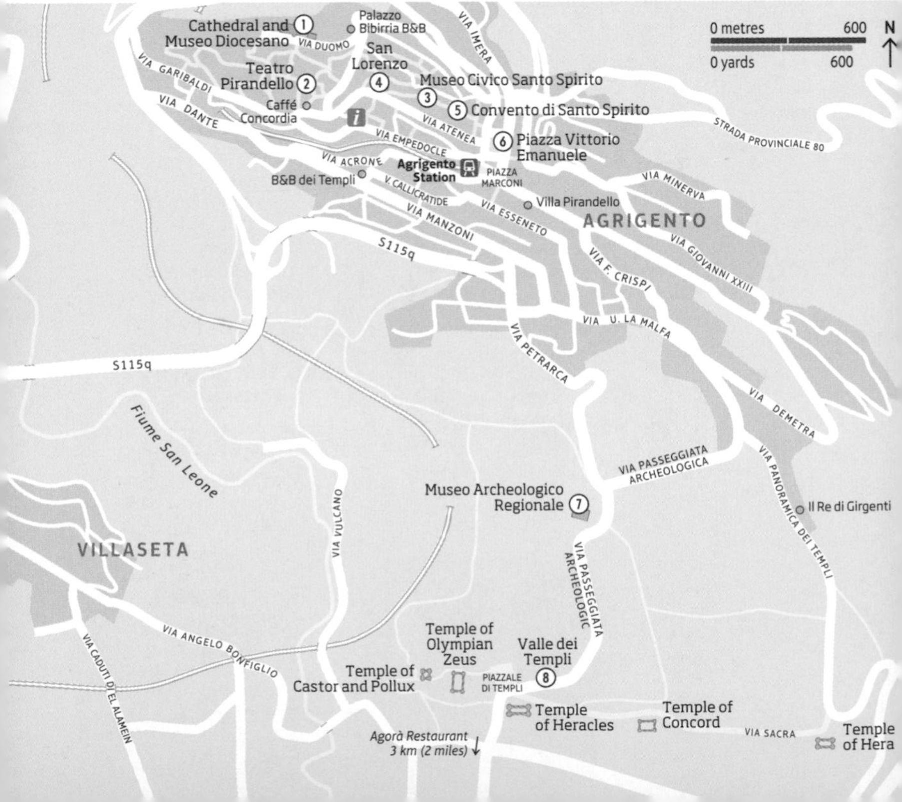

Cathedral and Museo Diocesano ①
Palazzo Bibirria B&B
San Lorenzo ④
Teatro Pirandello ②
Caffé Concordia
Museo Civico Santo Spirito ③
⑤ Convento di Santo Spirito
⑥ Piazza Vittorio Emanuele
Agrigento Station
Piazza Marconi
B&B dei Templi
Villa Pirandello
AGRIGENTO
VILLASETA
Museo Archeologico Regionale ⑦
Il Re di Girgenti
Temple of Olympian Zeus
Valle dei Templi ⑧
Piazzale di Templi
Temple of Castor and Pollux
Temple of Heracles
Temple of Concord
Temple of Hera
Agorà Restaurant 3 km (2 miles)
Via Duomo
Via Garibaldi
Via Dante
Via Imera
Via Atenea
Via Empedocle
Via Acrone
V. Callicratide
Via Manzoni
Via Esseneto
S115q
Strada Provinciale 80
Via Minerva
Via Giovanni XXIII
Via F. Crispi
Via U. La Malfa
Via Petrarca
Via Demetra
Via Passeggiata Archeologica
Via Panoramica dei Templi
Fiume San Leone
Via Vulcano
Via Angelo Bonfiglio
Via Caduti di El Alamein
Via Sacra
0 metres 600
0 yards 600
N

The modern city of Agrigento nestled on the southern coast of Sicily

Teatro Pirandello

Piazza Pirandello
fondazioneteatro pirandello.it

Founded in 1870 as the Teatro Regina Margherita, the theatre was renamed in 1946 after the famous Agrigento-born playwright, whose works feature prominently from November to April.

Museo Civico Santo Spirito

Via Santo Spirito 8
0922-590 371 Sat & hols

This museum, which is located next to the old Convento Suore Benedettine, houses medieval sculptures and an ethno-anthropological section. The nearby **Collegio dei Filippini** contains paintings from the 14th–20th centuries.

Collegio dei Filippini

Via Atenea 270 9am-1pm and 3:30-6:30pm Mon-Sat

INSIDER TIP
San Leone Music

To hear live music head to the San Leone quarter of Agrigento, a district paralleling the coastline, with a plethora of jazzy lounge bars and foot-thumping beachfront nightclubs where you can dance until dawn.

San Lorenzo

Piazza del Purgatorio
For special events only

Little remains of this church (also known as Chiesa del Purgatorio), which was rebuilt in the Baroque style in the 1600s. The two-stage façade has a delightful portal flanked by two large spiral columns and a large bell tower. Both the interior and exterior boast a series of allegorical statues representing the Christian virtues, executed in the early 18th century by Giuseppe and Giacomo Serpotta, and a *Madonna of the Pomegranate* attributed to Antonello Gagini.

Near the church, under a stone lion, is the Ipogeo del Purgatorio (Hypogeum of Purgatory), a network of subterranean conduits built in the 5th century BC to supply water to the city's various quarters.

EAT

Agorà Restaurant

A light and breezy lunch spot decorated in the hues of the sand and sea, with a well-curated menu of Sicilian classics.

Via Leonardo Sciascia 27c Thu agora restaurant.it

Il Re di Girgenti

Low-lit, eclectic decor, great food and knockout views of the Valley of the Temples.

Via Panoramica dei Templi 51 Tue; Nov ilredigirgenti.it

Caffè Concordia

Exquisitely decorated tearoom with a wide selection of beverages.

Piazza Luigi Pirandello 36 Mon 0922-25894

STAY

Palazzo Bibirria B&B
In the heart of Agrigento's historic centre, this thoroughly charming boutique accommodation is well positioned to explore the sights of the city on foot. The Sicilian breakfast, a feast of sweets and savouries, includes gluten-free options on request.

Via Duomo 60
palazzobibirria.it

Villa Pirandello
A Sicilian-English family runs this B&B, housed in a 19th-century villa where Luigi Pirandello's wife once lived. Simple, bright rooms and a sunny terrace, with the Terra restaurant in its shady garden.

Via Francesco Crispi 34
villapirandello.com

B&B Dei Templi
A good budget option. Five basic and orderly rooms are housed in a compact, modest apartment building five minutes from the railway station. It's similar to a hostel, but with private bathrooms. Guests share a common kitchen area and a small washing machine is provided.

Via Callicratide 164
bbdeitempli.it

Convento di Santo Spirito

Salita Santo Spirito
0922-20664 Daily

This stunning abbey complex is of ancient origin. The church and adjacent Cistercian monastery were founded in the 13th century by Countess Prefoglio of the powerful Chiaramonte family. They were altered several times, particularly the façade, which, however, still maintains a Gothic portal and rose window. For many centuries the church was the most important in the Agrigento area and was known as the Badia Grande. In the 18th century the nave was decorated with lavish stuccowork that mirrors the shapes of the church. A series of high-relief panels depict scenes from Christ's childhood.

Next to the church is the monastery, whose elegant cloister is well worth a visit. The building is now city property and houses a civic museum. The impressive chapterhouse is lined with Gothic arcades.

Piazza Vittorio Emanuele

This large, lively, traffic-filled square connects the old town of Agrigento with the newer part, which developed during the 19th century. The two main areas, Girgenti to the west and Rupe Atenea to the east, were once separated by a valley that was filled in during the late 19th century, blocking

Located in a panoramic spot with beautiful views over the Valle dei Templi, the Museo Archeologico Regionale exhibits finds excavated from around Agrigento.

↑ Admiring the courtyard of the 13th-century Convento di Santo Spirito

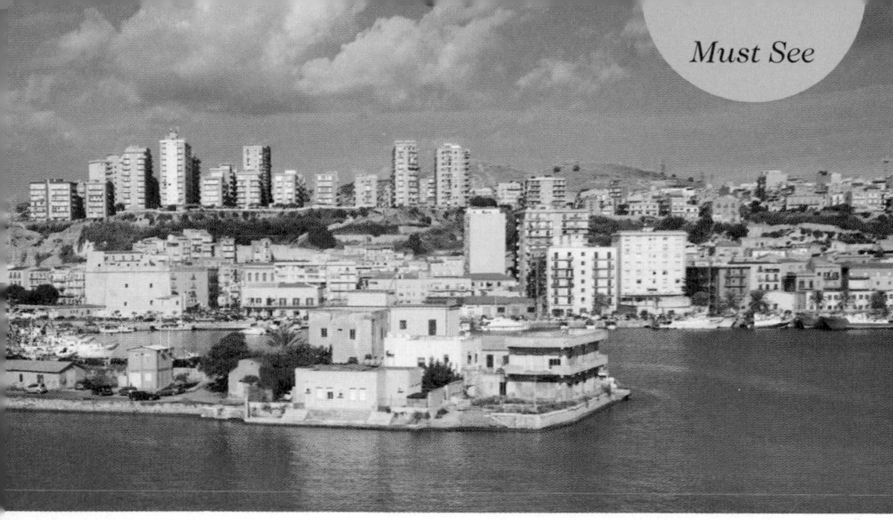

Bastione di Carlo V in Porto Empedocle, near Piazza Vittorio Emanuele

what was traditionally known as "Empedocles' opening", through which the north wind blew, cooling the valley below.

Towards the sea is the parish of Kaos, near Villaseta, worth visiting to see the **Birthplace of Luigi Pirandello**, the house of the great dramatist and novelist and winner of the Nobel Prize for Literature in 1934. It now functions as a museum, displaying numerous memorabilia, photographs, letters and manuscripts. The urn containing Pirandello's ashes can be found in a crack in a rock next to an old fallen pine, facing the sea.

Nearby, Porto Empedocle was once an important outlet for mining activity. In the old harbour is the Bastione di Carlo V (Rampart of Charles V), while there is a constant bustle of fishing boats around the more industrialized area.

Heading roughly north from Agrigento and turning off SS189 at the Comitini crossroads, 2 km (1 mile) of dirt road to the south takes you to a place famous for a curious geological phenomenon: little volcano-shaped cones, known as the Vulcanetti di Macalube, emit methane gas bubbles and brackish mud in a landscape made sterile by this volcanic activity.

Birthplace of Luigi Pirandello

Contrada Caos, Villaseta
0922-511 826 9am-7:30pm daily

7 Museo Archeologico Regionale

Contrada San Nicola
0922-183 9996
9am-7:30pm daily

Part of the Convento di San Nicola and located in a panoramic spot over the Valle dei Templi, the excellent Museo Archeologico Regionale exhibits finds excavated from around Agrigento. Among the items on display are a remarkable Attic vase, the Krater of Dionysus, and the 5th-century BC marble statue of a young athlete known as the Ephebus of Agrigento.

One of the many Attic vases held at the Museo Archeologico Regionale

THE ORANGES OF RIBERA

The principal home of orange-growing is the plain around Mount Etna *(p210)*, however oranges play an important role in the southwestern corner of Sicily, too. In Ribera, an agricultural town where the statesman Francesco Crispi was born, they grow a special type of navel orange that was brought to Sicily from America by returning emigrants. These enormous and delicious oranges are celebrated in an annual orange festival, with cooking workshops and exhibitions, and during which the public gardens are filled with impressive sculptures made of fruit.

8

VALLE DEI TEMPLI

Agrigento Ruins: 8:30am-8pm daily; Museo Archeologico: 9am-7:30pm Mon-Sat, 9am-1:30pm Sun & pub hols parcodeitempli.net

Straddling a low ridge to the south of Agrigento, the Valle dei Templi (Valley of the Temples) is one of the most impressive complexes of ancient Greek buildings outside Greece and a prime example of the magnificence of Magna Graecia (Greater Greece). The valley was once at the heart of ancient Akragas (modern-day Agrigento), which the Greek poet Pindar described as "the fairest city inhabited by mortals". It became a UNESCO World Heritage Site in 1997.

Founded in 581 BC by colonists from Gela, Akragas was one of Sicily's richest and most powerful cities – visitors reported that its citizens had ivory furniture, abundant silver and gold, and even made elaborate tombs for their pets. The city was especially well known for breeding horses, which consistently won in the Olympic Games. After being besieged by the Carthaginians in 406 BC, Akragas was taken by the Romans in 261 BC, who sold the population into slavery and renamed the city Agrigentum. It remained in Roman control until the fall of the Empire. Today, you can explore the ruins of seven major temples, a series of minor shrines and a fascinating archaeology museum on the site.

The thick brush of the Valle dei Templi at the Temple of Concordia, where Igor Mitoraj's statue *Fallen Icarus* lies (*inset*) ↑

EARLY CHRISTIAN CATACOMBS

The Valle dei Templi is famous for its splendid monuments of the Magna Graecia civilization, but it also has early Christian ruins. The Ipogei of Villa Igea (also known as the Grotta di Frangipane), between the Temple of Heracles and the Temple of Concord, were cut out of the rock to house the bodies of the first Christians here. A series of niches, closed off by stone slabs, alternated with chapels that still bear traces of wall paintings.

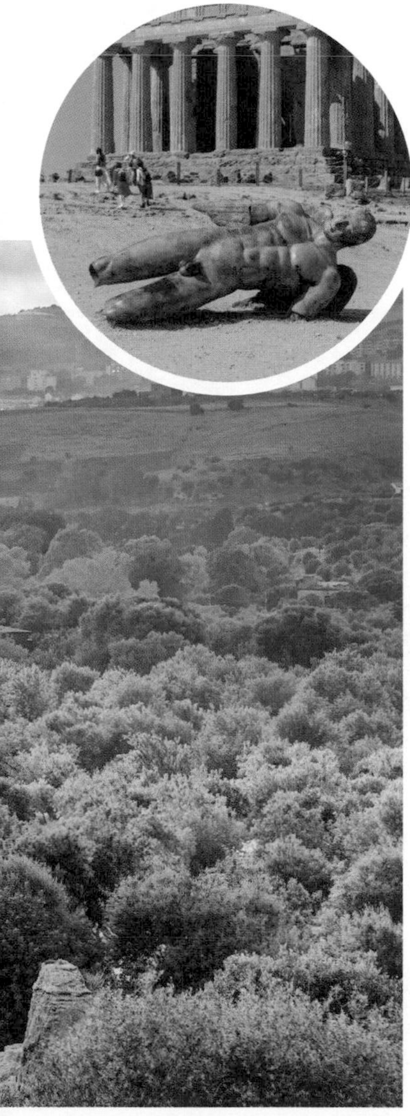

Valley Highlights

Museo Archeologico

▶ The Archaeological Museum was opened to the public in 1967. The 13 rooms display objects ranging from prehistoric times to the early Christian period, but the emphasis is on Greek and Roman finds such as vases, statues and sarcophagi. There is also a Telamon (pillar in the form of a male statue) from the Temple of Olympian Zeus.

Temple of Olympian Zeus

Only fragmentary ruins remain of this 5th-century-BC temple - the largest Doric temple ever built. It was once supported by 38 giant Telamons, one of which is now on display in the Museo Archeologico.

Temple of Heracles

▶ These eight columns belonged to the oldest temple dedicated to Heracles, worshipped by both the Greeks and the Romans. The archaic 6th-century-BC Doric structure has an elongated rectangular plan.

Temple of Concord

With its 34 columns, this is one of the best-preserved Doric temples in the world, partly thanks to alterations made in the 4th century, when it became a Christian basilica. It was restored to its original Classical form in 1748.

Temple of Hera

Relatively well-preserved, this 5th-century-BC temple was restored in Roman times, and 25 of the original 34 columns are still standing.

Temple of Castor and Pollux

▶ This temple's four surviving columns and partial roof, a symbol of the Valley of the Temples, were restored in the 19th century.

2

VILLA ROMANA DEL CASALE

E5 5 km (3 miles) SW of Piazza Armerina Apr-Oct: 9am-7pm daily (Nov-Mar: to 5pm) villaromanadelcasale.it

It is thought that this huge, sumptuous villa, with its public halls, private quarters, baths and courtyards, once belonged to Maximianus Herculeus, Diocletian's co-emperor, from AD 286 to 305.

This famous villa is one of the most fascinating archaeological attractions in Sicily. The exceptionally beautiful mosaics that decorated the rooms of the landowner's apartments have been preserved through the centuries, thanks to a flood that buried them in mud in the 12th century. The villa was discovered in the late 19th century. A logical sequence for a visit is as follows: the thermae, the large peristyle, the long corridor with hunting scenes, and lastly the owners' private apartments.

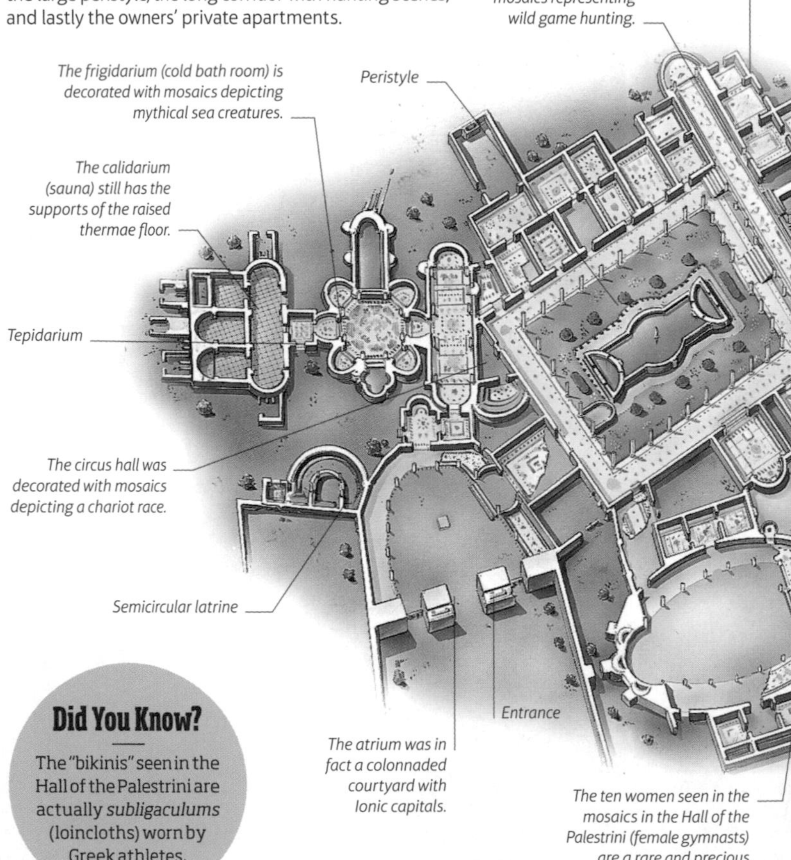

The vestibule in the private apartments of the villa's northern area has a large mosaic depicting Ulysses and the cyclops Polyphemus.
This passageway contains splendid mosaics representing wild game hunting.
The frigidarium (cold bath room) is decorated with mosaics depicting mythical sea creatures.
Peristyle
The calidarium (sauna) still has the supports of the raised thermae floor.
Tepidarium
The circus hall was decorated with mosaics depicting a chariot race.
Semicircular latrine
Entrance
The atrium was in fact a colonnaded courtyard with Ionic capitals.
The ten women seen in the mosaics in the Hall of the Palestrini (female gymnasts) are a rare and precious record of the Roman fashions of the time.

Did You Know?

The "bikinis" seen in the Hall of the Palestrini are actually *subligaculums* (loincloths) worn by Greek athletes.

Visitors admiring the superb mosaics uncovered at the villa

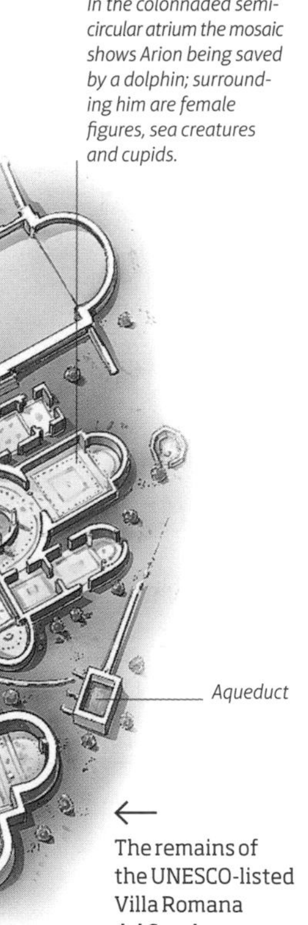
In the colonnaded semi-circular atrium the mosaic shows Arion being saved by a dolphin; surrounding him are female figures, sea creatures and cupids.
Aqueduct
The mosaics in the triclinium (dining room) feature the Labours of Hercules and other mythological subjects.

The remains of the UNESCO-listed Villa Romana del Casale

EXPERIENCE MORE

3

Piazza Armerina

E5 Enna
Via Gen. Muscarà 47a; www.piazzaarmerina.org

Situated in the middle of an area inhabited since the 8th century BC, Piazza Armerina developed in the Middle Ages, a period marked by frequent clashes between the local population – strongly influenced by centuries of Arab domination – and their Latin conquerors. After the huge devastation wrought in the 12th century by continuing battles between these two factions, Piazza Armerina was recreated around the Colle Mira hill (in the middle of the present-day Monte quarter) and was populated by a colony of Lombards from Piacenza. A new, massive defensive wall system was built in the late 14th century, but the town soon spread well beyond its fortifications into the surrounding hills and slopes.

In the heart of town is a large Aragonese castle, built by King Martin I in the late 14th century, whose massive towers dominate the Cathedral. Dedicated to Our Lady of the Assumption, the Cathedral is flanked by the campanile (bell tower) of another church which had been built on the same site in the 14th century. Inside, look out for the choir, built in 1627, and a wooden crucifix painted in the late 15th century. Entry to the cathedral also affords access to the adjacent Museo Diocesano, which has a small but impressive collection of vestments, monstrances and reliquaries on display.

Beyond the Duomo, the town has a great deal else to offer. Piazza Garibaldi is the heart of town life, boasting the Baroque Palazzo del Senato and two palatial mansions belonging to the barons of Capodarso. The whole of the historic centre, with its many charming medieval alleys, steps and lanes, deserves further exploration on foot.

Not far from the centre, at the end of Via Tasso, is Chiesa del Priorato di Sant'Andrea, founded in 1096 and then acquired by the Knights of the Order of the Holy Sepulchre. This magnificent example of Sicilian Romanesque architecture has a commanding view over a valley. Do not miss seeing the series of 12th- to 14th-century frescoes inside (visits are allowed only on Sundays during Mass).

Piazza Armerina's Duomo overlooking the half-medieval, half-Baroque old town

Castello di Falconara

D5 By appt only
castello difalconara.it

Not far from Licata is the village of Falconara, famous most of all for the impressive castle towering above the sea from the top of a rocky bluff. The Castello di Falconara was built in the 15th century. It is usually closed, but you can make an appointment to view with the custodian.

Towards Licata is the Salso river, the second longest in Sicily. Its name derives from the many outcrops of rock salt that make its waters salty (*salso* means saline). The river flows through the Sommatino plateau and down a series of gullies before meandering across the coastal plains.

Enna

E4 From Catania and Palermo STR Piazza Colajanni 6; www. ennaturismo.it

At 931 m (3,054 ft) the mountain town of Enna is the highest provincial capital in Italy. In antiquity Enna was first Greek, then Carthaginian and finally Roman. It remained a Byzantine stronghold even after the Arab conquest of Palermo, and was then conquered by general Al-Abbas Ibn Fadhl in 859; it was wrested from the Muslims only in 1087. From that time it was repeatedly fortified around the strongholds of Castello di Lombardia and Castello Vecchio (present-day Torre di Federico). The defensive walls, no longer visible, were the basis of the town's plan, while all the principal sites of religious and civic power were constructed on what is now Via Roma.

The town's exceptional position means splendid views. Going up Via Roma, you first come to Piazza Vittorio Emanuele, site of San Francesco d'Assisi, the only original part of which is the fine 15th-century bell tower. In Piazza Colajanni you will see the façade of Palazzo Pollicarini, which has many Catalan Gothic features, as well as the former church of Santa Chiara.

In 1307 Eleonora, wife of Frederick II of Aragón, founded the Cathedral of Enna. The building was destroyed by fire in the

EASTER WEEK

Easter celebrations of the *Misteri*, or statues of the Stations of the Cross, are of great importance. At Enna they begin on Palm Sunday and last until Easter Sunday the following week. Each day processions make their way through the streets of Enna, including a huge torchlit procession on Good Friday. The celebrations culminate on Easter Sunday, when the Resurrected Christ and the Virgin Mary statues meet in Piazza Duomo.

The Castello di Falconara near Licata, watching over Mediterranean shores

mid-1400s and subsequently rebuilt. The Cathedral is richly decorated with an assortment of statues and paintings.

The **Museo Regionale Interdisciplinare di Enna** has a fine display of prehistoric, Greek and Roman archaeological items found in the town, in the area around and near Lake Pergusa. But the pride and joy of Enna are its fortresses. The **Castello di Lombardia** is one of the grandest in Sicily. A tour here includes the three courtyards, the Torre Pisana and the Rocca di Cerere. In the public gardens is the octagonal **Torre di Federico II**, the only remaining part of the original defences.

Museo Regionale Interdisciplinare di Enna
0935-507 63 04
9am-7pm daily

Castello di Lombardia
Piazza Mazzini 8
0935-500 875
10am-7pm daily

6 Morgantina

E5 8am-1hr before sunset Mon-Sat STR, Via Generale Muscarà 47a, Piazza Armerina, 0935-680 201; Morgantina archaeological site, 0935-879 55

Situated about 4 km (2 miles) from Aidone, the ancient city of Morgantina was founded by the Morgeti, a population from Latium who settled here around 1000 BC. The city was then occupied by Greek colonists. Its golden age, when it was a strategic trade centre between the north and south of Sicily, was in the Hellenistic and Roman periods. From the top of the hill visitors have a fine view of what remains of the theatre, the city streets and the agora.

STAY

Castello di Falconara

This 14th-century fortress-turned-hotel more than hints at the grandeur of its old-world charm and affluence. Hugging a rocky cliff, 16 rooms are sprinkled about the manor house, some of which are part of a luxurious apartment that sleeps 13. Along with beach access, a lake-sized swimming pool and a sea-facing veranda, this historic Sicilian castle promises a stay fit for royalty.

D4 Strada Statale 115, KM 245, Butera, Caltanissetta castellodifalconara.it

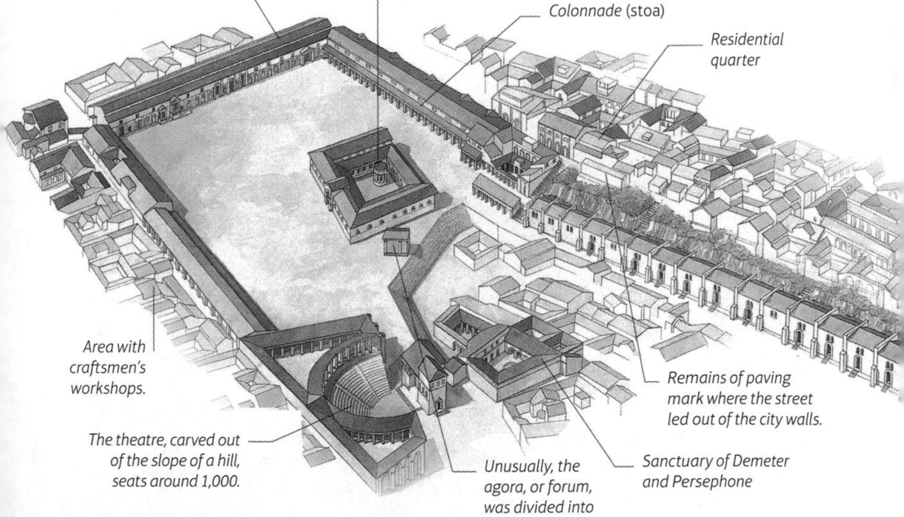

The Gymnasium, a large area for athletic exercises

The market lay in the middle of the upper agora.

Colonnade (stoa)

Residential quarter

Area with craftsmen's workshops.

Remains of paving mark where the street led out of the city walls.

The theatre, carved out of the slope of a hill, seats around 1,000.

Sanctuary of Demeter and Persephone

Unusually, the agora, or forum, was divided into two parts.

Reconstruction of the city of Morgantina as it appeared around 300 BC

7

Caltanissetta

D4 From Catania & Palermo Proloco, Largo Barile; www.proloco caltanissetta.com

One of the earliest traces of a settlement in this area is the **Abbazia di Santo Spirito**, a Norman abbey commissioned by Roger I and his wife Adelasia in the late 11th century and consecrated in 1153. In common with other hill towns in the interior, Caltanissetta was surrounded by medieval walls and then expanded towards the monasteries, built around the town from the 15th century on. The centre of a thriving mineral-rich area, it became prosperous after the Unification of Italy thanks to the sulphur and rock salt mines. It was during this period that the look of the town changed with the construction of buildings and public works.

In the heart of town, in Piazza Garibaldi, are the Baroque San Sebastiano and the Cathedral (dedicated to Santa Maria la Nova and San Michele). A brief walk down Corso Umberto I will take you to Sant'Agata – or Chiesa del Collegio – built in 1605 for the Jesuits of Caltanissetta, next to their seminary. The rich decoration inside includes a marble statue of *St Ignatius in Glory* on the left-hand transept altar, the altarpiece *San Francesco Saverio* in a side chapel and a canvas of the *Martyrdom of Sant'Agata*. Not far from the Castello di Pietrarossa, probably a former Arab fortress, is the **Museo Archeologico**, where the sections are given over to archaeology and modern art.

The **Museo Mineralogico, Paleontologico e della Zolfara**, established by the local Mineralogy School, S. Mottura, has a fine and extensive collection of minerals and fossils.

In common with other hill towns in the interior, Caltanissetta was surrounded by medieval walls and then expanded towards the monasteries.

Abbazia di Santo Spirito

Via di Santo Spirito 57 0934-566 596 9am-noon & 4-7pm daily

Museo Archeologico

Contrada Santo Spirito 0934-567 062 9am-1pm & 3:30-7pm daily Last Mon of month

Museo Mineralogico, Paleontologico e della Zolfara

Viale della Regione 71 0934-591 280 9am-1pm & 3-7pm Mon-Sat, by request Sun

8 

Licata

D6 From Syracuse, Palermo & Catania, via Caltanissetta; 0922-868 227 Town hall; Proloco; www.proloco licata.it

One of the chief market garden towns in southern Sicily, Licata lies on the coast, at the mouth of the river Salso. It was built in the

↑ The interior of Chiesa Matrice di Santa Maria la Nova, or Black Christ's Chapel, in Licata

Did You Know?

Licata is the largest European exporting centre of sulphur.

Greek period and under Roman rule became the port for the shipment of local produce. Evidence of the town's former wealth can be seen in the many rock-hewn Byzantine churches. After the period of Arab rule, in 1234 Frederick II made it part of the public domain, building fortresses that have disappeared over the centuries since, including Castel Nuovo, which was destroyed by the Turks at the end of the 1561 siege. Licata again became a part of history on 10 July 1943, when Allied troops landed nearby and advanced northwards in their conquest of Italian territory as part of Operation Husky during World War II.

The centre of town life is Piazza Progresso, where there is the Art Deco Municipio or Town Hall, designed in 1935 by Ernesto Basile, which houses some interesting artworks, including a statue of the *Madonna and Child* and a 15th-century triptych. Also worth visiting is the **Museo Archeologico**, which has exhibits of prehistoric artifacts from the Palaeolithic to the Bronze Age, archaic Greek and Hellenistic archaeological finds, and a series of medieval statues representing the Christian virtues. Along Corso Vittorio Emanuele, which leads towards the coast, there are some beautiful patrician mansions such as Palazzo Frangipane, which has an 18th-century façade decorated with reliefs. On the Corso Vittorio Emanuele you can also see the Chiesa Matrice di Santa Maria la Nova, which, according to local legend, the Turks tried to burn down in 1553. Founded in the 1500s, it houses a 16th-century crucifix and a 17th-century Flemish nativity scene.

Caltanissetta Cathedral's blue cupola and bell towers rising above the town skyline

DRINK

The region along the slopes of Mount Sant'Oliva has long been famous for its unique wines. Be sure to take some time to tour the area's vast, undulating wineries, where the vines are blessed with warm sun, cool sea breezes and rich, chalky soil. Afterwards, make your way to the wineries' tasting cellars to sample some of the wines for yourself.

Quignones Casa Vinicola
D6 Contrada Sant'Oliva, S.S. 123-Km 31.900, Licata
quignones.it

Feudi del Pisciotto
E5 Contrada del Pisciotto, Nescemi, 20 km (12 miles) SW of Caltagirone
winerelaisfeudidelpisciotto.com

Tenuta dell'Abate
D4 C.da Giffarrone Abate, Caltanissetta
tenutadellabate.it

A lively area on the waterfront for eating and shopping is the new Marina di Cala del Sole. A popular mooring with visitors arriving by boat, the Marina is the centre of Licata's sailing scene, with bars, cafés, a mall and a multiplex cinema, as well as useful tourist facilities.

Museo Archeologico
Via Dante, Badia di Licata
0922-772 602 9am-1pm Tue-Sat (Tue-Thu: also 3-6pm)

9

Palma di Montechiaro

C5 Town hall; 0922-799 001

Founded in 1637 by Carlo Tomasi, the Prince of Lampedusa, the small coastal town of Palma owes its name to the palm tree on the coat of arms of the De Caro family, relatives of the Tomasi. The town was the property of the Tomasi di Lampedusa family up to the early 19th century, but the family name became really famous only after the publication of the novel *Il Gattopardo (The Leopard)* in 1958, written by Giuseppe Tomasi di Lampedusa.

Palma was created with a town plan, partly the inspiration of the renowned 17th-century astronomer Giovanni Battista Odierna, and loosely based on that of Jerusalem. The layout revolves around Piazza Provenzani, with the Sicilian Baroque church of Santissimo Rosario and a Benedictine monastery. Further up is the monumental stairway leading to Piazza Santa Rosalia, with the Chiesa Madre, built in the late 1600s with an impressive two-stage façade flanked by twin bell towers. On Sundays and holidays this square is the hub of town life.

As you walk through town you will encounter a number of interesting Baroque buildings. A few miles away, not far from the sea, are the evocative ruins of Castello di Montechiaro, founded, according to tradition, by Federico III Chiaramonte. Although it is now closed for restoration, it is nonetheless worthwhile visiting the site of this 15th-century castle because of the wonderful views of the coastline from its walls. It's best to head here just before the sun sets for a delightful evening treat.

1863

The year Montechiaro was added to the name of Palma.

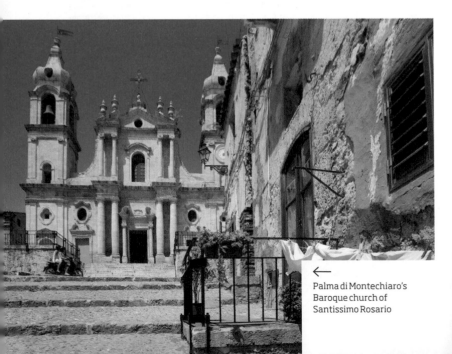

Canicattì

D5 Town hall; 0922-734 111/734 508; Proloco Largo Aosta; 377-236 43 87

The large agricultural town of Canicattì owes its fame to the production of dessert grapes (a festival in celebration is held each autumn). Known to Arab geographers as *al-Qattà*, this town became a part of documented Sicilian history in the 14th century, when it was registered as the fief of the Palmieri family from Naro. The late 18th century marked a period of prosperity and growth under the Bonanno family, who commissioned numerous buildings and public works.

In the centre of town are the Castello Bonanno and the Torre dell'Orologio, both rebuilt from ruins in the 1930s. Economic prosperity is confirmed by the many churches – San Diego, rebuilt in the Baroque period with stucco decoration; the Chiesa del Purgatorio, with a statue of the Sacred Heart; the Chiesa del Carmelo, rebuilt

←

Palma di Montechiaro's Baroque church of Santissimo Rosario

EAT

Bonfissuto Pasticceria

This pastry shop has gained a loyal following for its award-winning Christmas Panettone made with Sicilian ingredients like chocolate from Modica, pistachios from Bronte and strawberries from Ribera.

D5 Viale della Vittoria 72, Canicattì bonfissuto.com

↑ Naro's small Chiaramonte castle sits above the city with views over the hills and sea

in the early 20th century with funds donated by the local sulphur mine workers – and civic works such as the Fountain of Neptune and the Teatro Sociale. The Chiesa Madre is dedicated to San Pancrazio and it was rebuilt in the early 20th century. The current façade is the work of Francesco Basile and among its many interesting sculptures and paintings is the *Madonna delle Grazie*, sculpted in the 16th century in Byzantine style. Along the main street in the upper town there are three monasteries.

Naro

C5 Pro Loco; 0922-953 021/009

Naro lies on a hill in the middle of a water-rich area. Its name derives from ancient Greek and Arab origins – the Greek word for river is *naron*, and *nahr* is the Arab translation of the same.

A "resplendent" royal city during the reign of Frederick II Hohenstaufen, it was fortified at different times. Besides the Baroque churches and the remains of monasteries, there are the ruins of the medieval Chiaramonte castle (which is always closed), 14th-century Santa Caterina and the 16th-century Chiesa Madre.

Prizzi

C4 Town hall, Corso Umberto I 64; 091-834 4611

The slopes of wind-blown Mount Prizzi, overlooking the surrounding valleys, have been inhabited since ancient times. There was once a fortified Arab town here, but present-day Prizzi mostly reflects the vast influence of the Middle Ages. The maze of alleys winding up the slopes to the summit of Mount Prizzi (960 m/3,150 ft) is crowned by the ruins of the interesting medieval castle. As you stroll along the narrow streets you will see San Rocco, a large stretch of open space with Santa Maria delle Grazie, and the 18th-century Chiesa Madre, dedicated to St George and bearing a fine statue of the Archangel Michael.

IL GATTOPARDO (THE LEOPARD)

Giuseppe Tomasi di Lampedusa's famous novel *Il Gattopardo (The Leopard)* was a great success when it was published posthumously in 1958, selling over 100,000 copies. It was later made into a highly acclaimed film by Luchino Visconti. The novel was published thanks to the efforts of novelist Giorgio Bassani, who met Tomasi di Lampedusa in 1954, three years before he died. Most of the novel is set in Palermo, but there are recognizable descriptions of the villages and landscape in this part of Sicily, with which the author had strong bonds.

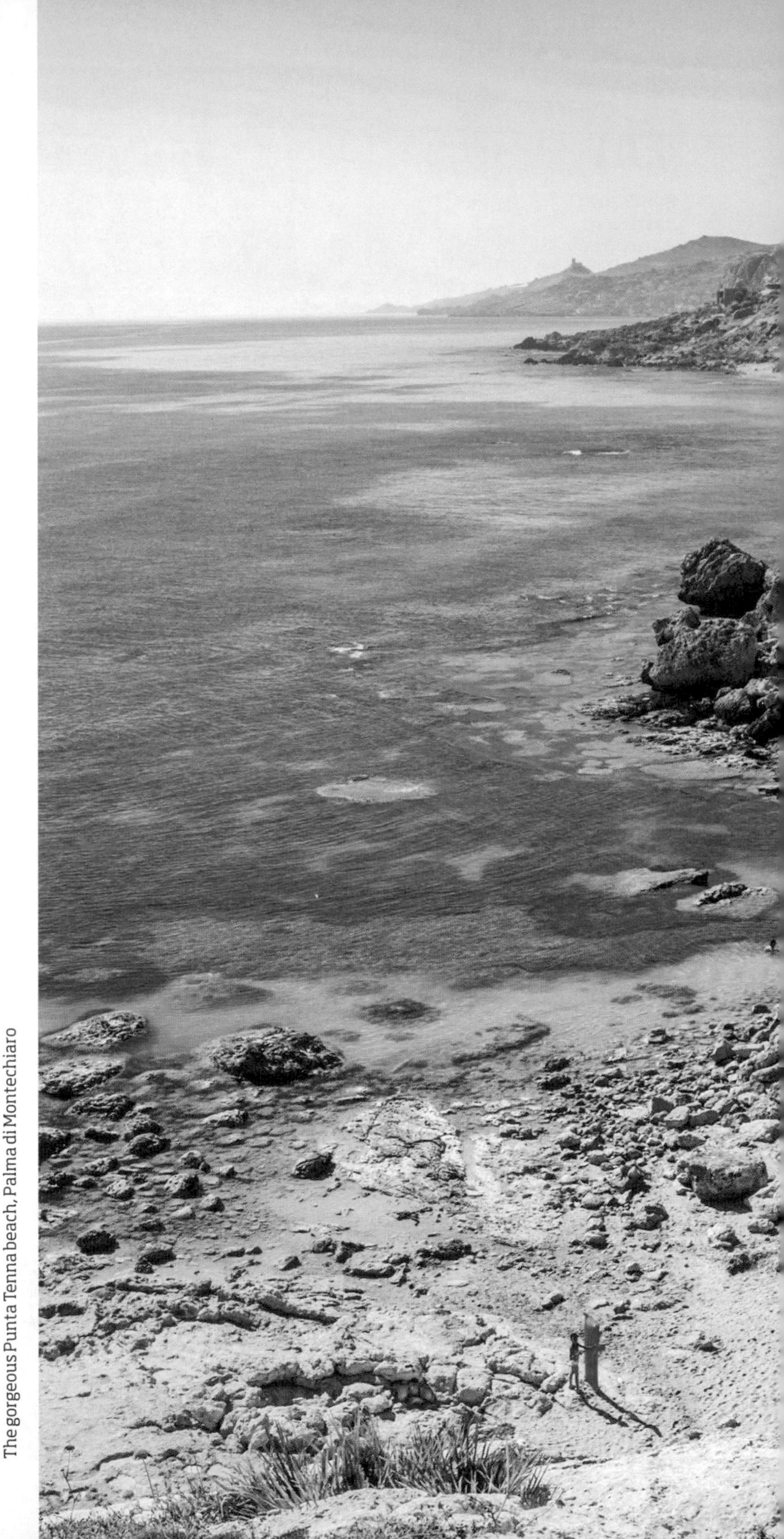

The gorgeous Punta Tenna beach, Palma di Montechiaro

↑ Expansive views over Sicilian valleys from the Cammarata hillside

13

Cammarata

 **C4 FS From Palermo & Agrigento i Town hall, via Roma; 0922-907 233**

The earliest historical records for this town date from the Norman period, when Roger I donated the fief to Lucia de Cammarata. The Chiesa Madre, San Nicolò di Bari, and the Dominican monastery, whose church was rebuilt in the 1930s, are all worth a visit. But the fascination of Cammarata lies in the overall layout: a labyrinth of alleys and steps – narrow or wide, depending on the natural slope of the rock – offering an unforgettable view of the valleys below this medieval hill town.

GREAT VIEW
Trail Monte Cammarata

Follow the signposted route from the centre of the town of Cammarata to Monte Cammarata, home to a vast, forested nature reserve with awe-inspiring views.

14

Racalmuto

 **C5 FS From Catania and Palermo (via Caltanissetta) i Town hall; 0922-940 000**

The town of Racalmuto (the name derives from the Arab *rahalmut*, or destroyed hamlet) was founded by Federico Chiaramonte, head of the powerful Sicilian Chiaramonte family, over an existing fortification. For centuries the growth of the town went hand in hand with the development of various monastic orders (Carmelite, Franciscan, Minor and Augustines), but the place still bears traces of the typical Arab layout marked by courtyards and alleys.

For centuries Racalmuto thrived on the mining of rock salt and sulphur. The town is also famous as being the birthplace of popular author Leonardo Sciascia. Today it is a renowned agricultural centre, especially known for its dessert grapes.

In the middle of town, in Piazza Umberto I, is the 17th-century Chiesa Madre dell'Annunziata, its interior decorated with lavish stucco, as well as San Giuseppe and the ruins of the 13th-century Chiaramonte castle, which is unfortunately closed to the public but worth a visit regardless. Steps lead to Piazza del Municipio, with the Santa Chiara Convent, now the Town Hall, and the Teatro Regina Margherita, founded in 1879 by Dionisio Sciascia. Further up the hill, at the far end of the steps, is the Sanctuary of Santa Maria del Monte, where an important annual festival is held on 11–14 July. Inside the sanctuary is a statue of the Virgin Mary from 1503. Other churches worth visiting are the Carmelite, which is home to a number of canvases by Italian painter Pietro D'Asaro, the Itria and San Giuliano, which was once the chapel of the Sant'Agostino Convent. A short walk from the centre takes you to Piazza Fontana, with a stone drinking trough, and, further along, Piazza San Francesco, where there is the monastery complex of the Conventual friars, rebuilt in the 1600s.

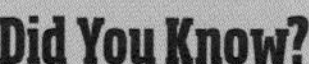

Did You Know?

Mussomeli's castle was considered impregnable, partly due to its hard-to-scale limestone rock.

15 Eraclea Minoa

B5 Digs: Cattolica Eraclea 9am-1 hr before sunset daily cattolica eracleaonline.it

This settlement was founded during the Mycenaean age and then developed by Spartan colonists who arrived in the 6th century BC and gave it its present name. After being fought over by Agrigento and Carthage, Eraclea became a Roman colony.

Today it is just a stone's throw from the craggy coast jutting out into the sea. Eraclea Minoa is a combination of a lovely setting and atmospheric ruins. The theatre is well preserved – excavations began in the 1950s – and hosts special performances of Greek theatre, although the overall impression is marred somewhat by the plastic used to protect it in bad weather. All around the theatre are the ruins of the ancient city with its defence system, as well as some necropolises.

16 Mussomeli

C4 comunedi mussomeli.it

In the 14th century, Manfredi III Chiaramonte founded the town of Mussomeli and the large fortress that still towers over it. The castle, called **Castello Manfredano** or Chiaramontano in honour of its founder and built over the remains of a Hohenstaufen fortification, was altered in the 15th century by the Castellar family. It has a second walled enclosure in the interior as well as the Sala dei Baroni, with noteworthy portals. From the outer walls there are panoramic views of the valleys and hills of Sicily's interior.

Castello Manfredonico
0934-992 009
9:30am-noon Tue-Sun (summer: also 3:30-6pm)

↓ Mussomeli's Manfredano Castle and its interior *(inset)*

CINEMA PARADISO

In 1989 the film *Cinema Paradiso*, by the Sicilian director Giuseppe Tornatore, won an Oscar for the best foreign film. It tells the story of the arrival of cinema (the "Nuovo Cinema Paradiso") in an isolated village in Sicily and the effect it has on the main character, a young boy. *Cinema Paradiso* was filmed in the streets and squares of Palazzo Adriano and used many of the locals as extras, conferring fame on the village. The weeks the film unit and the people of Palazzo Adriano spent working together are commemorated on a majolica plaque on a corner of Piazza Umberto I.

Caltabellotta

B4 Town hall, Piazza Umberto I 7; 0925-952 013

Visible from most of the hilly area of Sciacca, the rocky crest of Caltabellotta (950 m/ 3,116 ft) has been inhabited for millennia, as can be seen in the many ancient necropolises and hypogea. The site was fortified at different stages until the arrival of the Arabs, who gave the castle its definitive form, calling it *Kal'at-at-al ballut* (rock of the oak trees). The county capital, Caltabellotta witnessed the signing of peace between Charles I of Valois and Frederick II of Aragón in 1302, who took over the whole of Sicily. Perched on the ridge above the houses of the Torrevecchia quarter are the ruins of the Norman castle and San Salvatore, while on the other side of the rock is the Chiesa Madre, now being restored, founded by Roger I to celebrate his victory over the Arabs. On the western slope, the Hermitage of San Pellegrino, which consists of a monastery and a chapel, dominates the town.

Palazzo Adriano

C4 Pro Loco, Piazza Umberto I; 328-376 8592

Almost 700 m (2,296 ft) above sea level, on the ridge of Cozzo Braduscia, is Palazzo Adriano, founded in the mid-15th century by Albanian refugees who had fled from their Turkish conquerors. Central Piazza Umberto I is home to two important churches: the Greek Orthodox Santa Maria Assunta, built in the 16th century and then rebuilt; and Santa Maria del Lume, which is Catholic and was founded in the 18th century. In the middle of the square, bordered by Palazzo Dara, now the Town Hall, and Palazzo Mancuso, there is a lovely octagonal fountain sculpted in 1607. Further up the hill, in the oldest part of Palazzo Adriano, the red dome of the 15th-century

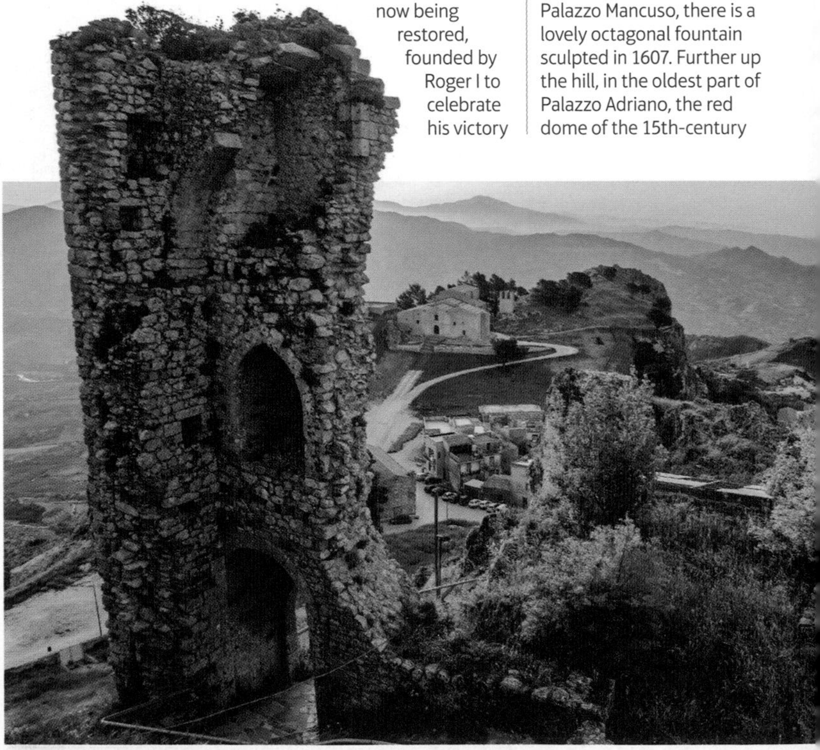

San Nicolò overlooks the alleyways of this quarter, which were built around the castle that stood here before the town was founded.

Sciacca

B4 From Palermo and Trapani STR, Corso Vittorio Emanuele 80; AAR Terme di Sciacca, Via Agatocle 2; www.termesciaccaspa.it

From a distance, Sciacca seems to be overwhelmed by Monte San Calogero, with its thermal waters and steam vapours, which have made the town famous over the centuries. Although the hot springs had been used since prehistoric times, Sciacca was founded as a mere military outpost for Selinunte during the interminable warfare with the city of Agrigento, and was called *Thermae Selinuntinae* (Selinunte baths) by the Romans. It developed rapidly under Arab rule (Sciacca derives from *as-saqah*) and many traces of their culture can be seen in the old Rabato and Giudecca-Cadda quarters, with their blind alleys and maze of roofed courtyards. The town was further fortified by the Normans, who quickly recognized its strategic importance in controlling the trade routes.

In the middle of town is Palazzo Steripinto, built in Catalan-Gothic style in 1501 with a rusticated façade. The church of Santa Margherita has a splendid Gothic portal. Do not miss the cloister of the former Convent of San Francesco and the unfinished Baroque façade of the Chiesa del Carmine, with its 14th-century rose window. In central Piazza Don Minzoni stands the Cathedral, dedicated to Santa Maria Maddalena. It was rebuilt in 1656, but retains three Norman apses.

The main attractions in Sciacca, however, are Monte San Calogero and its thermal pools. From the large square at the summit, with the sanctuary dedicated to the evangelist San Calogero, who in the 5th century eliminated pagan rites in the mountain caves, the panorama is breathtaking. The summit is almost 400 m (1,312 ft) high, and on a clear day there is a commanding view from Capo Bianco to Capo Lilibeo, with the limestone ridge of Caltabellotta in the background and Pantelleria island before you. The older spas are on the slopes of the mountain, while new ones have been built closer to the seaside.

Sciacca is also known for its ceramics, mentioned in antiquity by Diodorus Siculus. Local production thrived during the period of Arab rule, as well as in the 16th century. The fine tradition is being maintained today by local craftsmen.

← Spectacular views over the landscape from the mountain town of Caltabellotta

↑ Walking down the colourful streets of Sciacca, over the port

STAY

Verdura Resort Rocco Forte

Inspired by the landscape, the rooms of this stylish golf, tennis, and spa hotel were designed by Olga Polizzi and Flavio Albanese to showcase the sensational Mediterranean views.

B4 Strada Statale 115 Km 131, Sciacca roccofortehotels.com

Siculiana

C5 From Palermo and Trapani to Castelvetrano, then bus Town hall, Piazza Basile 23; 0922-818 011

The present-day town of Siculiana was built on the site of an Arab fort destroyed by the Normans in the late 11th century. The new lords – the Chiaramonte family from Agrigento – rebuilt the fortress in the 1300s and it was altered several times afterwards. Despite all the changes, Siculiana has retained some Arab features. In central Piazza Umberto I is the Baroque Chiesa Madre, dedicated to San Leonardo Abate, dominating the square at the top of a flight of steps. In the old centre, divided into large blocks, you can glimpse entrances to courtyards and alleys, which were once part of the covered Arab town.

Lampedusa

B7 From Porto Empedocle STR Agrigento; www.comune.lampedusaelinosa.ag.it

The largest island in the Pelagie (the archipelago that includes Linosa and the small island of Lampione), Lampedusa is 200 km (124 miles) from Sicily and 150 km (93 miles) from Malta. The Greek name *Pelaghiè* reflects their chief characteristic – isolation in the middle of the sea. Inhabited for a little more than a century – from the time Ferdinand II of Bourbon sent a group of colonists and prisoners there – Lampedusa was soon deforested, which in turn brought about the almost total degradation of the soil and any possibility of cultivating it. Human settlements have also led to a dramatic decrease in local fauna, and the Baia dei Conigli nature reserve was set up to create a safe refuge for sea turtles *(Caretta caretta)*. The island's main beaches are Cala Maluk, Cala Croce, Baia dei Conigli, Cala Galera and Cala Greca, and diving is one of the many popular sports here. Near the town of Lampedusa (which was almost completely destroyed in 1943) is the Madonna di Lampedusa Sanctuary, where on 22 September the Bourbon takeover is commemorated.

FIRE AT SEA

The tiny island of Lampedusa, caught in the crosshairs of an international catastrophe, is the setting for the 2017 Oscar-nominated documentary *Fire at Sea*. Directed by Gianfranco Rosi, the film is a moving portrait of Europe's migrant crisis as seen through the eyes of the desperate refugees making the harrowing Mediterranean crossing, and of the locals of Lampedusa - specifically a young boy suffering from anxiety and a small-town doctor who cares for the sick migrants and counts the dead.

Boats anchored in the stunning blue waters around Lampedusa

Pantelleria

A7 ✈ ⛴ i Town hall; Pro Loco; www.comune pantelleria.it

Pantelleria, the largest island off the Sicilian coastline, is closer to the Tunisian coast (Capo Mustafà is 70 km/ 44 miles away) than to Capo Granitola in Sicily (100 km, 62 miles). Despite its isolation, Pantelleria was colonized by the Phoenicians and then by the Greeks. It was controlled by the Arabs for almost 400 years and it was then conquered and fortified in 1123 by Roger I.

The strong wind that blows here all year round is responsible for a style of building called *dammuso*, a square, whitewashed peasant's house with walls almost 2 m (6 ft) thick and tiny windows in order to provide the best insulation.

Water is scarce on the island, so the roofs of these homes are shaped to collect rainwater. The coastal road is 53 km (33 miles) in length; it starts at the town of Pantelleria and goes past the archaeological zone of Mursia (with a series of megalithic structures called *sesi* in local dialect) and then up to high ground. The main sights here are Punta Fram, Cala dell'Altura and Punta Tre Pietre, where another road takes you to the little port of Scauri. The coast is steep and craggy with some inlets (like the Balata dei Turchi, once a favourite landing place for Saracen pirates, or the lovely Cala Rotonda) up to the Punta Tracino promontory – with a striking rock formation in front of it – which separates the Tramontana and Levante inlets.

The natural arch, Arco dell'Elefante (which looks like an elephant drinking from the sea with his trunk), near Cala Levante is one of the most beautiful viewpoints on the island, particularly in late afternoon or early-evening light. After the village of Gadir and the lighthouse at Punta Spasdillo the road descends to the Cala Cinque Denti inlet or the Bagno dell'Acqua hot springs and then back to its starting point. Life revolves around Piazza Cavour and the new Chiesa Madre, both facing the sea. Renting a bicycle is a very pleasant way of getting to know the island and the local way of life.

DRINK

Tunez Beach Bar

With an unbeatable location, this open-air bar overlooking the waters of Cala Croce draws crowds with its sunset *aperitivo* buffet.

B7 Contrada Cala Croce, Lampedusa 8am-midnight Mon-Sat (from 12 noon Sun)

23

Linosa

B6 ⛴ i STR Agrigento; Consorzio Albergatori 35° Parallelo; www.comune. lampedusaelinosa.ag.it

Ancient Aethusa, 40 km (25 miles) from Lampedusa, is a small volcanic island where life centres around the village of Linosa, with its brightly coloured houses. Thanks to the naturally fertile volcanic soil, agriculture thrives on the island. One of the best ways of exploring Linosa is by leaving the road behind and rambling around craters and the fenced-in fields.

Brightly coloured houses line the streets of the quiet town of Linosa

Washing hanging from an apartment building in Syracuse

SYRACUSE, VAL DI NOTO AND THE SOUTH

Dominated by Mount Etna, southern Sicily's permanent backdrop, this area is a curious mixture of fertile land and intensive cultivation, ancient monuments and utter neglect. Many towns and monuments built by the ancient Greeks still survive, most notably in the town of Syracuse, birthplace of Archimedes.

Southern Sicily, which the Arabs called the Val di Noto, presents another facet of the region. One of Sicily's most important sights is the stony-tiered Greek theatre in Syracuse. The tradition of performing ancient Greek plays was revived in 1914, and now every summer the great works of the ancient tragedians come to life in their natural setting.

Inland, the rebuilding of towns following the earthquake of 1693 resulted in a number of Spanish-influenced Baroque gems combined with Sicilian decorative and structural elements. The churches, buildings and balconies of Ragusa, Modica, Scicli, Noto and Chiaramonte are a triumph of the Sicilian Baroque style, with majestic steps, detailed ornamentation and curving façades.

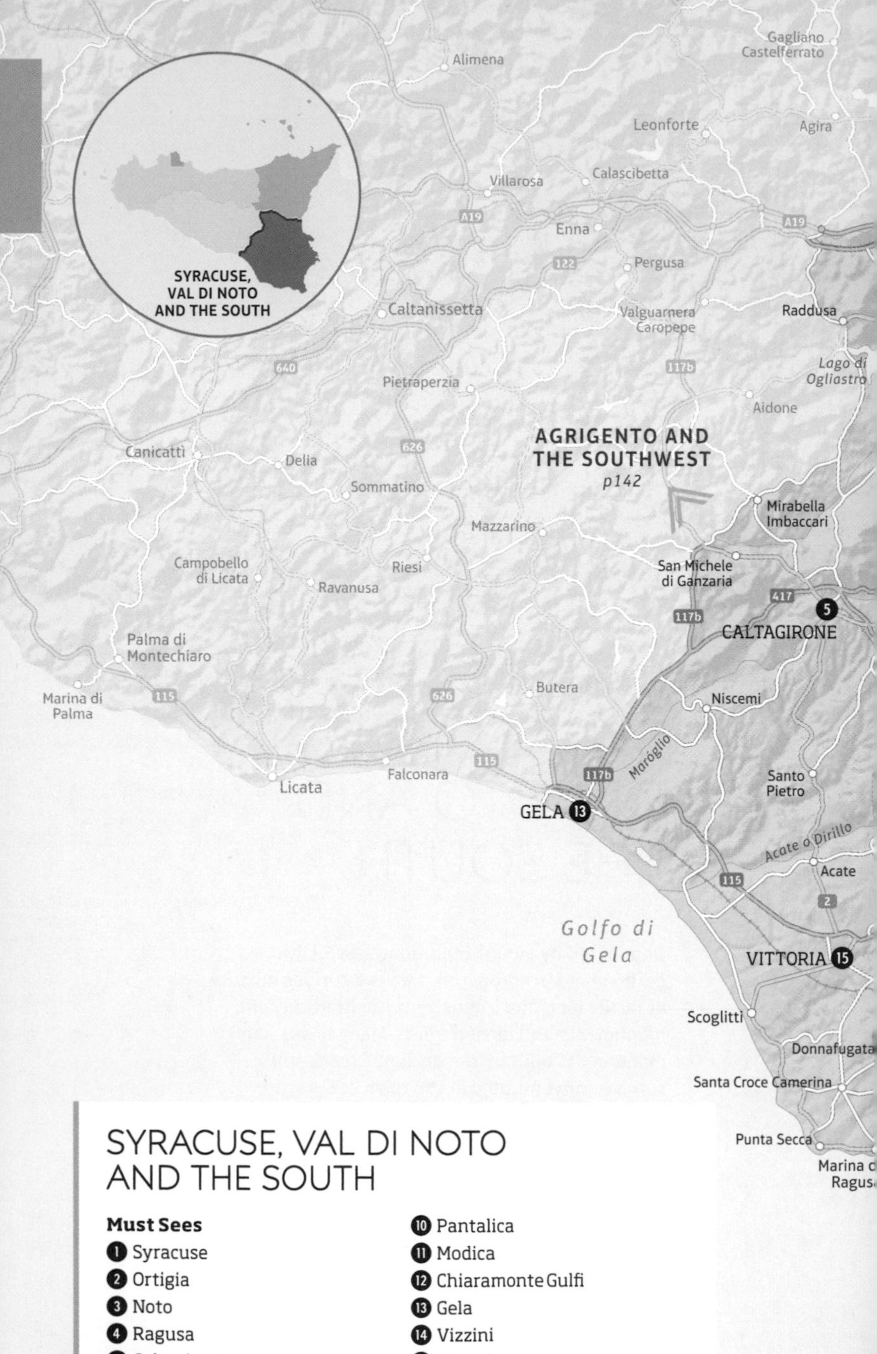

SYRACUSE, VAL DI NOTO AND THE SOUTH

Must Sees

1. Syracuse
2. Ortigia
3. Noto
4. Ragusa
5. Caltagirone

Experience More

6. Palazzolo Acreide
7. Lentini
8. Megara Hyblaea
9. Augusta
10. Pantalica
11. Modica
12. Chiaramonte Gulfi
13. Gela
14. Vizzini
15. Vittoria
16. Pachino
17. Capo Passero
18. Cava d'Ispica
19. Scicli

MOUNT ETNA, THE AEOLIAN ISLANDS AND THE NORTHEAST
p198
Naples
Rifugio Sapienza
Giarre
Zafferana Etnea
Adrano
Pozzillo
Regalbuto
Pedara
Acireale
Aci Trezza
Aci Castello
Misterbianco
Catania
Castel di Iudica
Dittaino
Gerbini
Aeroporto di Catania-Fontanarossa
Golfo di Catania
Gornalunga
Piana di Catania
Ramacca
Vaccarizzo
Ferro
Palagonia
Lago di Lentini
Agnone Bagni
Capo Campolato
Brucoli
Scordia
7 LENTINI
Militello
Carlentini
Mineo
Villasmundo
Capo Santa Croce
9 AUGUSTA
Francofonte
Grammichele
Monti Iblei
MEGARA HYBLAEA 8
Golfo di Augusta
Melilli
Sortino
14 VIZZINI
Priolo Gargallo
Licodia Eubea
Penisola Magnisi
10 PANTALICA
Buccheri
Anapo
Capo Santa Panagia
Monterosso Almo
Solarino
Buscemi
Castello Euríalo
Floridia
1 SYRACUSE
2 ORTIGIA
CHIARAMONTE GULFI
12
6 PALAZZOLO ACREIDE
Giarratana
Canicattini Bagni
Capo Murro di Porco
Aeroporto di Comiso
Val di Noto
Ognina
Cavagrande del Cassibile
Cassibile
Lago Santa Rosalia
Comiso
Noto Antica
Frigintini
RAGUSA 4
Tellaro
Avola
NOTO 3
Calabernardo
MODICA 11
18 CAVA D'ISPICA
Golfo di Noto
Modica Sorda
Rosolini
Isola Vendicari
Irminio
Jungi
19 SCICLI
Ispica
Riserva di Vendicari
Donnalucata
Marzamemi
Pozzallo
16 PACHINO
Sampieri
Punta Religione
Portopalo di Capo Passero
Isola Capo Passero
17
CAPO PASSERO
Punta delle Formiche
Mediterranean Sea
0 kilometres 15
0 miles 15
N
Malta

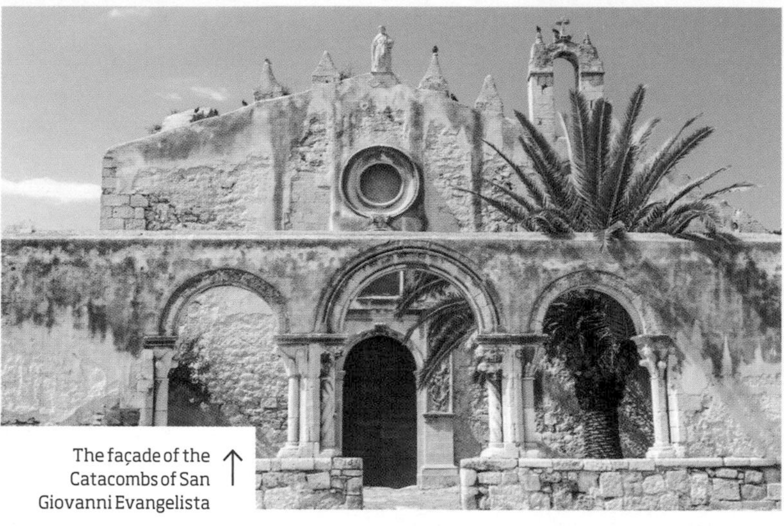

The façade of the Catacombs of San Giovanni Evangelista ↑

1

SYRACUSE

 **G6** **Interbus (interbus.it); AST (0916-208 111)** **Via Duca degli Abruzzi; www.siracusaturismo.net**

For three centuries from around 500 BC, Syracuse was the most powerful city in the Mediterranean, birthplace of Archimedes and home to Pythagoras and Plato. The city's history, from prehistoric to Baroque, is still clearly visible. Most of the relics of ancient Syracuse lie in the bustling mainland city, notably the Greek Theatre, the archaeological museum and the Roman catacombs.

①

The Neapolis Archaeological Zone

Viale Paradiso 14 0931-66206 9am-3pm Tue-Sun (summer: to 6pm) Mon

The Neapolis Archaeological Zone was established in 1955 with the aim of grouping the antiquities of Syracuse within one site, enabling visitors to make an uninterupted tour of the city's most remote past. Not far from the ticket office for the park is medieval San Nicolò dei Cordari, built over a reservoir cut out of the rock, which was used to clean the nearby Roman amphitheatre.

②

Altar of Hieron II and Roman Amphitheatre

A short walk down from the Archaeological Zone's main entrance brings you to these, on your left. Although only the foundations of the Altar of Hieron II remain, its size is impressive. Dedicated to Zeus, it was used for public sacrifices in which as many as 400 bulls were put to death at one time.

A huge public work undertaken in the early years of the Roman Empire, the amphitheatre is only slightly smaller than the arena in Verona. The walls in the interior were part of the underground section, used to house stage scenery. Hidden beneath the tiers were corridors through which gladiators and wild beasts entered the arena.

300,000

The population of Magna Graecia Syracuse at the height of its power.

③

Catacombs of San Giovanni Evangelista

Via San Giovanni alle Catacombe 0931-646 94 Summer: 10am-1pm & 2:30-6pm Tue-Sun; winter: 9:30am-12:30pm & 2:30-5:30pm Tue-Sun (to 4pm in Dec) Mon, Jan-Feb

This underground complex, dating to the 4th century AD, housed hundreds of *loculi*, or rooms, used to bury the followers of the new Christian religion in Roman times. The main gallery leads to a series of round chapels that still bear traces of frescoes.

↑ Ancient sculpture at the Museo Archeologico Regionale Paolo Orsi

④

Castello Eurialo

Frazione Belvedere, 8 km (5 miles) from Syracuse ☎ 0931-711 773 ◷ 9am-6pm Mon-Sat (to 5pm in winter, 7pm in summer) Sun & hols

On the hill overlooking the city is the main work of military architecture in the Greek world, built by Dionysius the Elder in 402 BC. The fort was protected by two rock-cut moats and a tower on the eastern side, while a 15-m (49-ft) keep was built in the middle, and further towers overlooked the sea.

⑤

Museo Archeologico Regionale Paolo Orsi

Parco Landolina, Viale Teocrito 66 ☎ 0931-489 511 ◷ 9am-6pm Tue-Sat, 9am-1pm Sun & hols

Founded in 1967 (and opened to the public in 1988), in order to establish a proper home for the enormous quantity of material excavated from digs throughout southeastern Sicily, the Regional Archaeological Museum boasts a collection of over 18,000 pieces. The museum is named after the eminent archaeologist Paolo Orsi, head of the Antiquities Department of Sicily from 1888, who was instrumental in fostering interest in the island's past and was personally responsible for many important excavations and discoveries. The collections named after him have been reorganized since the museum moved from its Ortygia site. Two more sections have since been opened: Il Medagliere, a unique collection of coins and medals dating from the Greek period to the medieval era, and an area dedicated to the magnificent tomb of a Roman noblewoman that was discovered in the catacombs of San Giovanni Evangelista.

THE SICILIAN FLAG

Thought to be one of the oldest in the world, the Sicilian flag is characterized by a *trinacria*, the Greek symbol of three bent legs radiating from the head of Medusa. Each limb points to one of the three corners on the island, while the vivid red and yellow background is a nod to the towns of Palermo and Corleone, both instrumental in expelling the French Angevin in the 13th century.

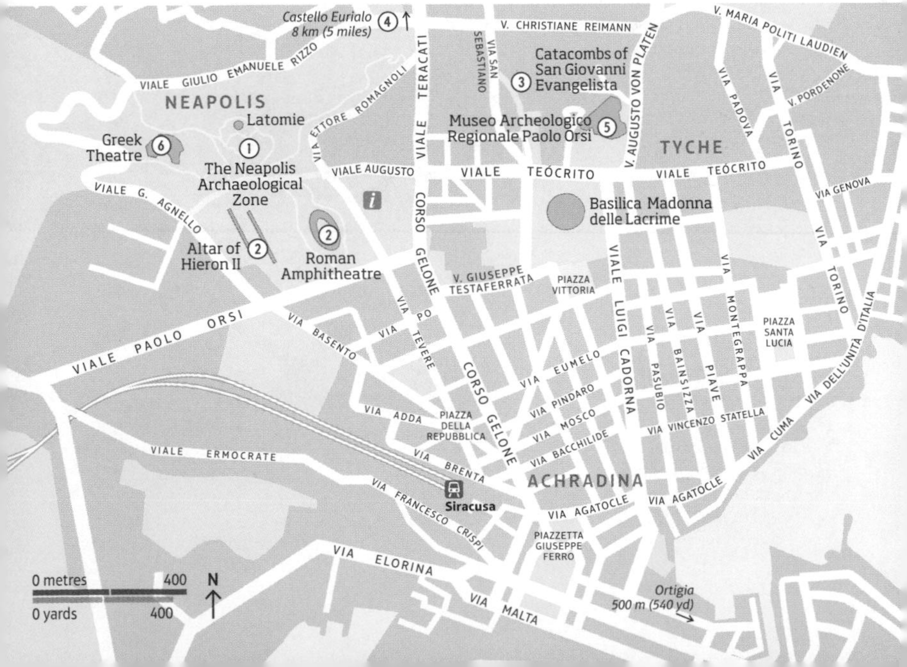

Castello Eurialo 8 km (5 miles) ④ ↑
V. Christiane Reimann
V. Maria Politi Laudien
Via San Sebastiano
Catacombs of San Giovanni Evangelista ③
Viale Giulio Emanuele Rizzo
Neapolis
Latomie
Via Ettore Romagnoli
Viale Teracati
Museo Archeologico Regionale Paolo Orsi ⑤
V. Augusto von Platen
Via Padova
Via Torino
V. Pordenone
Greek Theatre ⑥
① The Neapolis Archaeological Zone
Tyche
Viale Augusto
Viale Teócrito
Viale Teócrito
Viale G. Agnello
Corso Gelone
Basilica Madonna delle Lacrime
Via Genova
Altar of Hieron II ②
② Roman Amphitheatre
V. Giuseppe Testaferrata
Piazza Vittoria
Viale Luigi Cadorna
Via Montegrappa
Via Torino
Via Po
Via Pasubio
Via Bainsizza
Via Piave
Piazza Santa Lucia
Viale Paolo Orsi
Via Basento
Via Tevere
Via Eumelo
Via Dell'Unità d'Italia
Via Adda
Piazza della Repubblica
Corso Gelone
Via Pindaro
Via Mosco
Via Bacchilide
Via Vincenzo Statella
Via Cuma
Viale Ermocrate
Via Brenta
Achradina
Siracusa
Via Francesco Crispi
Via Agatocle
Via Agatocle
Piazzetta Giuseppe Ferro
Via Elorina
Via Malta
Ortigia 500 m (540 yd)
0 metres 400
0 yards 400
N

GREEK THEATRE

Viale Paradiso 14 9am-7:45pm Tue-Sun Mon indafondazione.org

Built in the 5th century BC, this is one of the most important examples of ancient theatre architecture anywhere. For centuries the Greek Theatre was the centre of Syracusan life, and was a much more complex construction than today's ruins might indicate.

Originally designed by the Greek architect Damacopos, the Teatro Greco was enlarged in the 3rd and 2nd centuries BC by Hieron II. From the 5th century BC onwards, the great Greek playwrights, including Aeschylus, wrote and staged their works in this magnificent setting. In 1520–31, Emperor Charles V had much of the stone transported to build the walls around Ortigia *(p176)*. The theatre is set within the Neapolis Archaeological Zone, which contains the ruins of several other impressive Greek and Roman structures, including the Altar of Hieron II, used for ritual sacrifices, and a 3rd-century Roman amphitheatre.

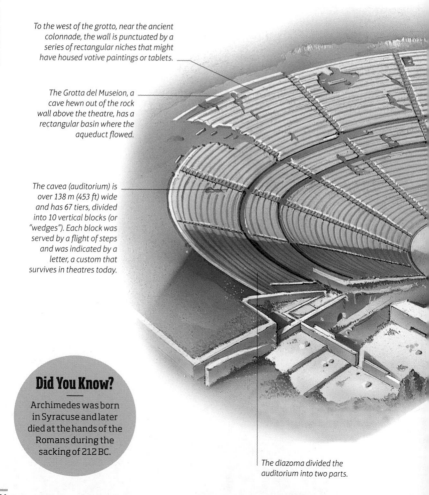

To the west of the grotto, near the ancient colonnade, the wall is punctuated by a series of rectangular niches that might have housed votive paintings or tablets.

The Grotta del Museion, a cave hewn out of the rock wall above the theatre, has a rectangular basin where the aqueduct flowed.

The cavea (auditorium) is over 138 m (453 ft) wide and has 67 tiers, divided into 10 vertical blocks (or "wedges"). Each block was served by a flight of steps and was indicated by a letter, a custom that survives in theatres today.

The diazoma divided the auditorium into two parts.

Did You Know?

Archimedes was born in Syracuse and later died at the hands of the Romans during the sacking of 212 BC.

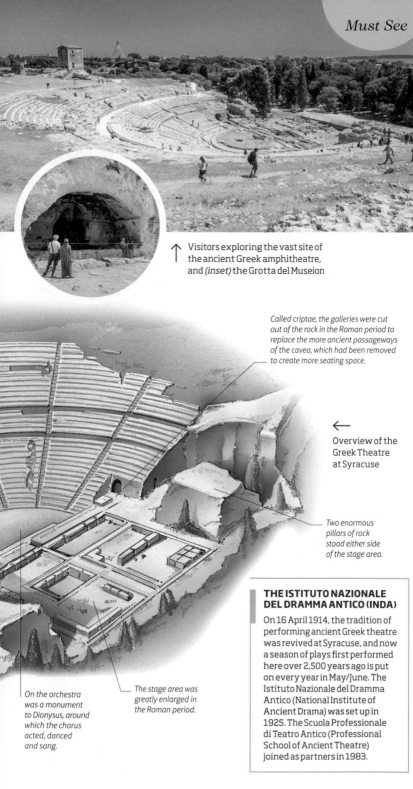

↑ Visitors exploring the vast site of the ancient Greek amphitheatre, and *(inset)* the Grotta del Museion

Called criptae, the galleries were cut out of the rock in the Roman period to replace the more ancient passageways of the cavea, which had been removed to create more seating space.

← Overview of the Greek Theatre at Syracuse

Two enormous pillars of rock stood either side of the stage area.

On the orchestra was a monument to Dionysus, around which the chorus acted, danced and sang.

The stage area was greatly enlarged in the Roman period.

THE ISTITUTO NAZIONALE DEL DRAMMA ANTICO (INDA)

On 16 April 1914, the tradition of performing ancient Greek theatre was revived at Syracuse, and now a season of plays first performed here over 2,500 years ago is put on every year in May/June. The Istituto Nazionale del Dramma Antico (National Institute of Ancient Drama) was set up in 1925. The Scuola Professionale di Teatro Antico (Professional School of Ancient Theatre) joined as partners in 1983.

↑ The Piazza del Duomo and Duomo illuminated in the evening

ORTIGIA

G6 Interbus (0931-66 710); AST (0931-46 27 11)
Via Ruggero VII 19; 0931-618 44

Traces of Siracusa's glorious past are everywhere in its historic centre, Ortigia, an offshore island where Baroque buildings of mellow golden sandstone twist and turn along a labyrinth of narrow medieval streets lined with pavement cafés, restaurants and stylish little shops. Intersperse sightseeing with lunch in the market, take a swim in one of the miniature lidos along Lungomare Levante, or enjoy a pre-dinner drink while watching the sun set over the Porto Grande.

Piazza del Duomo

This is quite possibly Sicily's most magnificent piazza, an immense theatrical space free of traffic, except for the occasional wedding car.
It is gorgeous at any time of day, but it is perhaps most magical at night, when its smooth pavement gleams like silk and the Baroque façades that surround it are illuminated. Relaxing with a coffee at one of the many cafés on the piazza is a fantastic way to enjoy the architecture and the atmosphere.

Duomo

Piazza del Duomo 4 0931-64 694 9am-7pm daily

Siracusa's Duomo is an ancient Greek temple that was converted into a church sometime during the 6th century. Twelve of the Doric temple's fluted columns are embedded in the Duomo's Norman wall. The Norman façade was destroyed in the earthquake of 1693 and replaced with the Baroque edifice.

Santa Lucia alla Badia

Via Santa Lucia alla Badia 2 11am-4pm Tue-Sun

The façade of Santa Lucia alla Badia, with its barley-sugar twist columns and intricate stonework, is one of Ortigia's prettiest. The church is home to one of Siracusa's most prized works of art, *The Burial of Santa Lucia* by Caravaggio. The canvas was not designed for this church but for the Church of Santa Lucia in the Borgata district, the location of the saint's martyrdom. Bathed in shafts of sunlight, dwarfed by stark, bare plaster walls, two gravediggers brace themselves to lower the corpse of the saint into her tomb, watched by a bishop and a group of mourners.

Temple of Apollo

Largo XXV Luglio

The ruins of the oldest temple in Magna Graecia were discovered in 1860 inside an old Spanish barracks. Built in the early 6th century BC, the

EAT

Fratelli Burgio

Siracusa's best delicatessen has a simple outdoor restaurant among the bustle of the market, where guests can feast on platters of gourmet cheeses, hams and salamis sourced from all over Italy, along with their own cured olives, *caponata*, sun-dried tomatoes and other delectable conserves.

Piazza Cesare Battisti 4 Sun fratelliburgio.com

temple is huge, and over the centuries it has served as a Byzantine church, a mosque and a military stronghold. Visiting in the 18th century, the French writer Vivant Denon reported finding one of the columns embedded in the wall of a bedroom of a house on the adjacent Via Resalibera. While renovating the building, the owner had hacked away part of the stone.

Fonte Aretusa

Largo Aretusa

Surrounded by papyrus plants and inhabited by a colony of ducks and bream, this fountain is fed by a freshwater spring that bubbles up under the sea. It is the origin of the myth of the nymph Arethusa, who escaped the advances of the river god Alpheios by turning into the spring, which disappeared beneath the Ionian sea and re-emerged here.

SWIMMING SPOTS IN ORTIGIA

The most popular place to swim in Ortigia is the big rock at Forte Vigliena (commonly known as Lo Scoglio, or "The Rock"); during the summer the local council "extends" it by erecting a platform for public use. There is also a small beach at Cala Rossa (at the foot of Via Roma). There are two popular lidos in Ortigia, one on the Lungomare Levante (at the foot of Via della Maestranze), the other below the Fonte Aretusa.

Palazzo Bellomo: Galleria d'Arte Regionale

Via Capodieci 14-16 0931-69 511 9am-7pm Tue-Sat, 2-7:30pm Sun

Palazzo Bellomo is a sprawling 13th-century building whose austere, minimalist façade dates from a time when Sicily was part of the Holy Roman Empire. The palace now houses a fine regional art museum. A highlight of the collection is Antonello da Messina's *Annunciation*, painted for a church in Palazzolo Acreide, with the Hyblaean mountains visible through the windows behind the angel.

3

NOTO

F6 Catania Fontanarossa (80 km/50 miles) FS
Corso Vittorio Emanuele 135; www.comune.noto. sr.it

The heart of the town is the main avenue, the modern Viale Marconi, which becomes Corso Vittorio Emanuele at the monumental Porta Reale (or Ferdinandea) city gate, and passes through Piazza XXIV Maggio, Piazza Municipio (a good starting point for a visit) and Piazza XXX Ottobre. Steps lead to the upper town, with marvellous views of the landscape around.

Cathedral

Corso Vittorio Emanuele

Noto's Cathedral was built in 1776 and dedicated to San Nicolò. It stands at the end of a spectacular three-flight staircase designed by Paolo Labisi, the façade bearing twin bell towers and a bronze portal. The interior has a wealth of frescoes and other decoration, especially in the side chapels.

In the winter of 1996, a loud rumble signalled the collapse of the Cathedral cupola. It was a great loss to Sicilian Baroque art and left a scar in the heart of Noto. However, the Cathedral has now been brought back to its former splendour following extensive restoration.

PICTURE PERFECT

Noto-gram

Old-town Noto will inspire any shutterbug. Popular Instagrammable locations include the Cathedral and the Teatro Comunale. The flower festival in May is a veritable explosion of colours and textures.

Palazzo Ducezio

Piazza Trigona 10am-1:30pm, 3-6pm daily

This palazzo, which stands opposite the Cathedral, was built in 1746. The façade is decorated with an impressive series of columns. The interior houses a huge drawing room decorated in Louis XV style, with gold and stucco decorative elements and a fine fresco on the vault by Antonio Mazza.

San Francesco All`Immacolata

Corso V. Emanuele 142
9am-12:30pm, 4:30-6:30pm daily

On the wide stretch of Piazza XXX Ottobre, a stairway leads to San Francesco, which was once part of a convent and is now a high school. The church was built in the mid-1700s and has a wooden statue of the Virgin Mary (1564) thought to belong to one of the churches in the old town, Noto Antica.

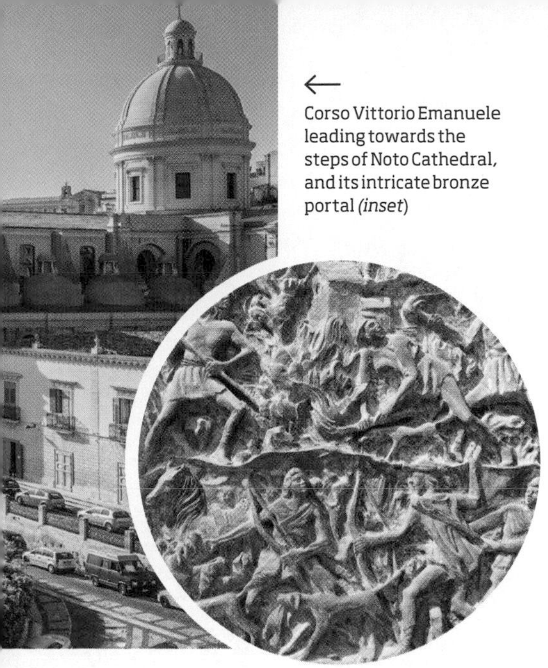

Corso Vittorio Emanuele leading towards the steps of Noto Cathedral, and its intricate bronze portal *(inset)*

Palazzo Trigona

⌂ Via C. B. Conte di Cavour

This palazzo is perhaps the most "classically" Baroque building in Noto. The façade, with its curved balconies, blends in with the adjacent religious and civic buildings, in line with the schemes of the architects who rebuilt Noto. The palace now operates as a high-end boutique hotel, offering three luxury suites.

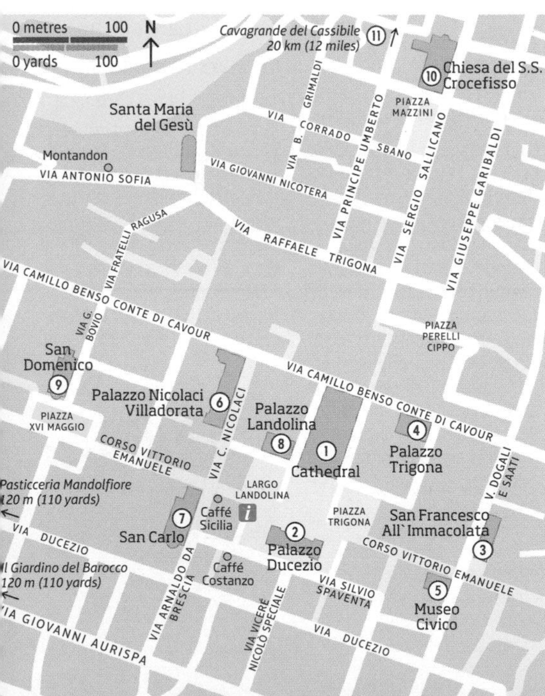

⑤

Museo Civico

⌂ Corso V. Emanuele 149
🕒 9:30am–1:30pm, 3:30–7:30pm Tue–Sun
📞 0931-836 462

The Civic Museum (some rooms of which are closed for restoration) features ancient and medieval material from the old town, Noto Antica, and from many nearby places.

EAT

Caffé Sicilia

The Assenza brothers, Carlo and Corrado, create innovative as well as classic ice creams - all according to season. Some of the finest Sicilian *gelato* in Noto.

⌂ Corso Vittorio Emanuele 125
Mon; Feb
caffesicilia.it

Caffé Costanzo

One of the most historic and reputable *gelaterias* in Italy, with a striking view of the Cathedral.

⌂ Via Spaventa 7
Wed 📞 0931-835 243

Pasticceria Mandolfiore

Famous for its delicious pastries, *gelato* and *granita*, this pastry shop sits opposite the impressive Chiesa Madonna del Carmine.

⌂ Via Ducezio 2
📞 0931-839836

BAROQUE ARCHITECTURE AND ART IN NOTO

After the devastating earthquake of 1693, a programme of reconstruction was introduced throughout eastern Sicily in the early 18th century. The architects entrusted with this task elaborated upon the achievements of 17th-century Baroque architecture and adopted recurrent features that can still be seen in the streets of Noto. The façades of both churches and civic buildings became of fundamental importance in the hands of these men. Some of them, like Rosario Gagliardi, who designed the churches of Santa Chiara, Santissimo Crocefisso and San Domenico in Noto, were originally craftsmen themselves. Their skills can be seen in the decorative detail in façades and balconies. Rebuilding made the large monasteries - which together with the mansions of the landed gentry were the economic and social backbone of 18th- and 19th-century Noto - even more grandiose than before.

Palazzo Nicolaci di Villadorata

Via Corrado Nicolaci
10am-1pm, 3pm-1 hr before sunset daily
palazzonicolaci.it

Built in the 18th century to house the Nicolaci family, the Palazzo Nicolaci del Principe di Villadorata is a fine example of Sicilian Baroque architecture. The façade has six balconies supported by corbels which are decorated – in keeping with the pure Baroque style – with complex wrought-iron work and grotesque and mythological figures: lions, sirens, griffons and cherubs. The interior has fresco decoration in the lavish rooms, the most striking of which is the Salone delle Feste (Hall of Festivities). The palazzo also houses the Biblioteca Comunale, or City Library, founded in the mid-19th century, which counts many old volumes and the architects' original designs for Noto among it collection.

San Carlo

Corso Vittorio Emanuele

The original Chiesa di San Carlo (also called Chiesa del Collegio, referring to the former Jesuit monastery next door) was destroyed during the 1693 earthquake. The current Sicilian Baroque construction, built in 1730, has an elegant convex façade (restored again in 1776) with three levels – Doric, Ionic and Corinthian. The impressive Latin cross–plan interior is filled with 16th–18th century frescoes, canvas paintings and sculptures. For a small fee, you can climb the church's august campinile (bell tower), which offers unparalled views of the town's skyline.

Taking a stroll along the balconies of Palazzo di Nicolaci Villadorata

Palazzo Landolina

Piazza del Municipio

To the right of the Cathedral is the 19th-century Palazzo Vescovile (Bishop's Palace), while to the left is Palazzo Landolina, residence of the marquises of Sant'Alfano, an old and powerful family of the Norman aristocracy who came to Noto during the reign of Roger I in the late 1th century. Once past the elegant Baroque

60,000

The number of people lost on Jan 11, 1693 when a 7.3 earthquake levelled the towns of the Val di Noto.

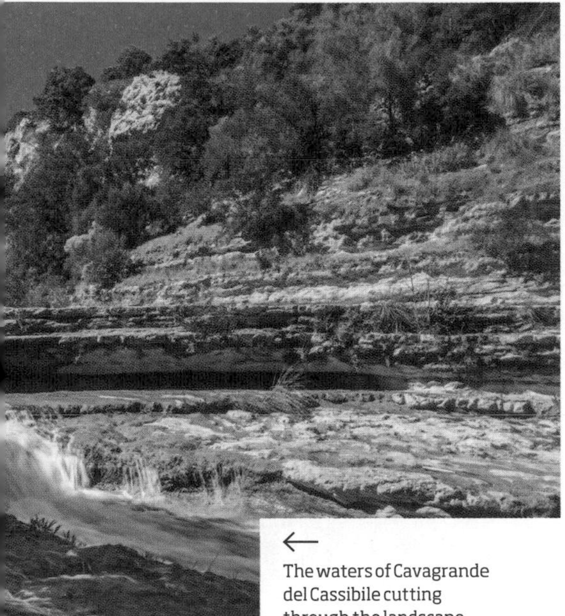

←

The waters of Cavagrande del Cassibile cutting through the landscape

façade, you enter a courtyard where two sphinxes flank the stairway leading to the upper floors, whose rooms feature many delightful frescoes.

San Domenico

Piazza XVI Maggio

Overlooking Piazza XIV Maggio, the Church of San Domenico is part of a group of buildings that includes the Dominican Convent (also worth visiting for the splendid host of friezes adorning the entrance). Much like other buildings of this kind, the convent was abandoned after the elimination of all congregational orders, decreed by the Italian government in 1866. The church's magnificent two-level (Doric and Ionic) façade, with its convex central area, was designed by the architect Rosario Gagliardi. The portal gives way to a rounded Greek cross–plan interior, which is crowned by five cupolas with fine stucco decoration.

Chiesa del S.S. Crocefisso

Piazza Mazzini 0931-891 622 Summer: 8am-noon, 5:30-8pm daily; winter: 8am-noon, 4:30-7pm daily

In the heart of Noto Alta, at the end of a stairway that begins at Piazza Mazzini, is this church, built at the end of the street that leads upwards from Piazza Municipio and the Cathedral. The façade – designed by Gagliardi but never finished – has a large Baroque door. The Latin cross–plan interior boasts a magnificent Renaissance statue by Francesco Laurana, known as the Madonna della Neve (Madonna of the Snow, 1471), which miraculously survived the 1693 earthquake. At the end of the left-hand aisle is Cappella Landolina. The Romanesque statues of lions also come from the old town. The church is surrounded by palazzi, convents and churches. Among others, the façades of Sant'Agata, the Badia della Santissima Annunziata and Santa Maria del Gesù are well worth a longer look.

Cavagrande del Cassibile

20 km (12 miles) N of Noto

North of Noto, near the little town of Avola, this breathtaking nature reserve has a 10-m-(33-ft-) long and 300-m-(984-ft-) deep gorge that cuts into the park's limestone walls – one of the largest canyons in Europe. It is a wonderful place to hike the panoramic Prisa-Carrubella nature trail and swim in natural pools beneath cascading waterfalls.

STAY

Montandon

Each room at this family-run B&B is large and airy, with its own private terrace. There's also a communal terrace for breakfast, where you can also prepare snacks or an *aperitivo*, a walled garden and a barbeque.

Via Antonio Sofia 50
b-bmontandon.it

Il Giardino del Barocco

This small *pensione* is set in a magnificent historic palace with a courtyard garden, offering an oasis of calm in the town centre.

Via Aurispa Giovanni 77 ilgiardino delbarocco.it

A SHORT WALK AROUND NOTO

Distance 1.2 km (0.8 miles) **Time** 15 minutes

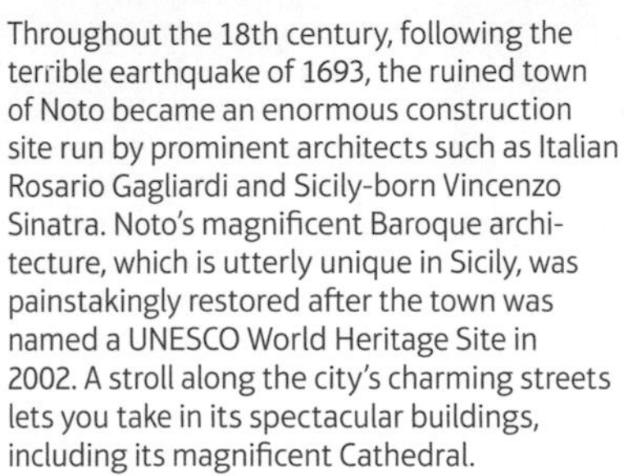

Throughout the 18th century, following the terrible earthquake of 1693, the ruined town of Noto became an enormous construction site run by prominent architects such as Italian Rosario Gagliardi and Sicily-born Vincenzo Sinatra. Noto's magnificent Baroque architecture, which is utterly unique in Sicily, was painstakingly restored after the town was named a UNESCO World Heritage Site in 2002. A stroll along the city's charming streets lets you take in its spectacular buildings, including its magnificent Cathedral.

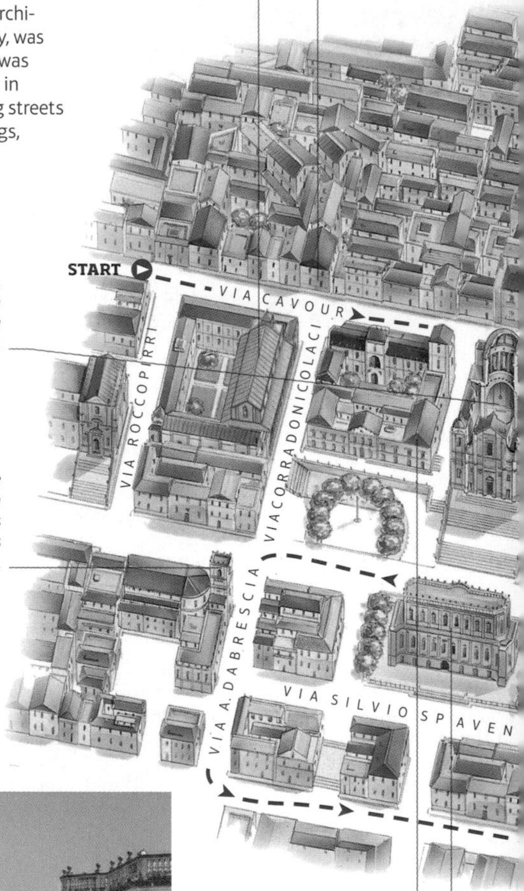

Montevergine church

Palazzo Nicolaci

START

VIA CAVOUR

VIA ROCCO PIRRI

VIA CORRADO NICOLACI

VIA A. DA BRESCIA

VIA SILVIO SPAVEN

Dedicated to San Nicolò, the Cathedral looks down on three flights of steps. It has a beautiful Baroque interior.

San Carlo al Corso is more formally known as San Carlo Borromeo. This church contains frescoes attributed to Carasi.

0 metres 100
0 yards 100
N

Palazzo Landolina (Sant'Alfano)

Palazzo Ducezio, now the Town Hall, has lovely round arches.

←

One of Noto's streets, lined with beautiful Baroque buildings

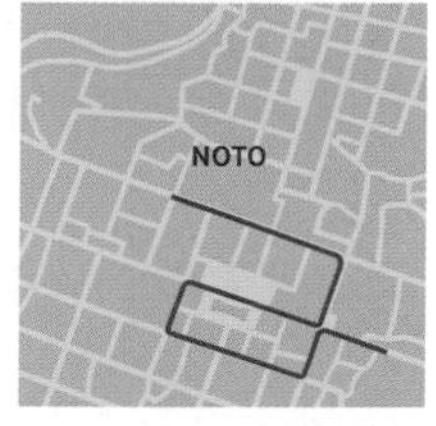

Locator Map
For more detail see p170

↑ The exterior of Santa Chiara church in Noto

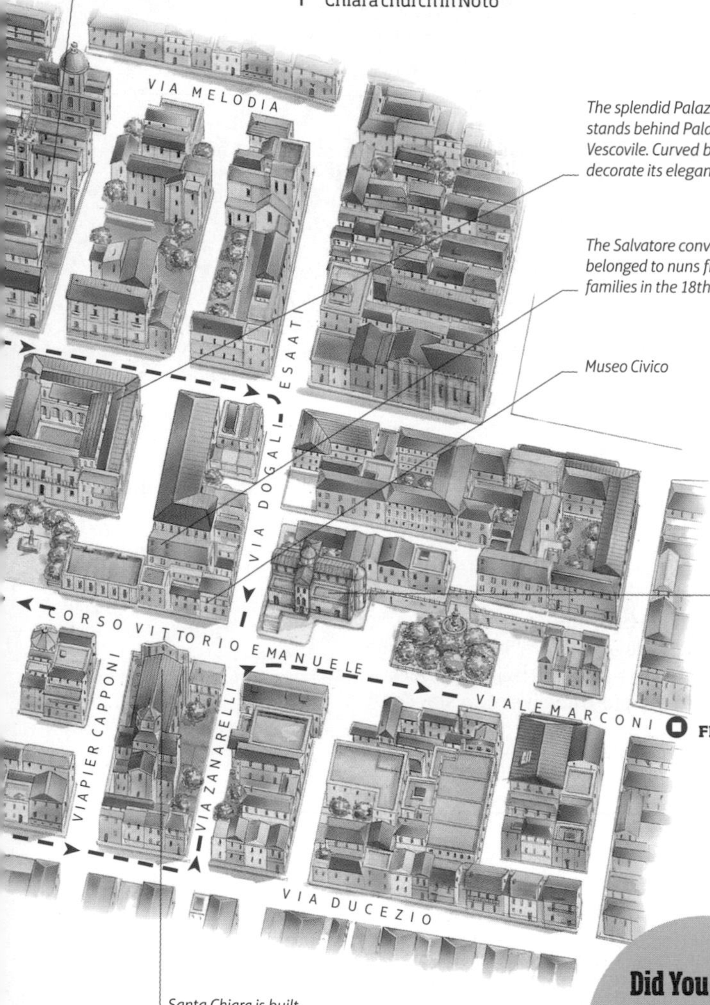

Palazzo Astuto

The splendid Palazzo Trigona stands behind Palazzo Vescovile. Curved balconies decorate its elegant façade.

The Salvatore convent belonged to nuns from noble families in the 18th century.

Museo Civico

San Francesco All'Immacolata has a Latin cross interior.

VIA MELODIA

VIA DOGALI

ESAATI

CORSO VITTORIO EMANUELE

VIA PIER CAPPONI

VIA ZANARELLI

VIALE MARCONI

FINISH

VIA DUCEZIO

Santa Chiara is built on an oval plan and is richly decorated.

Did You Know?

Noto was granted the title of *civitas ingeniosa* (ingenious city) in 1503.

4

RAGUSA

F6 Comiso Piazza Stazione Via Zama, Interbus-Etna Transporti (331-687 76 78) Piazza San Giovanni, Ragusa Superiore, www.comune.ragusa.gov.it

This ancient city was founded as Hybla Heraia when the Sicels moved into the interior to escape from the Greek colonists. A UNESCO World Heritage site, it is divided into two communities: new Ragusa Superiore, built on the plateau after the 1693 earthquake, and quiet, atmospheric Ragusa Ibla, a Sicilian Baroque jewel that is linked to the modern city by a rocky crest. A visit to Ragusa therefore involves two stages.

Cathedral

Piazza San Giovanni
0932-621 599
10am-noon, 4-6pm daily

Ragusa's splendid cathedral (Cattedrale di San Giovanni Battista) was built between 1706 and 1760 in the middle of the new town. It replaced a smaller building that had been hastily erected after the earthquake of 1693. The low and broad façade is an excellent example of Sicilian Baroque, with a rather grand monumental portal and some elegant sculptures of St John the Baptist, to whom the cathedral is dedicated, the Virgin Mary and St John the Evangelist. There is also an impressive porticoed terrace and a huge cusped bell tower. The ornate Baroque interior has a Latin-cross plan and fine stucco decoration.

The cathedral museum features seven exhibition rooms with holy relics, gold artefacts, liturgical clothes, jewellery and episcopal texts.

Museo Archeologico Ibleo

Via Natalelli 0932-622 963 9am-7pm daily

The Archaeological Museum is devoted to the cultures that have dominated the province of Ragusa. The first of its six sections features prehistoric finds from Modica, Pantalica

INSIDER TIP

Cook with Nonna

Learn all the tricks of the trade for making typical Ragusan recipes like ravioli with ricotta and cavatelli (a traditional handmade pasta) when you join up with Zuleima Ospitalità Diffusa a Ragusa Ibla *(www.zuleima.org)* for a fun, hands-on cookery course taught by a real Sicilian grandmother.

←

The Baroque jewel of Ragusa Ibla glowing on a hill at nighttime

and Cava d'Ispica. The second is given over to Kamarina, the Syracusan subcolony founded on the banks of the Ippari river on a coastal site not far from present-day Vittoria. Kamarina once enjoyed important trade links with ancient Ibla. Among the displays here are the statue of a warrior, the bronzes of Kamarina and Attic vases, all recovered during the excavations at Kamarina, organized and sponsored by the Syracuse Archaeological Office. The third section deals with the Siculi cultures, and is followed by an exhibit of Hellenistic finds. The fifth section focuses on the Roman epoch, while the last one illustrates the growth of this area in the Byzantine age, with finds from the ancient port of Caucana.

③

Santa Maria delle Scale

Discesa Santa Maria

This church stands at the top of a flight of 340 steps connecting Ibla and Ragusa, hence the name – *scale* meaning stairs. The church was built in the 14th century over a Norman convent and rebuilt after the 1693 earthquake. The original Gothic doorway and external pulpit of the bell tower are still intact.

ETHNOGRAPHIC MUSEUMS

Museo del Tempo Contadino
Via San Vito 158, Ragusa
Sun, Mon
Houses historic farm and kitchen tools, and lace and embroidery work.

Museo del Costume
Via Francesco Mormina Penna 65, Scicli Mon
Dedicated to the history and culture of the Iblean mountain communities.

Casa-Museo di Antonino Uccello
Via Machiavelli 19, Palazzolo Acreide
Exhibits of farmers' handmade objects.

Mulino ad Acqua Santa Lucia
Valle dei Mulini 10, Palazzolo Acreide
Reservations only
Antique water-powered grain mill complete with working millstones.

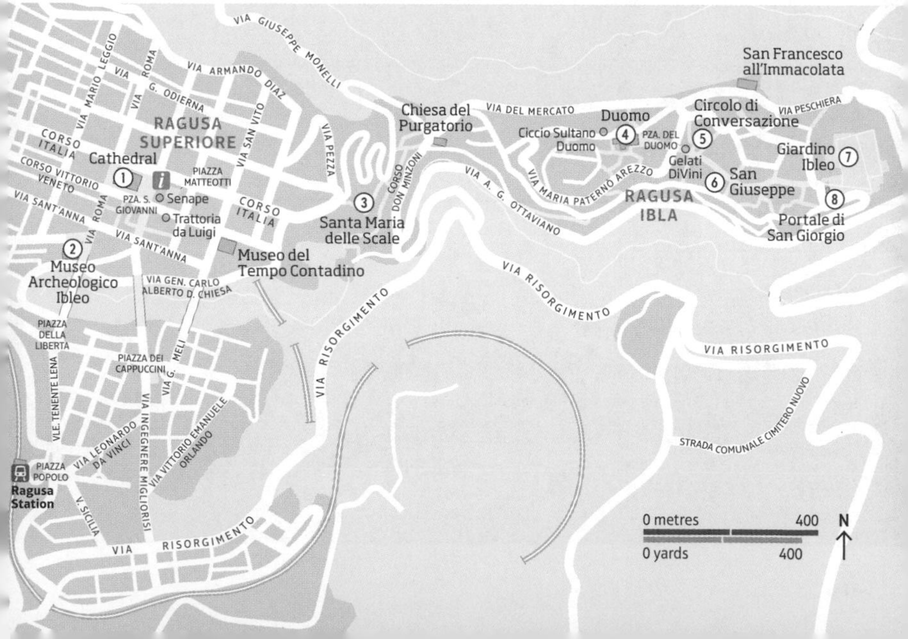

RAGUSA SUPERIORE
Cathedral ①
Museo Archeologico Ibleo ②
Santa Maria delle Scale ③
Museo del Tempo Contadino
Chiesa del Purgatorio
Duomo ④
Circolo di Conversazione ⑤
San Giuseppe ⑥
Giardino Ibleo ⑦
Portale di San Giorgio ⑧
San Francesco all'Immacolata
RAGUSA IBLA
Ciccio Sultano Duomo
Gelati DiVini
Senape
Trattoria da Luigi
Ragusa Station
VIA GIUSEPPE MONELLI
VIA ARMANDO DIAZ
VIA G. ODIERNA
VIA MARIO LEGGIO
VIA ROMA
VIA SAN VITO
VIA PEZZA
CORSO ITALIA
CORSO VITTORIO VENETO
VIA SANT'ANNA
PIAZZA MATTEOTTI
PZA. S. GIOVANNI
VIA GEN. CARLO ALBERTO D. CHIESA
PIAZZA DELLA LIBERTÀ
PIAZZA DEI CAPPUCCINI
VIA G. MELI
VLE. TENENTE LENA
VIA LEONARDO DA VINCI
VIA INGEGNERE MIGLIORISI
VIA VITTORIO EMANUELE ORLANDO
PIAZZA POPOLO
V. SICILIA
VIA RISORGIMENTO
CORSO DON MINZONI
VIA DEL MERCATO
VIA A. G. OTTAVIANO
VIA MARIA PATERNÒ AREZZO
PZA. DEL DUOMO
VIA PESCHIERA
STRADA COMUNALE CIMITERO NUOVO
0 metres 400
0 yards 400
N

EXPLORING RAGUSA

Ragusa's new town was designed to suit the needs of the emerging 17th-century landed gentry, while the feudal nobles preferred to stay in old Ibla, and it was laid out on an octagonal plan following the earthquake of 1693. The stunning landscape, the sandy beaches and the Baroque and Art Nouveau architecture makes the whole area seem like an open-air stage. The famous TV series *Il Commissario Montalbano (Inspector Montalbano)* showcases the sun-drenched province of Ragusa at its best.

Duomo (San Giorgio)

Piazza Duomo

Ragusa Ibla's Cathedral stands at the top of a stairway that begins at Piazza Duomo, the real centre of Ibla. It was built over the foundations of San Nicolò, which was destroyed by the 1693 earthquake. The new church was designed by Rosario Gagliardi and built in 1738–75. The huge façade is immediately striking, with its three tiers of columns which, together with the vertical lines of the monumental stairway leading to the church, accentuate the vertical thrust of the building. An impressive Neo-Classical cupola dominates the nave. Inside are paintings from different periods (including an 18th-century *Immaculate Conception* by Vito D'Anna) and 33 stained-glass windows.

The cathedral is the focus of the annual Festa di San Giorgio, held on the last Sunday of May, when thousands gather to see the equestrian statue of Saint George paraded around town.

Circolo di Conversazione

On Corso XXV Aprile you will find the Neo-Classical Circolo di Conversazione (Conversation Club), on your left. This private club has a plush interior steeped in the atmosphere of 19th-century Ibla.

San Giuseppe

Also along Corso XXV Aprile, at Piazza Pola, is the Baroque Chiesa di San Giuseppe, which is in many ways similar to the Duomo, its designer having been an apprentice to the architect Rosario Gagliardi,

18

The number of World Heritage monuments in Ragusa Ibla.

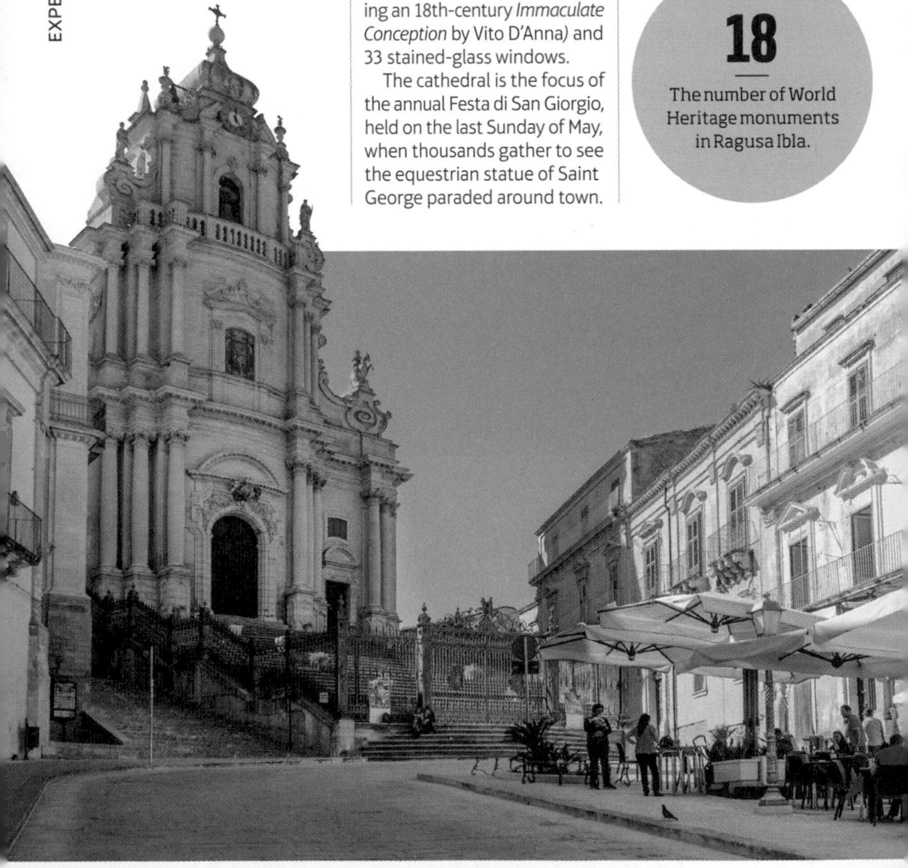

though his name is unknown. Its three-tiered façade is dotted with statues of Benedictine saints. The oval-shaped interior is dominated by a large cupola, decorated with a fresco of the *Glory of St Benedict*. Outside, turn left on Via Orfanotrofio towards Piazza Chiaramonte, where you will find the beautiful Chiesa di San Francesco all'Immacolata, which was built over Palazzo Chiaramonte and incorporates the 13th-century Gothic portal of the former nobleman's palace.

↑ Cherry blossoms hanging over the Giardino Ibleo

Giardino Ibleo

This delightful 19th-century public garden, the oldest of the four in Ragusa Ibla and occupying most of the eastern part of town, offers fine views of the surroundings, taking in the Iblei mountains and the valley of the Irminio river. It also boasts no less than three churches within its grounds: San Giacomo, San Domenico and the Chiesa dei Cappuccini, notable for its alluring 15th-century altarpieces, including one by Pietro Novelli.

Portale di San Giorgio

The splendid 14th-century Catalan-Gothic portal of the Church of Saint George – for the most part destroyed by the 1693 earthquake – survived to become the enduring symbol of Ragusa. Its lunette has a bas-relief of St George killing the dragon and, above, the eagles from the House of Aragon coat of arms.

← Al fresco dining in Piazza Duomo, overlooked by the Cathedral of St George

EAT

Ciccio Sultano Duomo

Gastronomic powerhouse and native son Ciccio Sultano is the talented chef behind this atmospheric, two-Michelin-star restaurant a stone's throw from Ragusa's splendid Baroque cathedral.

Via Capitano Bocchieri 31 Sun; Jan & Feb cicciosultano.it

Trattoria da Luigi

Flavoursome and fresh local food is served at this traditional trattoria. Book in advance to avoid disappointment - it's a favourite with locals and tourists alike.

Corso Vittorio Veneto 96 0932-624 016 Thu

Senape

A versatile café perfect for a coffee break in the afternoon and a casual dinner in the evening. Grab a table outside for piazza views.

Piazza San Giovanni 1 0932-248 661 7am-2am daily

Gelati DiVini

Tickle your tastebuds with a stunning array of ice-cream options at this friendly café. For a bit of a kick, try a scoop of the famous wine-flavoured *gelato*.

Piazza Duomo 20 10am-1pm daily

CALTAGIRONE

E5 From Catania and Gela (www.trenitalia.it) STR, Volta Libertini 4; 0933-538 09

In the history of this UNESCO World Heritage site, built between the Erei and Iblei hills, there is one element of continuity – ceramics. Prehistoric pottery has been found on the hills around the Arab Kalat al Giarin ("Castle of Vases"). The local potters were world-famous in the Middle Ages, and the tradition is maintained today.

Piazza Municipio

The former Piano della Loggia – now Piazza Municipio – is the heart of the city. In the piazza are the Town Hall and Palazzo Senatorio, formerly the city theatre, which is now home to the Galleria Sturzo.

Duomo di San Giuliano

Piazza Umberto I

The exterior of the Cathedral in Piazza Umberto I has a long history: first it was Norman, then Baroque, and was rebuilt in the 20th century. Inside, you will find a 16th-century wooden crucifix. Head towards the San Francesco bridge and you will come to the old Bourbon prison and the Chiesa di Sant'Agata.

Museo Civico

Via Roma 0933-31590 9:30am-1:30pm & 4-6:30pm Tue & Fri-Sun, 9:30am-1:30pm Wed & Thu

This museum in the former 17th-century Bourbon prison has prehistoric, Greek and Roman material, sculptures and ceramics from the 1500s to the present.

San Francesco d'Assisi

Heading south over Ponte San Francesco leads to the Church of Saint Francis of Assisi, also known as Chiesa dell'Immacolata (Church of the Immaculate), which was founded in the 13th century and rebuilt in Baroque style after the 1693 earthquake.

PICTURE PERFECT

A Flight of Fancy

La Scalinata de Santa Maria del Monte, the 142-step staircase clad in ceramic, is worth the visit. Point the viewfinder from ground level looking up or climb to the top and experiment with different angles and light. Don't forget to capture the intricate details of the majolica porcelains at close range.

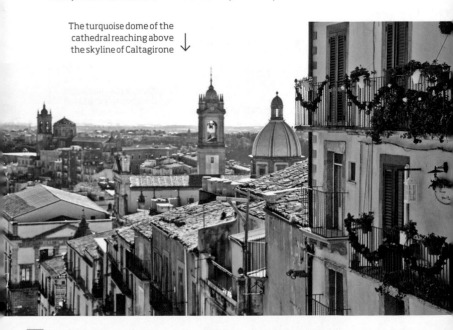

The turquoise dome of the cathedral reaching above the skyline of Caltagirone ↓

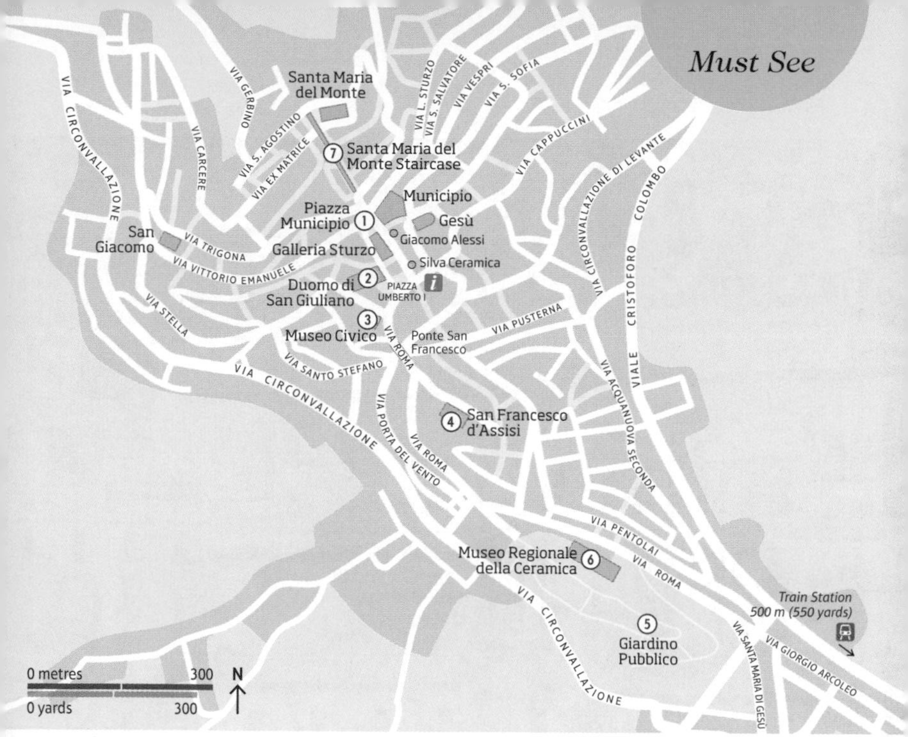

Santa Maria del Monte
Santa Maria del Monte Staircase
Municipio
Piazza Municipio
Gesù
Giacomo Alessi
Silva Ceramica
San Giacomo
Galleria Sturzo
Duomo di San Giuliano
Piazza Umberto I
Museo Civico
Ponte San Francesco
San Francesco d'Assisi
Museo Regionale della Ceramica
Giardino Pubblico
Train Station 500 m (550 yards)
Via Circonvallazione
Via Gerbino
Via Carcere
Via S. Agostino
Via Ex Matrice
Via L. Sturzo
Via S. Salvatore
Via Vespri
Via S. Sofia
Via Cappuccini
Via Circonvallazione di Levante
Viale Cristoforo Colombo
Via Trigona
Via Vittorio Emanuele
Via Stella
Via Pusterna
Via Roma
Via Santo Stefano
Via Acquanuova Seconda
Via Porta del Vento
Via Pentolai
Via Santa Maria di Gesù
Via Giorgio Arcoleo
0 metres 300
0 yards 300
N

Giardino Pubblico

Caltagirone's beautiful public gardens are best reached by going down Via Roma. The park was designed in the mid-1800s, and the long balustrade and the bandstand are richly decorated with ceramic tiles.

Museo Regionale della Ceramica

Viale Giardini Pubblici
0933-58418
9am-6:30pm

At the northwestern end of the public gardens is the Ceramics Museum, accessed via an 18th-century belvedere known as the "Teatrino". Exhibits include Bronze Age pots and Greek, Hellenistic and Roman kraters and figurines. The Middle Ages are represented by Arab vases and Sicilian pieces. The collection also has more recent pharmacy jars and glazed vases with religious figures.

Santa Maria del Monte Staircase

Back in the centre of town, one of the most impressive sights is the monumental Santa Maria del Monte staircase, with its 142 majolica-clad steps. The steps were built in 1606 to link the cathedral to Palazzo Senatorio. During the feast days of San Giacomo (24 & 25 July) the entire flight of stairs is illuminated with thousands of lamps, skilfully arranged to create dazzling patterns of light.

Back in the centre of town, one of the most impressive sights is the monumental Santa Maria del Monte staircase, with its 142 majolica-clad steps.

SHOP

Giacomo Alessi
A world-famous ceramicist, Alessi reinterprets the traditions and myths of ancient Sicily in his medieval tiles, gleeful dinnerware and lavish centrepieces, not to mention his iconic Moor's head vases and pine cone pieces.

Via Principe Amedeo 9
giacomoalessi.com

Silva Ceramica
In a courtyard off the piazza, Silva Ceramica produces imitations of antique designs, including pretty figurines, pots and tiles.

Piazza Umberto I 19
silvaceramica.com

Santa Maria del Monte staircase snaking through Caltagirone

EXPERIENCE MORE

Palazzolo Acreide

F6 Town hall; 0931-871 260

Originally named Akrai, this town, a UNESCO World Heritage site, has a history that dates back to ancient times, as well as some important Baroque churches and buildings – the Chiesa Madre di San Nicolò, Palazzo Zocco and the 18th-century Chiesa dell'Annunziata.

However, the most interesting sight to visit here is the peaceful plain with the **excavations at Akrai**. Located just outside of the town's centre, this fascinating archaeological site was inhabited in 664 BC, when the settlement was founded by the Syracusans. A small theatre stands by the entrance. The acropolis contains an agora, two latomie (the Intagliata and Intagliatella quarries), the ruins of the Temple of Aphrodite and the so-called Santoni, 12 rock-hewn statues that represents the iconic Anatolian mother goddess Cybele.

Excavations at Akrai
2 km (1 mile) from Akrai centre 0931-876 602 Times vary, call ahead

Lentini

F5 From Catania, Syracuse & Messina APT Siracusa, 0931-481 200 or 464 255; Pro Loco Lentini, Via Conte Alamo, 095-900 601

An ancient Siculan city initially named Xuthia, Lentini was conquered by the Chalcidians in 729 BC and fought against Syracuse with Athens' support. Defeated and occupied by the Romans, the city went into decline. In the Middle Ages it became an important agricultural centre. The local **Museo Archeologico** has finds from the ancient city, especially the Siculan and Greek epochs. The digs at Leontinoi, at the edge of town in the Colle Castellaccio area, can be reached via the ancient Porta Siracusana city gate. The various walls testify to the city's battle-worn history, and there are a number of ancient burial grounds inside the archaeological precinct.

Museo Archeologico
Via Museo 1 095-783 29 62 8:30am-7pm Tue-Sat, 8:30am-1:30pm Sun

8 Megara Hyblaea

F5 0931-450 82 11 Augusta station 9am-6pm daily (winter: to 3pm)

One of the first Greek colonies in Sicily was founded in 728 BC here at Megara. According to legend, the founders were the followers of Daedalus, who had escaped from Crete. Unfortunately, today the site is surrounded by the oil refineries of Augusta and in such an unattractive environment it is difficult to visit the ruins of the ancient city and gain any sense of atmosphere.

Watching a performance at Akrai's theatre, at Palazzolo Acreide

Exploring the exterior and interior *(inset)* of the necropolis of Pantalica

The Megara colonists who founded Megara Hyblaea were soon at war with Syracuse and Leontinoi, and a century later founded the city of Selinunte, in western Sicily. You should be able to see the ruins of the Hellenistic walls, the Agora quarter, and the remains of some temples, baths and colonnades. These excavations were led by the eminent archaeologist Paolo Orsi and the École Française of Rome. Information display boards will help you to get orientated.

Augusta

G5 From Catania, Syracuse, Messina Augusta town hall; 0931-980111

Augusta was founded on an island by Frederick II as a port protected by a castle. Under the Aragónese the city was constantly at war with Turkish and North African pirates. It was almost totally destroyed by the 1693 earthquake. In the early 1900s the city expanded and became a major petrochemical port, and this drastically changed the landscape. You enter the old town through the Porta Spagnola city gate, built by the viceroy Benavides in 1681, next to which are the ruins of the old walls. In the centre, the Baroque Chiesa delle Anime Sante, the Chiesa Madre (1769) and the Museo della Pizzaforte (Arms Museum, open Saturdays only) are worth a look.

Pantalica

F5 19 km/12 miles from Ferla, 45 km/28 miles from Syracuse 7am-7pm Sat & Sun (reservation)

Tombs, dwellings and temples line the walls of the limestone gorges at the confluence of the Bottiglieria and Anapo rivers. Pantalica, a UNESCO World Heritage Site since 2015, was the heart of the ancient kingdom of Hybla, which, in its heyday, used Syracuse as its port. The city was conquered by the Greeks when the coastal colonies became powerful in the 8th century BC, and Pantalica became important again during the early Middle Ages, when Arab invasions and constant wars led the locals to seek refuge in its inaccessible canyons. The cave dwellings and hermitages date from this period, as do the ruins of a settlement known as the "Byzantine village".

A WALK THROUGH PANTALICA

This archaeological site - the largest necropolis in Sicily - covers a large area, but the steep gorges mean there are few roads, and the only practical way of getting around is on foot. About 9 km (5 miles) from Ferla stands the Filiporto Necropolis, with more than 1,000 tombs cut out of the cliffs. Next is the North Necropolis; the last place to park is near the *Anaktoron*, the megalithic palace of the prince of ancient Hybla dating from the 12th century BC. The road ends 1 km (half a mile) further on. From this point, one path goes down to the Bottiglieria river, where steep walls are filled with rock-cut caves, and another takes you to the so-called "Byzantine village", the rock-hewn church of San Micidiario and the other necropolises in this area. It is not advisable to try to go to Pantalica from Sortino (the northern slope) as it is an extremely tiring walk regardless of your fitness level.

11

Modica

F6 From Syracuse
Town hall, Corso Umberto I, 141; 346-655 82 27

Inhabited since the era of the Siculi culture, Modica rebelled against Roman rule in 212 BC and, thanks to its strategic position, became one of the most important towns in medieval and Renaissance Sicily. It is now a UNESCO World Heritage site.

Modica Alta is built on a hill and is connected to the lower town, Modica Bassa, via flights of steps. Alleys and lanes evoke the walled town, which from 844 to 1091 was Mohac, an important Arab city.

A climb up the hill to see the Cathedral, the Duomo di San Giorgio, is worthwhile. It is dedicated to St George and was built by Count Alfonso Henriquez Cabrera on the site of a 13th-century church. The magnificent façade rises upwards with three ranks of columns. In the interior, there is a *polittico* by Bernardino Niger made of ten 16th-century wooden panels with scenes from the New Testament.

Corso Regina Margherita, the main street in Modica Alta, has many fine 19th-century palazzos. By going up Via Marchesa Tedeschi, you will come across the façade of Santa Maria di Betlem, a 16th-century church that was rebuilt after the 1693 earthquake. Inside is the Cappella del Sacramento, a splendid example of late Gothic-Renaissance architecture.

Interesting buildings along Corso Umberto I include the former Monastero delle Benedettine (a convent for Benedictine nuns now used as a courthouse), the fine 19th-century Teatro Garibaldi, the 18th-century Palazzo Tedeschi, Santa Maria del Soccorso and Palazzo Manenti. Also on Corso Umberto I a flight of Baroque monumental steps, flanked by statues of the Apostles, leads to the entrance of San Pietro. This church was built after the 1693 earthquake on the site of a 14th-century church. The *Madonna dell'Ausilio*, a Gagini-school statue, stands inside.

Fossils and majolica tiles are featured in the **Museo Civico Belgiorno**, alongside Greek and Roman ceramics and artifacts recovered from graves in the Modica area, including the archaeological site of Cava d'Ispica.

Museo Civico Belgiorno
Corso Umberto I, 149
346-655 81 05 10am-8pm Mon-Sun (to 1pm Sun)

Did You Know?

The seeds from carob trees found near Modica are known as "poor man's chocolate" and prized by chefs.

BAROQUE TOWNS OF THE VAL DI NOTO

In 1693 a devastating earthquake destroyed the entire southeast corner of Sicily. At the time, Sicily was under the rule of the Spanish Bourbons, and the architecture favoured was flamboyant, bold and extravagant. Many of the towns were rebuilt in this style and, as a result, this beautiful region of dramatic limestone gorges, flower-filled meadows and long sandy beaches is peppered with glorious Baroque towns.

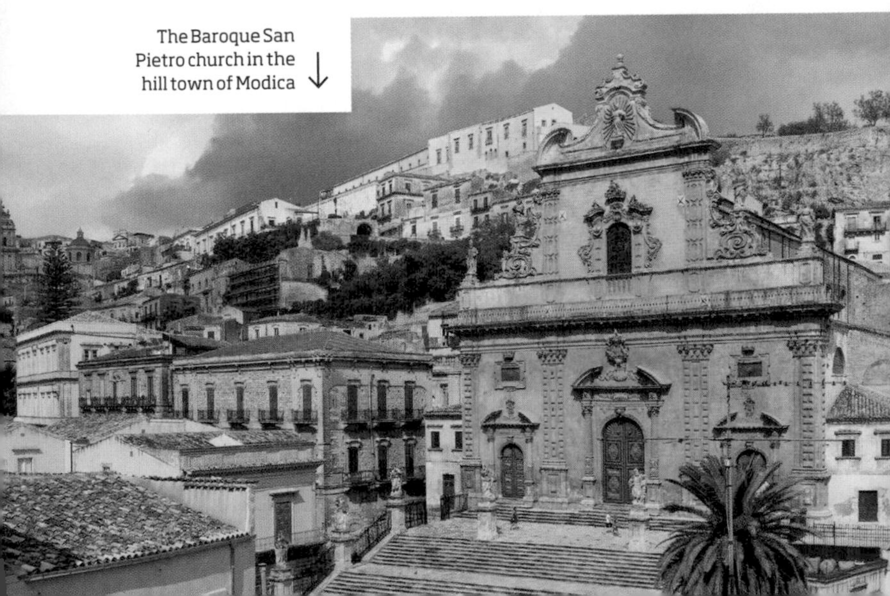

The Baroque San Pietro church in the hill town of Modica

→ Beautiful majolica-decorated steps pave this narrow street in Vizzini

Chiaramonte Gulfi

E6 comune.chiaramonte-gulfi.gov.it

This town was founded in the 14th century by Manfredi Chiaramonte, the Count of Modica, on the steep slopes of a rise and then developed towards the valley. The Chiesa del Salvatore and Matrice Santa Maria la Nova are in the centre, while the Madonna delle Grazie Sanctuary is on the outskirts.

Gela

E6 From Syracuse
STR; 0933-913 788

According to Greek historian Thucydides, Gela was founded in 688 BC. In the 6th century BC its inhabitants founded Agrigento. Extending over two slopes – the present-day Acropolis and the Capo Soprano area – the town was revived, after a long period of abandonment, by Frederick II. Today Gela is marred by ugly buildings, industrial plants and a strong anti-Mafia military presence. However, there are the archaeological sites: a long stretch of Greek **Fortifications at Capo Soprano** built by Timoleon and the sacred precinct and ancient Temple of Athena at the **Acropolis Excavations**, all good introductions before a visit to the **Museo Archeologico Regionale**.

Fortifications at Capo Soprano

0933-913788 9am-1 hr before sunset Mon-Sat

Acropolis Excavations

9am-1 hr before sunset
For lunch approx. 1-2pm

Museo Archeologico Regionale

Corso Vittorio Emanuele
0933-912 626 9am-6:30pm daily Winter: Sun (except first Sun of month)

EAT

Accursio

A Michelin-starred restaurant set within an old palazzo.

F6 Via Grimaldi 41, Modica accursioristorante.it

Teverna Nicastro

An old-fashioned joint in the old town, with tables on the steps outside.

F6 Via Sant' Antonino 30, Modica tavernanicastro.com

14

Vizzini

F5 Town hall; 0933-968 211

The fascination of Vizzini lies in the small streets and alleys of the old town, which has preserved its atmosphere and town plan – increasingly rare in Sicily because of modern urban growth. Also worth a look is the fine architecture of the Chiesa Madre di San Gregorio with its Gothic portal, which was taken from the destroyed Palazzo di Città.

Vittoria

E6 Pro Loco; 09338-2554 485

Founded by Vittoria Colonna in 1603, this agricultural town lies on the plain between the Ippari and Dirillo rivers. In the central Piazza del Popolo are the Teatro Comunale (1877) and Santa Maria delle Grazie, a Baroque church built after the disastrous 1693 earthquake *(p56)*.

↑ While away the hours at one of Marzamemi's waterside restaurants

Pachino

F7 Town hall; 0931-803 557

The town of Pachino, founded in 1758 by the princes of Giardineli and populated by a few dozen families, has evolved into a large agricultural and wine-producing centre. Despite inroads made by modern architecture, there are still some traces of the original town plan: a series of courtyards and alleys reveals an Arab influence. Pachino is also synonymous with a variety of small red tomato used for sauces and salads, which has become familiar throughout the country (it has even acquired DOC status). Besides the *pachini* tomatoes, the area – close to seaside resorts and the Vendicari nature reserve with sandy, isolated beaches – is famous for the production of red wine.

SHORT HIKES IN PACHINO'S VENDICARI RESERVE

Blue Route
Set out from Eloro beach and end at Calamosche, the most famous beach in the reserve.

Green Route
Explore Cittadella Maccari to the *tonnara*, passing the Trigona and a Byzantine necropolis.

Orange Route
From Vendicari's main entrance, pass the *tonnara*, Sveva Tower and Vendicari beach to end at Calamosche.

Capo Passero

F7

At the southern tip of Sicily, on the Capo Passero headland, lies the small town of Portopalo di Capo Passero, a centre for agricultural produce and fishing. Portopalo, together with the nearby town of Marzamemi, has become a popular summer tourist spot. Just off the coast is the small island of Capo Passero, which, because of its strategic position, has always been considered an excellent observation point. Proof is provided by the 17th-century watchtower, which replaced a series of military installations and fortifications, some of which were of ancient origin.

The southernmost point on the beautiful headland is Capo delle Correnti. Opposite the point a lighthouse stands on an island called Isola delle Correnti. Near here – or more precisely, close to Portopalo – Allied troops landed on 10 July 1943 with the aim of establishing a bridgehead on Sicily.

North of Portopalo you can see a tuna fishery *(tonnara)* and a fish processing plant. In nearby Marzamemi the town also grew up around a tuna fishery and the residence of the noble Villadorata family, who are still the proprietors of the local *tonnara*.

The waters of the central Mediterranean are still heavily populated by large schools of tuna fish that migrate annually. Enticed towards the *tonnara*, the fish become trapped in a complicated network of tuna fishing nets. Tuna caught using this traditional method is prized and considered highly superior to tuna caught out on the open sea.

Off the coast is the small island of Capo Passero, which, because of its strategic position, has always been considered an excellent observation point.

18

Cava d'Ispica

F6 Syracuse-Ispica Times vary, check website cavadispica.org

An ancient river carved the Cava d'Ispica out of the rock and the gorge has developed into an open-air monument. The sides of the canyon are perforated with the tombs of a necropolis, places of worship and cave dwellings where religious hermits went through mystical experiences. It was an Egyptian hermit, Sant'Ilarione, who initiated the monasticism in the canyon, which was used only as a burial site in antiquity.

You can access the Cava d'Ispica from SS115 from Ispica to Modica, taking a right-hand turn-off at Bettola del Capitano before following the branch for 5.5 km (3.5 miles) as far as the Cavallo d'Ispica mill. Improved access has also made it possible to visit the Larderia Necropolis, although since the establishment of a new enclosure, it is much more difficult to gain an overall idea of the complex of caves that have made Cava d'Ispica such a world-famous attraction for decades. While the Larderia Necropolis is an impressive network of catacombs (there is also a small museum), not far from the entrance you can visit – on request – the Grotta di San Nicola, a cave with a Byzantine fresco of the Madonna, or the small Byzantine church of San Pancrazio, in a claustrophobically narrow enclosure. Despite the difficult terrain, the unfenced part of the gorge is also well worth visiting. Every step of the way you will be well rewarded for the strenuous climb.

Scicli

F6 From Syracuse From Noto Town hall; 0932-839 111; Palazzo Spadaro; 0932-839 608

The town lies at the point where the Modica river converges with the valleys of Bartolomeo and Santa Maria la Nova. Scicli, a UNESCO World Heritage site, once played a major role in controlling communications between the coast and the uplands. It was an Arab stronghold and then became a royal city under the Normans. It was totally rebuilt after the 1693 earthquake, and Baroque streets, façades and churches emerged from the devastated town.

For visitors arriving from Modica along the panoramic San Bartolomeo valley, the first stop is San Bartolomeo followed by the new town centre, built on the plain after the old hill town was abandoned. In the centre is the church of Santa Maria la Nova, rebuilt several times and now with Neo-Classical features, and Palazzo Beneventano with its Baroque motifs. The Chiesa Madre in Piazza Italia is worth visiting for its papier-mâché *Madonna dei Milici* and the Baroque street Via Mormino Penna. Higher up are the ruins of San Matteo, the old cathedral, at the foot of the ruined castle built by the Arabs. The town is also often used as a film set.

STAY

Albergo Diffuso

At this innovative "scattered hotel", stay in accommodation in 11 different houses around the centre.

F6 Via Mormino Penna 15, Scicli sciclialbergodiffuso.it

→ Driving along the beautiful Baroque Palazzo Beneventano in Scicli

VENDE
OMEGA

The bustling city of Catania with Mount Etna forming a backdrop

MOUNT ETNA, THE AEOLIAN ISLANDS AND THE NORTHEAST

In 734 BC the first colonists from Greece landed on this coast and founded Naxos, the first of a series of powerful colonies in Sicily that gave rise to a period of prosperity and cultural sophistication. However, thanks to the presence of Mount Etna, the Ionian coast of Sicily has often had to deal with violent volcanic eruptions. These, together with devastating earthquakes, have destroyed almost all traces of the splendid Greek cities in this area, with the exception of the ancient theatre in Taormina, which was rebuilt in the Roman era.

One of the most catastrophic volanic eruptions here was in 1669, when the molten lava even reached the city of Catania and the sea. The lava flows have formed Etna's distinctive landscape, however, and flowers and festoons of black lava now adorn many of the churches and buildings in Catania and the surrounding towns.

The dramatic views, mild climate and wealth of architectural beauty have made this coast a favourite with visitors. The first of these were people who undertook the Grand Tour in the 1700s and made their first stop at Messina, just as many modern travellers do today.

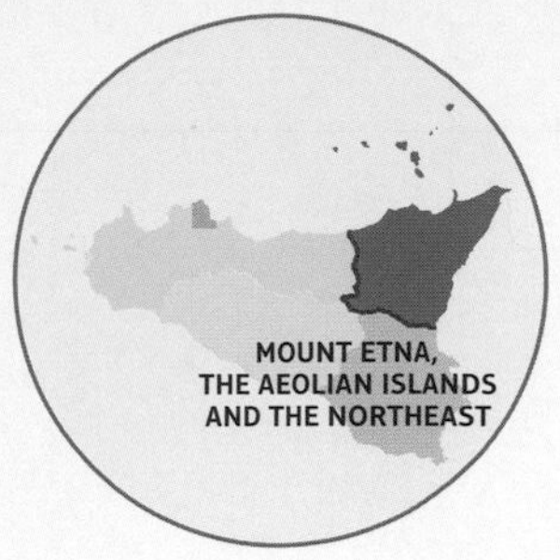

MOUNT ETNA, THE AEOLIAN ISLANDS AND THE NORTHEAST

Must Sees

1 Catania
2 Taormina
3 Mount Etna
4 Messina
5 Aeolian Islands

Experience More

6 Adrano
7 Motta Sant'Anastasia
8 Agira
9 Paternò
10 Regalbuto
11 Aci Castello
12 Mascalucia
13 Centuripe
14 Acireale
15 Aci Trezza
16 Bronte
17 Zafferana Etnea
18 Randazzo
19 Linguaglossa
20 Castiglione di Sicilia
21 Giardini-Naxos
22 Capo d'Orlando
23 Giarre
24 Tyndaris
25 Milazzo
26 Patti
27 The Nebrodi Mountains

Isola Stromboli
Ginostra
San Vincenzo
Stromboli, Salerno
Isola Panarea
San Pietro
Pollara
Malfa
Santa Marina Salina
Isola Salina
Rinella
Acquacalda
Quattropani
Lipari
Isola Lipari
Porto Levante
Isola Vulcano
Gelso
Capo di Milazzo
Baronia
Spartà
Torre Faro
Divieto Tirrena
Ganzirri
Spadafora
Villa S. Giovanni
Golfo di Patti
MILAZZO 25
Gioiosa Marea
San Giorgio
CAPO D'ORLANDO 22
MESSINA 4
Rometta
TYNDARIS 24
Barcellona Pozzo di Gotto
Gazzi
Brolo
PATTI 26
Falcone
Castroreale Terme
Contesse
Sant'Angelo di Brolo
Castroreale
Mili San Pietro
Monti Peloritani
Reggio di Calabria
Galati Marina
Castell'Umberto
Mazzarrà Sant'Andrea
Monte Poverella 1,279 m (4,195 ft)
Frazzano
Scaletta Zanclea
Alì
Ucria
Novara di Sicilia
Pizzo di Verná 1,286 m (4,218 ft)
Mandanici
Longi
Tortorici
Alì Terme
Stretto di Messina
Floresta
Antillo
Roccalumera
Casalvecchio Siculo
Furci Siculo
27 THE NEBRODI MOUNTAINS
Monte Colla 1,611 m (5,285 ft)
Sant'Alessio Siculo
Forza d'Agro
Francavilla di Sicilia
CASTIGLIONE DI SICILIA 20
RANDAZZO 18
Alcàntara
Castello di Maniace
Passopisciaro
Mazzarò
2 TAORMINA
Maletto
LINGUAGLOSSA 19
21 GIARDINI-NAXOS
Troina
BRONTE 16
MOUNT ETNA 3
Fiumefreddo di Sicilia
Naples
Sant' Alfio
Simeto
Rifugio Citelli
Riposto
Rifugio Sapienza
Milo
23 GIARRE
ZAFFERANA ETNEA 17
Santa Venerina
Ionian Sea
ADRANO 6
Pozzillo
Biancavilla
Pedara
13 CENTURIPE
Nicolosi
Viagrande
14 ACIREALE
Belpasso
Aci Catena
12
15 ACI TREZZA
PATERNÒ 9
MASCALUCIA
11 ACI CASTELLO
Etnaland
Misterbianco
1 CATANIA
MOTTA SANT'ANASTASIA 7
0 kilometres 15
0 miles 15
N
Aeroporto di Catania-Fontanarossa

↑ Piazza Duomo with the cathedral and Fontana dell'Elefante

1

CATANIA

F4 Via Vittorio Emanuele II 172; www.comune.catania.it

Etna looms high over Catania. The earthquake in 1693 completely destroyed the city, and its centre was entirely reconstructed from Etna lava. The 18th-century rebuilding created imposing Baroque edifices, set on broad, straight streets and unevenly shaped squares, a precaution for earthquakes. Today Catania is a big, bustling and rather austere city with a compact historic centre.

①

Piazza Duomo

The heart of city life lies at the crossing of Via Etnea and Via Vittorio Emanuele. The square boasts many fine Baroque buildings: Palazzo del Municipio (Town Hall), the former Chierici Seminary, the Cathedral and Porta Uzeda, the city gate built in 1696 to connect Via Etnea with the port area. In the centre is the Fontana dell'Elefante, a fountain sculpted in 1736 by Giovanni Battista Vaccarini. On a pedestal in the basin is an elephant made of lava, on the back of which is an Egyptian obelisk with a globe on top. The latter, a late Roman sculpture, has become the city's symbol.

②

Cathedral

Piazza Duomo
10:30am-noon & 4-5:30pm daily
cattedralecatania.it

The principal church in Catania is dedicated to the city's patron saint, Agatha. It still has its three original Norman apses and transept. The façade, with two tiers of columns, is fully Baroque thanks to the design by Vaccarini, who is also responsible for the left-hand side of the cathedral. The majestic interior has a cupola, a tall transept and three apses. On the second pilaster to the right is the Tomb of Vincenzo Bellini; on the first one to the left, a 15th-century stoup. A door in the right-hand transept leads to the Norman Cappella della Madonna, home to the remains of Aragonese rulers.

Palazzo Biscari

Via Museo Biscari 10-16
7am-1pm & 3-7pm by appt palazzobiscari.com

This is the largest private palazzo in 18th-century Catania. Construction was begun by Prince Paternò Castello on an embankment of the 16th-century city walls. Work continued for nearly a century and involved some of the leading architects of the time. The most interesting side of the building faces onto Via Dusmet, with a large terrace decorated with putti (winged

Did You Know?

According to Homer's *Odyssey*, the rock stacks on the Ionian coast were thrown there by Polyphemus the Cyclops.

infants), telamons (pillars in the form of male statues) and garlands sculpted by Antonino Amato. The building is partly private and partly used as city administrative offices.

Badia di Sant'Agata

Via Vittorio Emanuele II
7:30am-noon daily

This masterpiece of Catanian Baroque architecture was built in 1735–67 and designed by Giovanni Battista Vaccarini. The façade is a play of convex and concave surfaces. The octagonal interior, a triumph of Rococo decoration, is equally impressive.

Teatro Bellini

Via Perrotta 12
9am-noon Tue-Sat
teatromassimobellini.it

Named after the Catania-born composer Vincenzo Bellini, this theatre is renowned the world over for its incomparable acoustics, lavish decor and top-quality performances. Beyond the impressive 19th-century Neo-Baroque façade is an equally extravagant theatre, whose ceiling features a fresco of Bellini surrounded by his main operas.

Museo Civico Belliniano

Piazza San Francesco 9 095-715 05 35 9am-7pm Mon-Sat, 9am-1pm Sun 1 Jan, 1 May, 25 Dec

Vincenzo Bellini's birthplace is now a museum filled with mementos, signed scores, musical instruments and dioramas of scenes from some of his operas.

Pescheria

Situated at the beginning of Via Garibaldi, the Fontana dell' Amenano fountain is fed by the waters of the underground Amenano river. Sculpted in 1867, the fountain is the focal point of a colourful fish market, the Mercato della Pescheria, which occupies the nearby streets and small squares every morning. At the end of Via Garibaldi is the monumental Porta Garibaldi city gate, built of limestone and lava in 1768 to celebrate the wedding of Ferdinand IV.

SHOP

Libera Bafe

This enchanting bookshop strewn with papier-mâché puppets also has a quiet corner where parents can have tea while their little ones join in with crafts and sing-alongs.

Via Monte Sant'Agata 18/20 Sun bafe.it

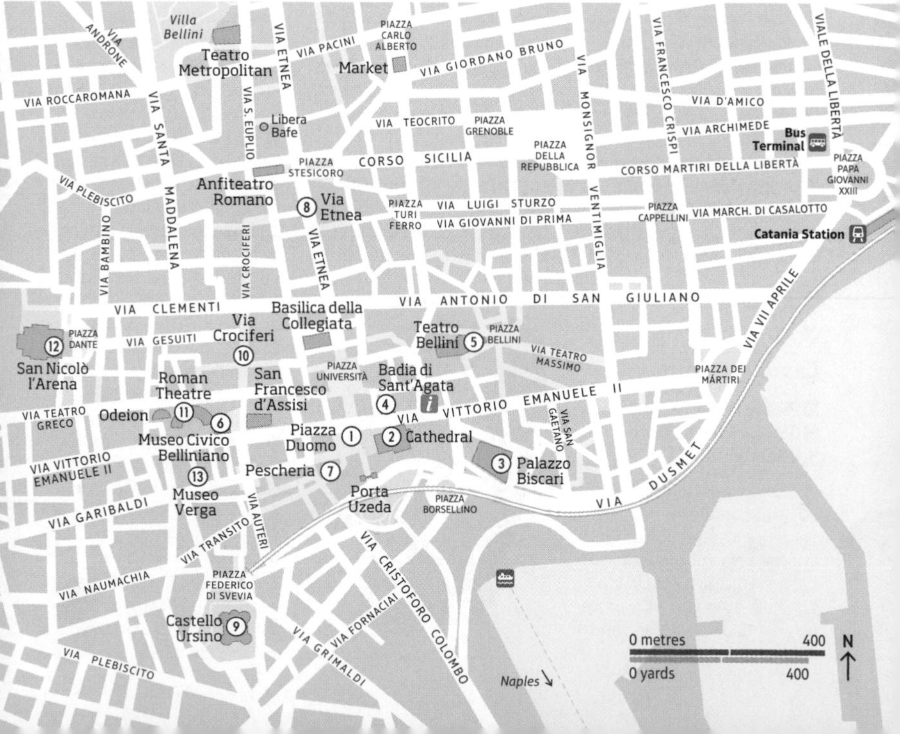

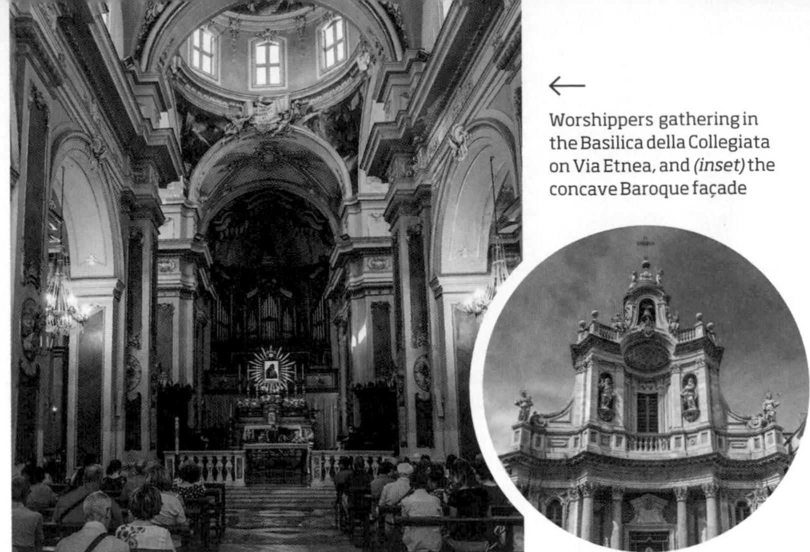

Worshippers gathering in the Basilica della Collegiata on Via Etnea, and *(inset)* the concave Baroque façade

Via Etnea

Catania's main street goes up a slight incline and connects the most important parts of the city. Partly closed to traffic, Via Etnea has the most elegant shops and cafés in town. Halfway along the street lies Piazza Stesicoro, with the ruins of the Roman amphitheatre, built in the 2nd century AD. Nearby is the vast Piazza Carlo Alberto, occupied by Catania's huge central market (Mon–Sat). Back on Via Etnea is the Basilica della Collegiata, built in the early 1700s and one of the most important late Baroque works in the city. Near the end of Via Etnea is Villa Bellini, a public garden with subtropical plants and busts of famous Sicilians.

(9)

Castello Ursino

Piazza Federico di Svevia 095-345 830 9am-6pm daily

This castle was built in 1239–50 by Riccardo da Lentini for Frederick II and is one of the last few vestiges of medieval Catania. The Castello Ursino originally stood on a promontory overlooking the sea and was part of a massive defence system that once included the Motta, Anastasia, Paternò and Adrano castles. As a result of lava flow from Mount Etna, it now stands some way inland, and it was one of the few buildings to survive the 1693 earthquake. On its eastern side, a five-pointed star is visible above a large window; its origins are somewhat mysterious, though it is thought to have a cabalistic meaning. In a niche on the façade is a sculpture of the Swabian eagle seizing a lamb with its claws, a symbol of Hohenstaufen imperial power. In the inner courtyard, where the kings of Aragon administered justice, there is a display of sarcophagi, columns and other pieces. The upper rooms house the Museo Civico, which has a fine art gallery with many important medieval and Renaissance paintings and a vast collection of archaeological artifacts, including ancient Greek sculpture, Attic vases and 4th-century mosaics.

Via Crociferi

This street is lined with lavishly decorated Baroque palazzi and churches. The road begins at Piazza San Francesco, with the Baroque San Francesco d'Assisi. In the interior are the so-called candelore, carved and gilded wooden constructions which symbolize the various artisans' guilds in the city. In February the candelore are carried in procession as part of the celebrations honouring St Agatha, the city's patron saint. Outside the church is the Arco di San Benedetto, an arch connecting the fine Badia Grande abbey, designed by Francesco Battaglia, and the Badia Piccola, attributed to Giovanni Battista Vaccarini.

The Ancient Greek "Biscari head" (c 500 BC) in the Museo Civico at Castello Ursino

To the left is San Benedetto, where the wooden portal carries scenes of the life of St Benedict, and San Francesco Borgia, at the top of a double flight of steps flanked by the former Jesuit College. Opposite stands San Giuliano, a masterpiece of Catanian Baroque architecture also designed by Vaccarini.

Roman Theatre

Via Vittorio Emanuele 226 095-715 05 08 9am-7pm daily

Built of limestone and lava on the southern slope of the acropolis, the theatre had a diameter of 87 m (285 ft) and could seat up to 7,000 people. Although there was probably a Greek theatre on this site at one time, the present ruins are entirely Roman. The theatre was badly damaged in the 11th century, when Roger I authorized the removal of the marble facing and limestone blocks for use as building material for the cathedral. What remains of the theatre today are the cavea, the edge of the orchestra and part of the backstage area. Next to the theatre is the small semicircular Odeion, made of lava and used mainly for competitions in music and rhetoric. The entrance to the Odeion is near the top tiers of seats in the Roman theatre.

INSIDER TIP
Pompelmo

The Pompelmo is a popular summertime cocktail made with equal parts Amaro dell'Etna liqueur, Prosecco and San Pellegrino grapefruit soda. If you're feeling bounteous, order one at the glitzy, over-the-top Morgana Lounge Bar *(Scesa Morgana 4)*.

San Nicolò l'Arena

Piazza Dante 095-715 99 12 9am-5pm daily (Aug: 11am-6pm daily)

San Nicolò was built on the site of a Benedictine monastery damaged in the 1669 eruption. After collapsing in the 1693 earthquake, the church was rebuilt in the 1700s. It now houses the faculty of letters of the University of Catania. The nave has two aisles, separated from the central section by huge piers. In the transept is one of the largest and most accurate sundials in Europe, built in the mid-1800s by the German baron Wolfgang Sartorius von Waltershausen. The 24 slabs of inlaid marble show the signs of the zodiac, days of the year and the seasons. At noon, sunlight falls from the roof, marking the day and month.

Museo Verga

Via Sant'Anna 8 095-715 05 98 9am-1pm, 2-5:30pm Mon-Fri

The apartment where the great Sicilian author Giovanni Verga lived for many years and died in 1922 is on the second floor of a 19th-century building; it now operates as a museum with period furniture and personal mementos. At the entrance you can find reproductions of manuscripts, the originals of which are kept at the University of Catania's regional library. The library in Verga's house boasts over 2,500 books, ranging from works by the Italian Futurist Marinetti to the Russian author Dostoevsky. The bedroom is quite simple, with a bed, a dressing table, a wardrobe and a few portraits of Verga.

↓ The sunken ruins of the Roman Theatre in Catania

2

TAORMINA

G3 Catania Fontanarossa, 70 km (43 miles) 5 km (3 miles) from Giardini-Naxos SAIS (www.saistrasporti.it) STR, Palazzo Corvaja; www.taorminainforma.it

On a bluff above the Ionian Sea, at the foot of Monte Tauro, Taormina is Sicily's most famous tourist resort. Immersed in luxuriant subtropical vegetation, it was a favourite stop for those on the Grand Tour and the preferred summer residence of aristocrats and bankers, from Wilhelm II of Germany to the Rothschilds. In its time the town has been Siculan, Greek and Roman, but its medieval layout gave it today's look.

INSIDER TIP
Shopping Etiquette

DO greet shopkeepers with a simple *buongiorno* or *buona sera*. DON'T bring food or drink into a store. DO ask before handling merchandise. Credit cards are usually accepted, but DO carry cash *(contanti)* in small denominations and coins *(monete)* to pay for items under €20.

Greek Theatre

Via Teatro Greco 0942-23220 9am-1 hr before sunset daily

Set in a spectacular position, Taormina's Greek Theatre is one of the most famous Sicilian monuments in the world. It was built in the Hellenistic age (3rd century BC) and then almost entirely rebuilt by the Romans in the 2nd century AD, when it was repurposed as an arena for gladiatorial combat. From the cavea (the tiered seating area), carved into the side of the hill, the view takes in Giardini-Naxos and Mount Etna. The upper part of the theatre is surrounded by a double portico. The theatre originally had a diameter of 109 m (358 ft) and a seating capacity of 5,000. Behind the stage area stood a wall with niches and a colonnade. Some of the Corinthian columns are still standing.

Palazzo Corvaja

Piazza Vittorio Emanuele 0942-23243 8:30am-10pm daily

Taormina's grandest building dates from the 15th century, although it was originally an Arab tower. The austere façade, topped with crenellation, is given some elegant flourishes in the form of the mullioned windows and the limestone and black lava decorative motifs. The courtyard stairway, decorated with reliefs of the *Birth of Eve* and the *Original Sin*, takes you to the *piano nobile*, where the Sicilian parliament met in 1411 and where Queen Blanche of Navarre and her retinue lived for a short period. Some of the rooms are open to visitors. The palazzo also houses the local tourist information bureau and a small museum – the Museo Siciliano di Arte e Tradizione Popolari. Next to the palazzo are the Baroque Santa Caterina and the ruins of the Odeion, a small Roman theatre.

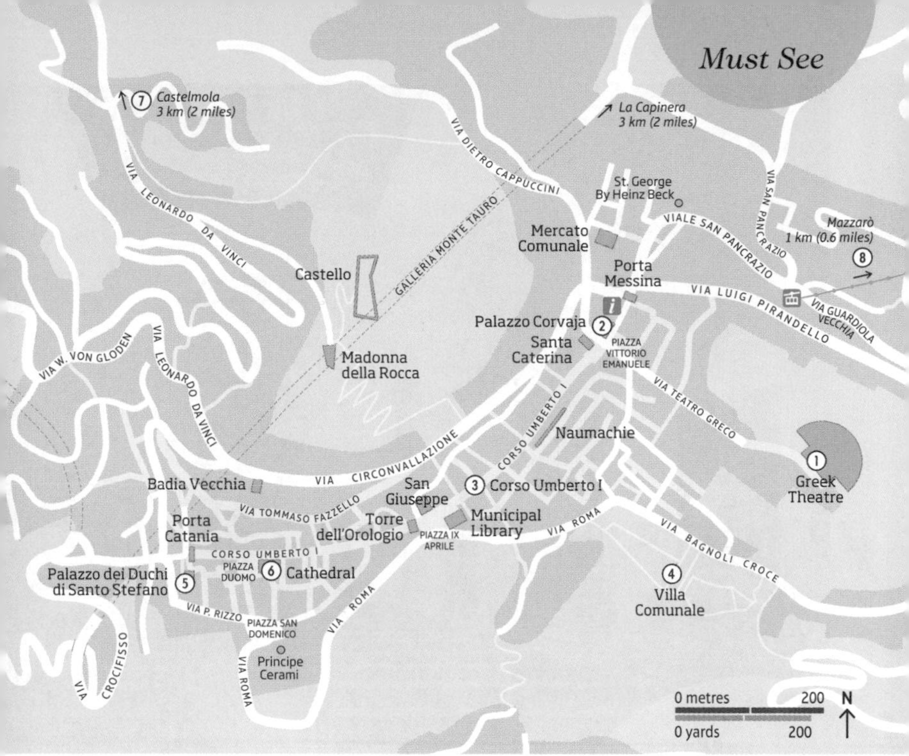

Corso Umberto I

The main street in Taormina begins at Porta Messina and ends at Porta Catania, a gate crowned by a building that bears the municipal coat of arms. The street is lined with shops, *pasticcerie* and cafés famous for their glamorous clientele. Halfway down the Corso is Piazza IX Aprile, a panoramic terrace with the churches of Sant'Agostino (now the Municipal Library) and San Giuseppe, as well as the landmark Wünderbar, where you can try the cocktails that Liz Taylor and Richard Burton were so fond of. A short distance away is the Porta di Mezzo gate with the 17th-century Torre dell'Orologio, or clock tower. Dotted above and below Corso Umberto I you will find several stepped alleyways and lanes that pass through quiet, characterful areas. One such alley leads to the Naumachie, a massive Roman brick wall dating back to the Imperial age, with 18 arched niches that once supported a huge cistern.

Taormina's ancient Greek Theatre, with Mount Etna looming in the distance

Villa Comunale

Via Bagnoli Croci
Summer: 9am-1 hr before sunset daily ; winter: 8am-sunset daily

Dedicated to Duke Colonna di Cesarò, this public garden was bequeathed to Taormina by Florence Trevelyan, an English aristocrat who fell in love with the town. Situated on a cliff with a magnificent view of Etna, the garden is filled with Mediterranean and tropical plants. A characteristic part of the garden is the arabesque-decorated tower, similar to a Chinese pagoda, once used for bird-watching.

Set in a spectacular position, Taormina's Greek Theatre is one of the most famous Sicilian monuments in the world.

Palazzo dei Duchi di Santo Stefano

Via De Spuches 9am-1pm & 3:30-8pm daily (winter: 3:30-6:30pm)

This 13th-century masterpiece of Sicilian-Gothic architecture near Porta Catania was the residence of the De Spuches, the Spanish dukes of Santo Stefano di Brifa and princes of Galati, two towns on the Ionian coast near Messina. The influence of Arab masons is clearly seen in the wide black lava frieze, alternating with rhomboidal white Syracusan stone inlay. Note the trilobated arches and the double lancet windows on the façade. The interior and the palace gardens are given over to the Fondazione G. Mazzullo, who set up a permanent exhibition of the works of sculptor Giuseppe Marzullo.

Cathedral

Piazza Duomo 0942-23123 8:30am-8pm daily arcipreturataormina.org

The Cattedrale di San Nicola di Bari was first built in the 13th century but has been altered a number of times – in the 15th, 16th, 18th and 20th centuries – and its austere façade crowned with crenellation has earned it the moniker the "Fortress Cathedral". The 17th-century portal is decorated with a medallion pattern, and over this are a small rose window and two windows with pointed arches. In the nave you'll find some gorgeous works of art: *The Visitation* by Antonio Giuffrè (15th century), a polyptych by Antonello Saliba of the *Virgin Mary and Child*, and an alabaster statue of the Virgin Mary by the Gagini School. In the middle of Piazza Duomo is a delightful Baroque fountain, and beyond that the Palazzo del Municipio (Town Hall), one storey of which is lined with Baroque windows.

Castelmola

visitsicily.info/castelmola

A winding 5-km- (3-mile-) long road northwest of town leads to this charming village perched on a rocky hill behind Taormina. Today little remains of the Norman castle that once stood here, but in antiquity this was a vital bastion against Arab attacks.

The interior and *(inset)* exterior of Cathedral of St Nicolò di Bari

An alternative route to Mazzarò is to take the steps which descend from the centre of Taormina, passing through gardens of bougainvillea in bloom.

Exploring the village only takes a few hours, but there are a good few churches, cafés, restaurants, and alleyways. For a more unusual experience, pop into Bar Turrisi and wonder at the vast collection of phallus-themed art that decorates every room from floor to ceiling. A few choice spots around the village also offer one of the most spectacular panoramic views in the world, taking in the Ionian coast, Mount Etna, Giardini-Naxos, the Strait of Messina and the Calabrian coast, not to mention bustling Taormina below – best enjoyed with a glass of wine at sunset.

HIDDEN GEM
Letojanni Beach

Get away from the glitterati and head to Letojanni, a relaxed seaside resort 7 km (4 miles) north of Taormina, marked by golden sandy beaches and plenty of free beach lidos and private clubs (*stabilimenti*) for those who want a little extra in the way of facilities.

Mazzarò

This small town might well be called Taormina's beach. It can be reached easily by cable car from Taormina or via the road leading to the Catania–Messina state road N114. An alternative route to Mazzarò is to take the steps which descend from the centre of Taormina, passing through gardens of bougainvillea in bloom.

Taking off from the crystal-clear waters of the bay, you can go on excursions to other sights along the coast: Capo Sant'Andrea, with the Grotta Azzurra, a spectacular marine grotto, can be visited by boat; to the south are the stacks of Capo Taormina and the beach at Villagonia; and to the north are Isola Bella, one of the most exclusive places in the area, and the beaches at the Baia delle Sirene and the Lido di Spisone. Further on is the beach at Mazzeo, a long stretch of sand that reaches as far as Letojanni and continues up to Lido Silemi.

EAT

Principe Cerami

Boasts an opulent dining room and a seaside terrace.

Piazza San Domenico 5
Mon san-domenico-palace.com

€€€

La Capinera

Creative fresh fish dishes and a sophisticated atmosphere.

Via Nazionale 177, Spisone-Taormina Mare
Mon (except Aug)
pietrodagostino.it

€€€

St. George By Heinz Beck

Blending English manor-house style with Sicilian embellishments.

Viale San Pancrazio 46
Wed-Mon Nov-Mar
theashbeehotel.com

€€€

Small leisure boats anchored in the crystal-clear waters of Mazzarò Bay

3

MOUNT ETNA

F4 Catania 095 791 47 55 (to hire a guide) Linguaglossa or Randazzo; Circumetnea railway from Catania to Riposto To Nicolosi Via Martiri d'Ungheria 36/38, Nicolosi; www.parcoetna.ct.it

Fundamental to Sicily's nature and landscape, Mount Etna is Europe's largest active volcano and dominates the whole of eastern Sicily. Feared and loved, Etna is both snow and fire, lush vegetation and black lava. Around the crater you can still see the remnants of numbers of ancient vents. Further down is the eerie, barren landscape of the Valle del Bove.

To the Greeks, Etna was home to Hephaestus, god of fire, and the Arabs knew it as Mongibello (Mountain of Mountains). Today, Parco dell'Etna offers breathtaking views, great hiking and, in season, skiing, and the occasional eruption of red sparks and lava. In 2013, Mount Etna became a UNESCO World Heritage Site.

A protected area 58,000 ha (143,260 acres) in size, Mount Etna offers many opportunities for excursions. A popular route is from Zafferana to the Valle del Bove, the spectacular hollow whose shape was changed by the eruptions in 1992. The hike up to the large craters at the summit is not to be missed. Start off at the Rifugio Sapienza and Rifugio Citelli hostels and Piano Provenzana. A trip around the mountain is also thrilling: from the Sapienza to the Monte Scavo camp, Piano Provenzana and the former Menza camp. There are also several lava grottoes.

↑ Hikers traversing the sandy black landscape around the volcano

↑ A lone skier pausing on the icy slopes beneath the volcano's peak in winter

Etna's Dramatic Eruptions

Etna is a relatively "recent" volcano, emerging some two million years ago. Some of its most devastating eruptions were in 1381 and 1669, when the lava reached Catania. The most recent ones took place in 2001 and 2002. Some of the worst eruptions from the last century are shown here.

Timeline

1928

▲ Lava flow from an unusually low fissure cut off the railway at the base of the mountain and wiped out the village of Mascali in just 2 days.

1971

▼ Lava flow on Etna's east bank endangered several small villages, as well as destroying the Etna Observatory.

1991–3

▲ Earth barriers, controlled explosions and concrete blocks dropped from helicopters were used to stop lava reaching Zafferana.

2001–2

▼ Lava flow caused extensive damage to Rifugio Sapienza and came within 4 km (2.5 miles) of Nicolosi.

25

The approximate percentage of the Sicilian population that lives on the slopes of Mount Etna.

↑ Mount Etna, the most active volcano in Europe, spewing lava and ash into the sky

The vivid crater on the slopes of Mount Etna

2.5 km

Or 1.5 miles, the distance of the Strait of Messina, separating Sicily from mainland Italy.

4

MESSINA

G2 STR Via dei Mille 270; www.discovermessina.it

Comfortably situated between the eastern and western Mediterranean, Messina has always acted as a meeting point, and over the centuries it has been populated by various communities from maritime Europe. The city's layout is quite easy to understand if you arrive by sea. The defences of Forte San Salvatore and Lanterna di Raineri are your introduction to Messina. The main streets are Via Garibaldi, which skirts the seafront, and Via I Settembre, which leads from the sea to the centre of town. The Botanic Garden and the Montalto Sanctuary are located on the hillside above the city.

Santissima Annunziata dei Catalani

Piazza dei Catalani
090-668-41 11
By appt only

Paradoxically, the devastating 1908 earthquake helped to "restore" the original 12th–13th-century structure of this Norman church, as it destroyed almost all the later additions and alterations. The nave has two side aisles and leads to the apse with its austere brick cupola.

Monument to John of Austria

In the square in front of the Annunziata church is a statue of John of Austria, the admiral who won the famous Battle of Lepanto (1571), with his foot on the head of the defeated Ottoman commander Alì Pasha. The work was sculpted in 1572 by Andrea Calamech.

The pedestal celebrates the formation of the Holy League and the defeat of the Turks in this historic naval battle. One of the sailors taking part was the great Miguel de Cervantes, author of *Don Quixote*, who recovered from his wounds in a Messina hospital.

Marina

In 1882, the author Frances Elliot wrote: "Nothing I have seen in Europe can compare with the Marina of Messina."

THE 1908 EARTHQUAKE

At 5:20am on 28 December 1908, an earthquake and a tsunami struck Messina at the same time, razing over 90 per cent of the buildings and killing 60,000 people. Reconstruction began immediately, and some of the remains of the old town were salvaged by being incorporated into a new urban plan based around the harbour.

Elegant and picturesque Messina marina, overlooked by mountains

For Elliot, Messina was "the gate of the promised land", boasting the largest natural harbour in the Mediterranean. The buildings that lined the marina before the earthquake were part of the Palazzata complex, also known as the Teatro Marittimo, a series of buildings that extended for more than a kilometre in the heart of the port area.

University of Messina

Piazza Pugliatti

The university was founded in 1548, closed by the Spanish in 1679 and reconstructed at last in 1927. Follow Viale Principe Umberto, and you will come to the Botanic Garden and the Montalto Sanctuary, with the Madonna of Victory standing out against the sky.

Fontana di Orione

This elegant 16th-century marble fountain stands next to the cathedral and incorporates statues representing the rivers Tiber, Nile, Ebro and Camaro (the last of which was channelled into Messina via the first aqueduct in the city specifically to supply the fountain with water).

Acquario Comunale

Piazza dell'Unità d'Italia
9am-1pm Wed & Thu
acquariomessina.it

The garden of the Villa Mazzini is decorated with busts and statues, and is also home to the Municipal Aquarium, where you can observe hundreds of species of Mediterranean sea life housed in tanks that are fed by sea water directly from the Strait of Messina. Next door is the Palazzo della Prefettura, in front of which is the Fountain of Neptune, sculpted in 1557 by Giovanni Angelo Montorsoli, which depicts the god of the sea vanquishing the monsters Scylla and Charybdis. The statues are actually 19th-century copies; the originals are on display in the Museo Regionale Interdisciplinare.

EAT

La Pitoneria

From an ordinary-looking storefront, *pitoni messinesi* (or *pitoni*) is served from early morning to late at night. Made of folded dough stuffed with endive, tomato, cheese and anchovy, it's flash-fried in hot oil to render it light and crispy.

Via Palermo 8/10
090-344 822 Tue

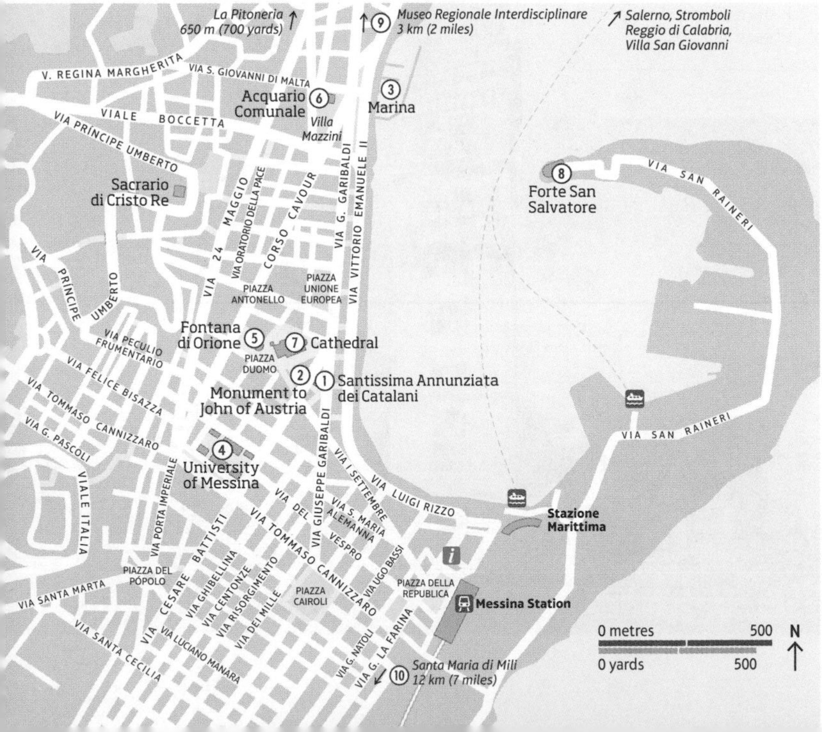

7

Cathedral

Piazza Duomo 090-774 895 7:30am-12.30pm & 4-7pm daily

Messina's cathedral is the heart of the town in every sense. Although it was reconstructed after the 1908 earthquake and the 1943 bombings, the cathedral has succeeded in preserving many of its medieval aspects. First built in 1197, you can still see the original central portal, installed in the early Middle Ages and decorated with two lions and a statue of the Virgin Mary and Infant Jesus. The side doors are decorated with statues of the Apostles and some marvellous inlays and reliefs. On the left-hand side of the façade is the monumental campanile (bell tower), which stands almost 60 m (197 ft) high and was built to house a unique object – the largest astronomical clock in the world, built in Strasbourg in 1933. At noon a number of mechanical figures move in elaborate patterns, geared by huge cogwheels.

Almost all of the impressive interior is the result of painstaking post-war reconstruction. The sculptures on the trusses in the central section of the two-aisle nave, a 15th-century basin and the 1525 statue of St John the Baptist by Gagini are all part of the original decoration. The doorways in the right-hand vestibule which lead to the Treasury are of note, as is the tomb of Archbishop Palmieri, sculpted in 1195. The magnificent organ in the transept was built after World War II, with five keyboards and 170 stops. The side aisles house many works of art, including several Gothic funerary monuments, most of which have been reconstructed.

BRIDGING THE STRAIT OF MESSINA

Communications with the mainland have always been an issue for Sicily, and for over 30 years the question of building a bridge over the Straits of Messina has been debated. In 1981 the Società Stretto di Messina was set up to design a single-span suspension bridge. A multitude of problems still needs to be tackled, however, one of which is the constant danger of earthquakes.

Forte San Salvatore

San Raineri Peninsula

Beyond the busy harbour area, at the very tip of the curved peninsula that protects the harbour, is Forte San Salvatore, built in the 17th century to block access to the Messina marina. On top of one of the tall towers in this impressive fort is a golden statue of the *Madonna della Lettera*: according to tradition, the Virgin Mary sent a letter of benediction to the inhabitants of Messina in AD 42.

On Via Garibaldi is the bustling Stazione Marittima, the boarding point for the ferries that connect Messina to Calabria on mainland Italy.

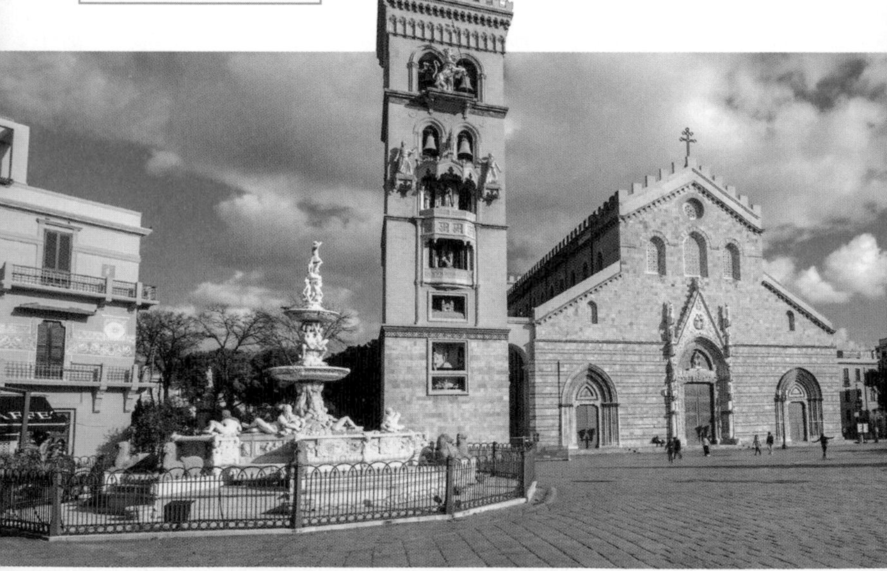

Although it was reconstructed after the 1908 earthquake and the 1943 bombings, the cathedral has succeeded in preserving many of its medieval aspects.

Museo Regionale Interdisciplinare

Viale della Libertà 465 090-361 292 9am-6:30pm Tue-Sat (last entrance 6:30pm), 9am-1pm Sun & hols (last entrance 12:30pm)

This fascinating museum near to Piazza dell'Unità d'Italia boasts a major collection of artworks salvaged after the catastrophic 1908 earthquake. In fact, most of the works come from the Civico Museo Peloritano, which was in the now destroyed Monastery of St Gregory. The museum has 12 rooms that present an overview of the artistic splendour of old Messina and include a number of famous paintings. At the entrance there are several 18th-century bronze panels depicting the *Legend of the Sacred Letter*. Some of the most important works include paintings from the Byzantine period and fragments from the duomo ceiling (room 1); the Gothic art in room 2; the examples of Renaissance Messina in room 3; the *Polyptych* that Antonello da Messina painted for the Monastery of St Gregory (room 4) and, in the same room, a *Madonna and Child* sculpture attributed to Francesco Laurana and a 15th-century oil on panel by an unknown Flemish artist.

Room 10 has two of the "pearls" of the museum, two masterpieces by Caravaggio, executed in 1608–1609: *The Raising of Lazarus* and *The Nativity*. This great artist's sojourn in Messina exerted an influence on several other artists, giving rise to a local Caravaggesque school, as can be seen in the canvases by Alonso Rodriguez, *St Peter & St Paul* and *Doubting Thomas*, on view in room 7.

Santa Maria di Mili

Strada Provinciale 38, Mili San Pietro By appt milisanpietro.it

If you head south from Messina for about 12 km (7 miles), you will reach the villages of Mili San Marco and, higher up in the Peloritani mountains, Mili San Pietro. Not far from the latter, in an area of wild landscape characterized by the deep Forra di Mili ravine, is the Santa Maria di Mili Sanctuary. Its church has been rebuilt several times and now has a 17th-century appearance. It was founded in 1090 by Roger I as proof of his renewed faith after taking Sicily from the Arabs. The Norman king later chose it as the burial site for his son. The 16th-century marble portal is crowned by a sculpture of the Madonna and Child. Above the two-aisle nave is a finely wrought wooden ceiling that dates from 1411. Once past the three arches marking off the apse, the ceiling becomes a series of small domes, a characteristic feature of religious architecture of the Norman period.

←

Messina's Duomo, and its astronomical clock, embedded in the bell tower *(inset)*

DRINK

Faro di Messina

Ruby red, intense and fruity, Faro di Messina DOC is made from a mix of native grape varieties that include Nerello Mascalese, Nerello Cappuccio, Nocera and Nero d'Avola. Traditionally hand-harvested in and around the villages of Faro and Faro Superiore, it is considered to be a "niche" wine with just over 20 hectares (50 acres) dedicated to its production.

Le Cassematte
Contrada Corso
lecasematte.it

Tenuta Rasocolmo
Strada Statale 113
tenutarasocolmo.com

5

AEOLIAN ISLANDS

F2 Milazzo Siremar: all year from Milazzo, summer only from Naples (www.siremar.it); Liberty Lines, all year from Milazzo & Naples (www.libertylines.it); in summer: connections from Messina & Palermo Corso Vittorio Emanuele 202, Lipari town; 090-988 00 95

Consisting of strikingly beautiful volcanic cliffs separated by inlets, sometimes quite deep, the Aeolian Islands (in Italian, Isole Eolie) are unique for their extraordinary rock formations and volcanoes, and for their history. Dominating the islands, especially in the winter, is the sea, with migratory birds nesting on the cliffs and frequent storms, which can reinforce a sense of isolation, even in this age of rapid communications.

The sun setting on the perfectly still waters of Marina Corta on Lipari ↑

The islands attract hordes of visitors every summer who come to bathe and dive, swim and sail, trek and indulge, yet despite the crowds, each island somehow manages to preserve its own individual character.

The best starting point for a visit to the varied Aeolian Islands is Lipari, the largest and most populous of the islands and with excellent boat services. Here you can decide what type of holiday you want – natural history excursions, taking in the alien landscapes of volcanic Stromboli and Vulcano, the exclusive tourist resort at Panarea among chic villas and yachts, or the timeless tranquillity of Alicudi and Filicudi, a far cry from the larger, busier islands.

PICTURE PERFECT
Movie Night

On Salina, after dinner in the tiny village of Pollara, wander over to the piazza, where the beloved film *Il Postino* is screened nightly - scenes from the movie were shot in the village.

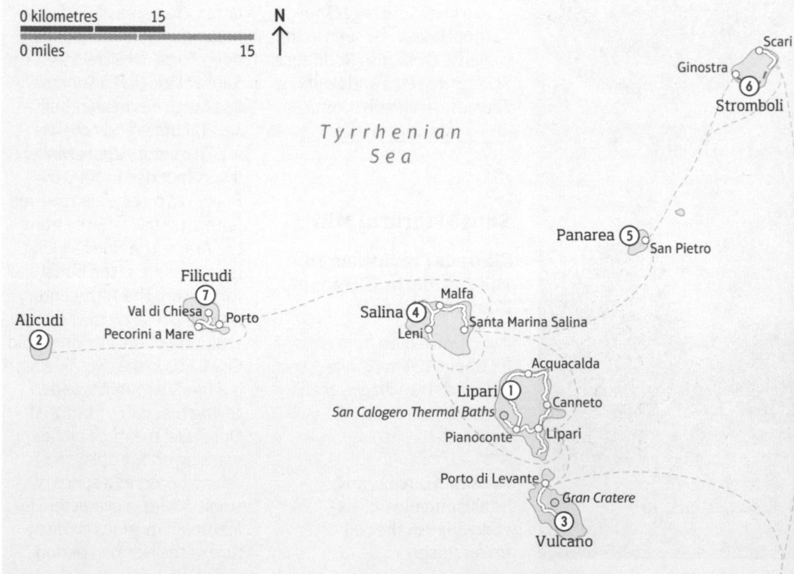

Lipari

The main Aeolian island is not large – a little less than 10 km (6 miles) long and barely 5 km (3 miles) wide, culminating in Monte Chirica, 602 m (1,974 ft) high. The volcanic activity of the past can be noted here and there in the hot springs and fumaroles. The town of Lipari has two landing places: Sottomonastero for ferries and Marina Lunga for hydrofoils. Inevitably, this is the busiest stretch of the seafront.

The old cathedral was built by the Normans in the 11th century and rebuilt after pirates destroyed the town in 1544. Next door to the cathedral is the **Museo Archeologico Eoliano**, which takes up part of the old castle, built by the Spanish (who incorporated the ancient towers and walls) in order to put an end to pirate raids. The first rooms in the museum are devoted to prehistoric finds. There is a large section featuring Classical archaeological finds, some discovered under water. Part of the museum is dedicated to volcanic activity, with detailed descriptions of the geological configuration of each island. Three further sights are the Belvedere Quattrocchi viewpoint, the ancient San Calogero thermal baths and Acquacalda beach, which was once used as a harbour for the ships that came to load the local pumice stone. The best way to explore is by scooter or bicycle, both of which can be rented in Lipari.

Museo Archeologico Eoliano

Via Castello 2 9am-7:30pm Mon-Fri, 9am-1:30pm Sat & Sun regione.sicilia.it/beniculturali/museolipari

Alicudi

This island was abandoned for the entire Middle Ages and was colonized again only in the Spanish period. Tourism is a relatively recent arrival, and there are no vehicles. The steps and paths are covered on foot (or donkey) and accommodation can be found in private homes. There is no nightlife, making this an ideal spot for those in search of a peaceful, relaxing break.

STAY

Hotel Tritone

A luxurious resort-style hotel with a great spa.

Via Mendolita, Lipari hoteltritonelipari.it

La Sirena

Chilled-out restaurant with rooms overlooking the beach, with fishing boats alongside.

Pecorini a Mare, Filicudi pensionelasirena.it

La Salina Borgo di Mare

Occupies a cluster of restored buildings by Lingua's lagoon.

Via Manzoni, Lingua, 12 km (7 miles) SE of Salina lasalinahotel.com

EAT

Da Filippino

Highly regarded restaurant situated in the scenic Town Hall Square. Dishes are based on the catch of the day and complemented by other ingredients local to the island.

Piazza Manzini, Lipari Nov-Jan filippino.it

Da Adelina

Intimate restaurant with a roof terrace overlooking the harbour and a menu of seasonal dishes, such as *moscardini* – tiny octopus with tomato, capers, fennel and chilli.

Via Comunale del Mare 28, Panarea Nov-Feb adelina-panarea.com

La Lampara

Atmospheric place where you dine under a pergola of climbing vines among huge pots of basil and rosemary.

Via V. Emanuele, Stromboli Lunch; Nov-Easter lalamparastromboli.com

Kasbah

Chic but unpretentious café with a beautiful garden serving an impressive array of pasta, meat and fish dishes.

Vico Selinunte 45, Lipari Thu-Tue (Jun-Sep: daily) Nov-Easter hoteltritonelipari.it

Vulcano

Close to Lipari is the island of Vulcano, dedicated to Vulcan, the Roman god of fire and metalworking. The only landing place is the Porto di Levante, from which a paved road, the Strada Provinciale 179, leads to the Faro Nuovo (new lighthouse), also known as Faro di Gelso, situated on the Punta dei Porci cape on the southern side of the island. Nearby are also the ruins of the old lighthouse (Faro Vecchio).

Vulcano consists of three old craters. The first, in the south between Monte Aria and Monte Saraceno, has been extinct for centuries; the Gran Cratere, on the other hand, is still active, the last eruption occurring in 1890. Vulcanello, the third crater, is a promontory on the northeastern tip of the island created almost 2,000 years ago by an eruption. The climb up to the middle crater is particularly impressive, and you can reach the top in less than an hour. Once there, it is worthwhile going down the crater to the Piano delle Fumarole to witness the "breath" of the volcano. Bathing and mud baths are available all year round at the spas near Porto di Levante, while hot springs heat the sea around the stack *(faraglione)*.

Salina

The second-largest Aeolian island has three main villages: Santa Maria di Salina, Leni and Malfa. Santa Maria overlooks the sea and is not far from the beach; it is connected to the other villages by a reliable minibus service which runs until late in the evening in the summer. Salina is also the site of a nature reserve, created to protect the ancient volcanoes of Monte dei Porri and Fossa delle Felci. The starting point for a visit is the Madonna del Terzito Sanctuary, the object of frequent colourful pilgrimages. Salina, and, in particular, the steep walls of the Pizzo di Corvo, is also a regular nesting ground for colonies of the rare Eleonora's falcon, which migrate to this spot every year from Madagascar. Among the local products is the highly prized sweet Malvasia wine.

Panarea

The smallest Aeolian island is surrounded by cliffs and stacks. Visitors land at the small harbour of San Pietro. At Capo Milazzese, in one of the most fascinating spots in the Aeolian Islands, archaeologists have uncovered the ruins

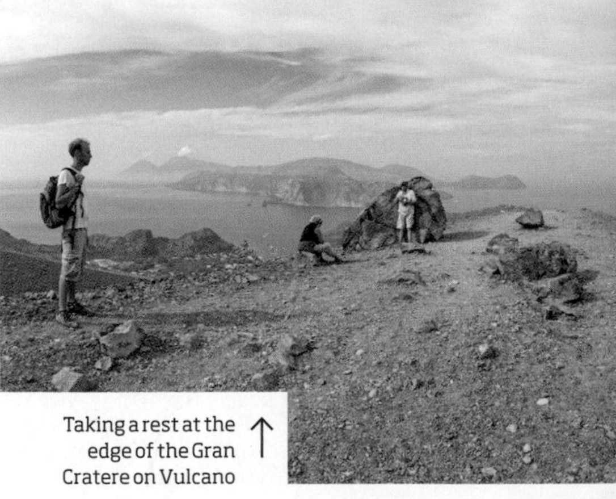

Taking a rest at the edge of the Gran Cratere on Vulcano ↑

of a Neolithic village, founded at Cala Junco. Fascinating finds such as Mycenaean pottery, tools and other items are on display in the local museum. A half-hour walk will take you to the village, starting off from San Pietro and passing through Drautto and the Spiaggia degli Zimmari beach. The island now has luxury tourist facilities.

Stromboli

The active crater of the north-easternmost island in the archipelago has been described by travellers for more than 2,000 years. Its stunning craggy coast (the deep waters are a favourite with swimmers and divers) and famous near-symmetrical volcano are unmistakable. For an excursion to the crater, start off from Piscità; you will first come to the old Vulcanological Observatory and then the top of the crater. The best time to go is around evening, as the eruptions are best seen in the dark. The climb is not always accessible, and the volcano can be dangerous. It is best to go with a guide and to wear heavy shoes (or hiking boots) and suitably hard-wearing clothing. There are also boats offering evening excursions to take visitors close to the Sciara del Fuoco lava field for the unforgettable spectacle of lava flowing into the sea. Boats to the island call either at Scari or Ginostra, but the island has other villages: San Vincenzo, Ficogrande and Piscità.

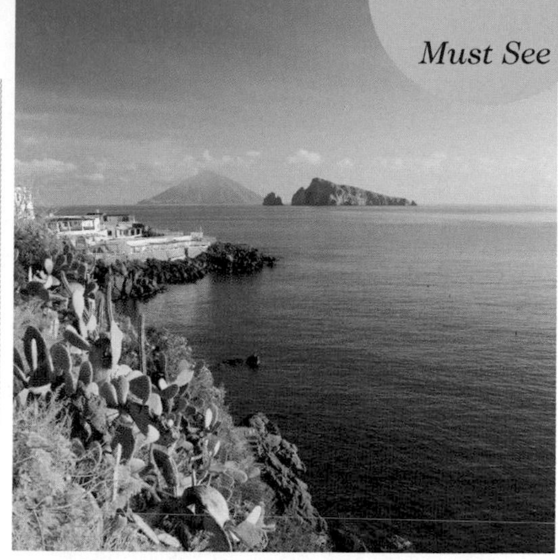

↑ View of volcanic Stromboli island from the north coast of Panarea island

⑦

Filicudi

Halfway between Salina and Alicudi, this remarkably quiet, undeveloped island has just three villages: Porto, Pecorini a Mare and Val di Chiesa. You can make excursions into the interior or, even better, take a boat trip around the island and visit the Faraglione della Canna basalt stack, Punta del Perciato, Grotta del Bue Marino and Capo Graziano.

Did You Know?

Stromboli has been erupting continuously for more than 20,000 years.

EXPERIENCE MORE

Adrano

F4 Ferrovia Circumetnea Pro Loco, Via Roma 56; 339-624 65 20

The city of Adrano dates back to the Greek period. A sanctuary dedicated to the local deity Adranos stood on a lava plateau facing the Valle del Simeto, where Sicilian hounds *(cirnecos)* were trained as hunting dogs. The city was founded in the Greek period by Dionysius the Elder, who chose this natural balcony to build a military stronghold. The centre of town is Piazza Umberto I, site of the Norman castle, a massive, quadrilateral 11th-century construction. The castle houses the Museo Archeologico, with an interesting collection of Neolithic pottery, Greek amphoras and millstones. A narrow stair, cut out of the Hohenstaufen wall in the Middle Ages, leads to the upper floors. Two have displays of archaeological items while the third houses the Art Gallery. The Chiesa Madre, built by the Normans and reconstructed in the 1600s, also stands in the same square.

INSIDER TIP
Lake Pozzillo

Pack a picnic and head to the shores of Lake Pozzillo, 28 km (17 miles) east of Adrano. The largest artificial basin in Sicily, with enticing views of Mount Etna it makes a nice spot to unwind.

Motta Sant'Anastasia

F4 Ferrovia Circumetnea Pro Loco, Via Castello 4; 336-830 25 34

Mount Etna forms an impressive backdrop to the ancient village of Motta.

From the top of the village, with the massive tower of the 12th-century Norman castle, the snow-capped volcano gleams through the winter, gradually darkening in spring and summer. Not far away from the castle is the Chiesa Madre (cathedral), which was also built in Norman times. At the foot of the old town is the heart of Motta Sant'Anastasia with its excellent *pasticcerie* (pastry shops), Baroque churches and a bustling atmosphere, placed as it is on a major route through the Catania region.

The town of Agira lit up at night against a backdrop of the majestic Mount Etna

Adrano's monastery and castle beneath a blanket of snow

Agira

E4 From Catania
Pro Loco, Piazza F Crispi 1; 0935-961 239

Because of its elevated position, Agira is clearly visible from a distance, with Mount Etna rising behind it. The ancient Siculan town of Agyron was colonized by the Greeks in 339 BC, and the ancient historian Diodorus Siculus was born here. The most interesting aspect of Agyron's modern-day counterpart is its Arab layout, with Norman churches and patrician residences with Arab-style portals. Centrally located Piazza Garibaldi is home to Sant'Antonio, which is well worth a visit to see its 16th-century wooden statue of San Silvestro and a painting on marble of *The Adoration of the Magi*. In the vicinity is Santa Maria del Gesù, with a crucifix by Fra' Umile da Petralia. In Piazza Roma is the lovely 16th-century façade of San Salvatore, with its bell tower covered with majolica tiles.

Paternò

F4 Ferrovia Circumetnea Via Ex Ospedale SS Salvatore

Surrounded by orchards of citrus fruit, this town lies at the foot of a castle, which has a stunning view of Mount Etna and the Simeto Valley. The massive square castle was built by Roger I in 1073, totally rebuilt in the 14th century and then restored twice in the 1900s. It lies up Via Matrice, which will also take you to the Chiesa Madre, the cathedral dedicated to Santa Maria dell'Alto. Originally Norman, the church was rebuilt in 1342.

Regalbuto

E4 From Catania
Pro Loco; 0935-910 514

This town was destroyed in 1261 by the inhabitants of Centuripe and rebuilt by Manfredi. The heart of the town is Piazza della Repubblica, with its multicoloured paving, while churches San Rocco, San Basilio and Santa Maria del Carmine are also worth a look. Nearby is the Lake Pozzillo dam, the largest artificial basin in Sicily, and a Canadian military cemetery with the graves of 490 soldiers who were killed in 1943.

THE CIRCUMETNEA RAILWAY

The carriages of the Ferrovia Circumetnea climb up the picturesque slopes of Mount Etna, passing through stretches of black lava and luxuriant vegetation. It takes about five hours to cover the 90 km (56 miles) or so between Catania and Giarre Riposto, the two termini, plus another hour to get back to Catania from Riposto via state rail. The rewards are magnificent views of terraced vineyards and almond and hazelnut groves, as well as the volcano itself.

↑ Enjoying a dip on the Riviera dei Ciclopi, near Aci Castello

11 Aci Castello

F4 AST Lungomare dei Ciclopi 137; www.prolocoacicastello.com

The name of this fishermen's village, a few kilometres from Catania, derives from the Norman castle built on the top of a basalt rock jutting into the sea. It was built in 1076 from black lava and in 1299 was the base for the rebel Roger of Luria. The castle was subsequently destroyed by Frederick II of Aragón after a long siege. Some rooms in the surviving parts are occupied by the Museo Civico, with archaeological and natural history collections relating to the Etna region (temporarily closed). There is also a small Botanical Garden. The town, with straight streets and low-rise houses, marks the beginning of the Riviera dei Ciclopi: according to Greek mythology, Polyphemus and his friends lived on Etna.

12 Mascalucia

F4 AST from Catania Pro Loco, Via Etnea 162; 095-754 26 01

On the eastern slopes of the volcano, just above Catania, to which it is connected by an uninterrupted series of villages and hamlets, is Mascalucia, a town of largish houses and villas. It is worth stopping here to visit the **Giardino Lavico** at the Azienda Trinità farmstead, a small "oasis" surrounded by modern building development on the slopes of Etna. The "lava garden" consists of an organically cultivated citrus grove, a 17th-century house and a garden filled with prickly pears, yuccas and other plants that thrive in the lava soil. The orchard's irrigation canals were inspired by Arab gardens. For helicopter trips over Mount Etna, make inquiries at the Azienda.

Giardino Lavico
Azienda Agricola Trinità, Via Trinità 34
095-727 21 56; open by appt

13 Centuripe

F4 0935-919 480
From Catania or Enna,

Known as "the balcony of Sicily" because of the wide views, Centuripe is especially pretty in February and March, when snow-capped Mount Etna forms a striking contrast with the blossom of orange and almond trees. An important Greek-Roman town, it was destroyed by Frederick II and rebuilt in the 16th century. A long tree-lined

Centuripe is especially pretty in February and March, when snow-capped Mount Etna forms a striking contrast with the blossom of orange and almond trees.

avenue leads to a viewing terrace called Castello di Corradino, with ruins of an Imperial Roman mausoleum.

Acireale

A F4 FS Catania Stazione, Centrale Piazza San Giovanni XXIII Messina-Catania i Via San Francesco di Paola; 340-145 4318

Acireale stands on a lava terrace overlooking the Ionian Sea in the midst of citrus orchards. Since Roman times it has been famous as a spa town with sulphur baths. The present name of the town refers to the myth, sung by Virgil and Ovid, of the cyclops Polifemo, the shepherd Aci and the nymph Galatea. It is the largest town on the eastern side of Mount Etna and has been destroyed time and again by eruptions and earthquakes. It was finally rebuilt after the 1693 earthquake, emerging as a jewel of Sicilian Baroque architecture. The heart of town is Piazza Duomo, with its cafés and ice-cream parlours. Acireale is dominated by its Cathedral, built in the late 1500s. The façade has two cusped bell towers covered with multi-coloured majolica tiles. The Baroque portal leads to the vast interior with its frescoed vaults. In the right-hand transept is the Cappella di Santa Venera, the patron saint of the town. On the transept floor is a meridian marked out in 1843 by a Danish astronomer. Piazza Duomo is also home to the Palazzo Comunale, with a Gothic door and a wrought-iron balcony, and Santi Pietro e Paolo, built in the 17th century. Close by is the Teatro dei Pupi, known for its puppet shows, and the Pinacoteca dell'Accademia Zelantea, with works by local painter Pietro Vasta, whose paintings also appear in the town's churches. The main street, Corso Vittorio Emanuele, crosses squares such as Piazza Vigo, with Palazzo Pennisi di Floristella and San Sebastiano.

Aci Trezza

A F4 i Lungomare dei Ciclopi 137; www.prolocoacicastello.com

This picturesque fishing village, part of Aci Castello, was the setting for Giovanni Verga's novel *I Malavoglia* and for Luchino Visconti's film adaptation, *La Terra Trema*. The small harbour faces a pile of basalt rocks, the Isole dei Ciclopi, now a nature reserve. On the largest island there is a biology and oceanography station. According to Homer, Polyphemus hurled the rocks at the sea in an attempt to strike the fleeing Ulysses, who had blinded him.

I MALAVOGLIA

Published in 1881 in Milan, *I Malavoglia* (*The House by the Medlar Tree*) is a masterpiece of italian realism by novelist Giovanni Verga. Set on the Riviera dei Ciclopi at Aci Trezza, it describes the harsh life of fishermen and their constant struggle with the sea. The Toscano family, "I Malavoglia", are "all good seafaring people, just the opposite of their nickname" (*malavoglia* means ill-will). In 1947 Luchino Visconti made a film inspired by the book, *La Terra Trema*.

Beautiful frescoes adorning the walls of Acireale's San Sebastiano ↓

2

percent of the world's pistachios come from Bronte and its surrounds.

Bronte

F4 Ferrovia Circumetnea Pro Loco, Via Laenza 1; www.proloco bronte.it

Situated on a terraced lava slope, Bronte was founded by Charles V. In 1799 Ferdinand IV of Bourbon gave the town and its estates to Admiral Horatio Nelson, who had helped him suppress the revolts in Naples in 1799. In 1860, after the success of Garibaldi's Red Shirts in Sicily, the peasants of Bronte rebelled, demanding that Nelson's land be split up among them, but their revolt was put down by Garibaldi's men. Despite many eruptions, Bronte has managed to retain its original character, with stone houses and steeply rising alleyways. The 16th-century Annunziata has a sandstone portal and, inside, an *Annunciation* (1541) attributed to Antonello Gagini. In the village of Piana Cuntarati, the Masseria Lombardo farm has been converted into an Ethnographic Museum which, among many interesting objects, has an Arab paper mill dating from the year 1000. Today Bronte is famous for the production of pistachios.

Around 12 km (7 miles) from Bronte is Castello di Maniace, a Benedictine monastery founded by Margaret of Navarre in 1174, on the spot where the Byzantine general Maniakes had defeated the Arabs. Destroyed by the 1693 earthquake, the site became the property of Horatio Nelson. Today it looks like a fortified farm, with a garden of exotic plants. The building itself is closed for restoration, but visitors can still explore the lovely grounds. Nearby is the medieval Santa Maria, with scenes from the Book of Genesis sculpted on the capitals of the columns.

→ Randazzo lies closer to the craters of Etna than any other town

↑ Bronte's Benedictine monastery, the Castello di Maniace, or Nelson's Castle

Zafferana Etnea

F4 AST bus from Catania Pro Loco, Via Garibaldi 317; 095-702 825

Famous for its honey, Zafferana Etnea lies on the eastern slopes of Etna and is one of the towns most often affected by recent lava flows. The most destructive eruptions occurred in 1852, when the lava reached the edge of town, and in 1992. The heart of Zafferana is its large tree-lined main square, dominated by the Baroque Chiesa Madre. The square is also the home of a permanent agricultural fair which, besides selling local wine and produce, has old farm implements on display.

Down the road towards Linguaglossa is Sant'Alfio, a town surrounded by vineyards and known for the huge 2,000-year-old tree called "Castagno dei cento cavalli" (Chestnut tree of 100 horses). According to legend, the leaves of this famous tree once protected Queen Jeanne d'Anjou and her retinue of 100 knights.

Randazzo

F3 Ferrovia Circumetnea Pro Loco, Piazza Municipio 7; www. prolocorandazzo.alter vista.org

Built of lava stone and set 765 m (2,509 ft) above sea level, Randazzo is the town closest to the craters of Mount Etna, but it has never been inundated with lava. In the

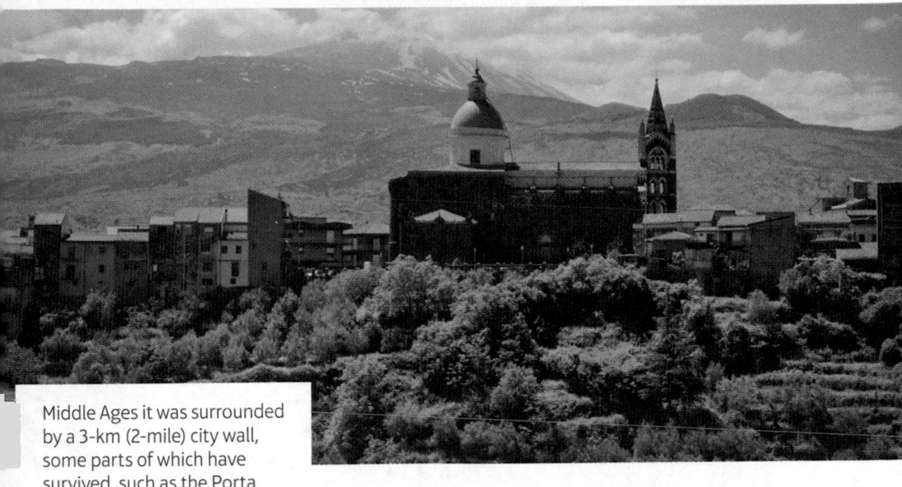

Middle Ages it was surrounded by a 3-km (2-mile) city wall, some parts of which have survived, such as the Porta Aragonese gate on the old road to Messina. The major monument and symbol of the town is Santa Maria, a basilica built in 1217–39: the towered apses with the characteristic ribbing are all that is left of the original Norman construction, while the double lancet windows and portals are Catalan. The nave with its black lava columns has multi-coloured marble altars and a marble basin sculpted by the Gagini School. Corso Umberto, the main street in Randazzo, leads to Piazza San Francesco d'Assisi, dominated by the Palazzo Comunale, once the monastery of the Minor Order, which has an elegant cloister with a cistern.

The narrow side streets have many examples of medieval architecture. The most characteristic of these is Via degli Archi, which has a lovely pointed arch and black lava cobblestone paving. In Piazza San Nicolò is the church of the same name, with a late Renaissance façade made of lava stone. In the interior there is a fine statue of San Nicola of Bari sculpted in 1523 by Antonello Gagini. The bell tower was damaged by an earthquake in 1783. Its reconstruction replaced the original cusp with a wrought-iron balcony. After a turn to the left, Corso Umberto crosses a square where San Martino stands. It has a beautiful bell tower with single lancet windows with two-coloured borders, and a polygonal spire. Opposite is the castle, which was a prison in the 1500s and is now the home of the Museo Archeologico Vagliasindi, with interesting Greek finds from Tissa, such as the famous vase depicting the punishment of the Harpies.

Linguaglossa

F3 Ferrovia Circumetnea Pro Loco, Piazza Annunziata 5; 095-643 094

Linguaglossa is the largest village on the northeastern slopes of Etna as well as the starting point for excursions to the volcano summit and for the ski runs. Its name derives from a 17th-century lava flow that was called *lingua glossa* (big tongue). The town's streets are paved with black lava and the houses have wrought-iron balconies. The Chiesa Madre, dedicated to Santa Maria delle Grazie, is worth a visit for its Baroque decoration and fine coffered ceiling. Linguaglossa is also home to the **Museo Etnografico**, a museum with geological and natural history exhibits as well as everyday objects and craftsmen's tools.

Museo Etnografico

Piazza Annunziata 8 095-643 094 9am-12:30pm & 4-7pm Mon-Sat (winter: to 6pm), Sun: am only

SHOP

The slopes of Mount Etna offer the opportunity to taste and buy unusual varieties of honey. Check out these shops to try the flavours.

Etna Honey

F4 Via Continella 7, Zafferana Etnea
By appointment only
etnahoney.it

Oro d'etna-l'Apicoltura

F4 Via S Giacomo 135, Zafferana Etnea
8:30am-6:30pm daily
orodetna.it

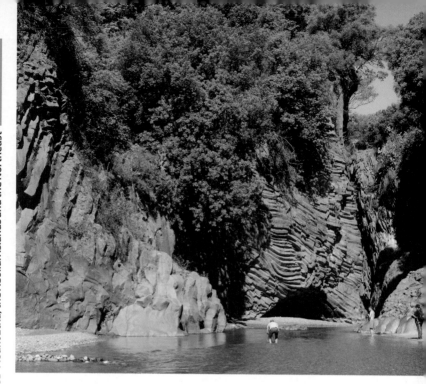

Castiglione di Sicilia

F3 Ferrovia Circumetnea Giardini-Naxos Town hall; 0942-980 211

This village, voted one of Italy's most beautiful, lies on a crag dominating the Alcantara Valley. Founded by the Greeks, many years later it became a royal city under the Normans and the Hohenstaufens, and the fief of Roger of Lauria at the end of the 13th century. Castiglione still retains its medieval layout, the narrow streets converging in central Piazza Lauria. From this point, moving up the hill, there are many churches. The first is the Chiesa Madre, or San Pietro, which still has a Norman apse; then there are the 17th-century Chiesa delle Benedettine and the Baroque Sant'Antonio and Chiesa Della Catena. At the top of the village is the Castel Leone, built by the Normans over Arab fortifications, with a view of the medieval bridge on the Alcantara river.

The Alcantara ravine, 20 m (66 ft) deep, cut out of black basalt by the rushing waters of the Alcantara river, is a compelling sight. If the weather is good, follow the gorge for about 150 m (500 ft), but only if you can manage without weatherproof gear. There is also a lift that you can take to avoid the long flight of steps that leads from the parking area to the ravine's entrance.

↑ Antefix from the Museo Archeologico in Giardini-Naxos

21

Giardini-Naxos

G3 Catania Fontanarossa, 66 km (41 miles) Autolinee SAIS STR, Lungomare Tysandros 54; 0942-510 10

Between Capo Taormina and Capo Schisò, Giardini-Naxos is a seaside resort near what was once the first Greek colony in Sicily. Thucydides relates that Naxos was founded in 735 BC by Chalcidians led by the Athenian Thucles, and Naxos became the base for all further colonization of the island. Naxos was destroyed by Dionysius of Syracuse in 403 BC. On the headland of Capo Schisò, amid lemon trees and prickly pears, is the **Museo Archeologico**. Of the two phases in the life of the city, the one which yielded the most important (if scarce) archaeological finds dates from the 6th and 5th centuries BC, with remains

The Alcantara river flowing between basalt cliffs near Castiglione di Sicilia

of the city walls and houses as well as stones from a temple possibly dedicated to Aphrodite. In the village of Giardini, by the beach, there are still some fine mansions on the oldest streets

Museo Archeologico
0942-51001 9am–1 hr before sunset daily
parconaxostaormina.com

Capo d'Orlando

F3 STR Unità Operativa 1, Via Amendola 20; 0941-912 784

Forming part of a region known for the intensive cultivation of citrus fruits, the Nebrodi mountains jut out into the sea at intervals. The coastal town of Capo d'Orlando lies at the foot of the Rupe del Semaforo cliff and the rocky hill after which the town was named. A climb of about 100 m (328 ft) will take you to the top of the cliff. There, in a large open space, stand the remains of a 14th-century fortress and Maria Santissima, a church built in the late 1500s and now home to a number of interesting paintings. However, the main reward for climbing up the hill is the marvellous panoramic view of the sea and of the fishing boats moving about in the pretty harbour below.

Giarre

F4 Ferrovia Circumetnea From Catania Town hall; Proloco, Piazza Monsignor Alessi; www.proloco giarre.it

Lying amid citrus groves extending down to the sea, the tiny town of Giarre is famous for its beautiful handmade wrought-iron products. The heart of Giarre is Piazza Duomo, dominated by the impressive Neo-Classical Duomo, which was built in 1794 and dedicated to Sant'Isidoro Agricola, the patron of Madrid. There are also many delightful patrician residences made of lava stone in the old town that are worth a close look at.

In the nearby village of Macchia is the informative **Museo degli Usi e dei Costumi delle Genti dell'Etna**, an ethnographic museum. One interesting exhibit that is worthwhile visiting here is a reproduction of a typical Etna farmhouse, with its traditional old kitchen and bread oven, well and washtub. Also on display in the museum are farm implements, looms, and fascinating period photographs and daguerreotypes.

Museo degli Usi e dei Costumi delle Genti dell'Etna
Lungotorrente Emanuele Filiberto, Macchia di Giarre
By appointment only
museogentietna.it

THE PELORITANI MOUNTAINS

The Monti Peloritani form a ridge between two seas peaking in Monte Poverello (1,279 m/4,195 ft) and the Pizzo di Vernà (1,286 m/4,218 ft). It is a fantastic area for excursions, often with stunning views of the sea and Mount Etna, in a landscape of knife-edge ridges and woods. Many of the mountain villages are interesting: Forza d'Agrò, dominated by a 16th-century castle; Casteluecchio Siculo, with its Arab-Norman Basilica dei Santi Pietro e Paolo; Savoca, with Capuchin catacombs; Ali, which has a strong Arab flavour; Itala, overlooking the Ionian Sea; and Mili San Pietro, with a basilica-monastery of Santa Maria.

The remains of the impressive ancient Greek Theatre at Tyndaris

Tyndaris

F3 From Messina STR, Piazza Guglielmo Marconi; 0941-241 136

Ancient Tyndaris was one of the last Greek colonies in Sicily, founded by the Syracusans in 396 BC, when the Romans were beginning to expand their territory in the Mediterranean. The town prospered under Roman rule and became a diocese during the early Christian period, and was destroyed by the Arabs. A visit to the archaeological site is fascinating because of the monuments and many details that give you an idea of everyday life in the ancient town.

Past the walls through the main city gate, not far from the **Madonna di Tindari Sanctuary** (which houses the famous Byzantine *Madonna Nera* or Black Madonna, honoured in a pilgrimage held every September), is the 60-m- (197-ft-) wide Greek Theatre. In the theatre area are the remains of a Roman villa and baths.

Next to the theatre is the Museo Archeologico, which has a large model of the Greek theatre stage and prehistoric finds. One unmissable sight is the view below the Promontory of Tyndaris: the Laguna di Oliveri, celebrated by the poet and Nobel Prize winner Salvatore Quasimodo.

Madonna di Tindari Sanctuary

Piazza Quasimodo
6:45am-12:45pm, 2:30-7pm daily (Jul-Aug: to 8pm)
santuariotindari.it

Milazzo

G2 From Messina & Palermo STR Piazza Duilio Caio 10; 090-922 27 90

Milazzo began to take its place in written history when Mylai was colonized by the Greeks in 716 BC. The Normans later chose this peninsula as their main coastal stronghold. The town was divided into three distinct zones in the Middle Ages – the walled town, the Borgo and the lower town – and it was expanded in the 1700s. The Salita Castello leads up to the ancient rock, which affords access to the walled town via a covered

SICILY'S FAUNA

Nebrodi Black Pig
A small breed raised in the forests of the Nebrodi mountains.

Girgentana Goat
From the Agrigento area, this goat is bred specifically for milk.

Sea Turtles
Rare sea turtles bury their eggs in the sands of the Belice Estuary and the Pelagie Islands.

San Fratellano Horse
A gorgeous horse indigenous to the Nebrodi mountains.

Cirneco dell'Etna
This native dog of Mount Etna is a natural hunter of small prey.

Milazzo's promenade with impressive views of the castle and sea

passageway. A doorway opens into Frederick II's Castle (1239), surrounded by a wall with five round towers and the great hall of the Sala del Parlamento (Parliament Hall). On the same rise is the old Duomo, the original 17th-century cathedral, which is used as a congress hall.

Do not miss the chance of an excursion to Capo Milazzo, where you will be rewarded with towers, villas and, at the foot of the 18th-century lighthouse, a marvellous view of the Aeolian Islands with Calabria beyond.

Patti

F3 From Messina and Palermo; 0941-892 021 STR Tyndaris; www.comune.patti.me.it

Past the rocky promontory of Capo Calavà on the slopes overlooking the sea is the town of Patti. Initially a fief of the Norman ruler Roger I, it was later destroyed during the wars with the Angevins and then frequently pillaged by pirates from North Africa. Patti is home to an 18th-century Cathedral built over the foundations of the former Norman church. Inside is a sarcophagus with the remains of Queen Adelaide, Roger I's wife, who died here in 1118.

Nearby in Marina di Patti are the ruins of a **Roman Villa** destroyed by an earthquake in the 4th century AD. This grand Imperial age building measures 20,000 sq m (215,200 sq ft) and comprises a peristyle, an apse-like room, thermal baths and many well-preserved mosaics.

Roman Villa
Via Papa Giovanni XXIII, Marina di Patti
0941-361 593 9am-7pm daily

The Nebrodi Mountains

E3 Parco Regionale dei Monti Nebrodi parcodeinebrodi.it

The Arabs occupied the Nebrodi mountains for centuries and referred to them as "an island on an island". The name comes from the Greek word *nebros*, or "roe deer", because of the rich wildlife found in this mountain range. The Parco Regionale dei Monti Nebrodi is a nature reserve with extensive forests and some pastureland, which is covered with snow in the winter. In the middle of the park is the Biviere di Cesarò lake, a stopover point for migratory birds and an ideal habitat for the *Testudo hermanni* marsh turtle. The tallest peak is Monte Soro (1,850 m/6,068 ft).

STAY

Locanda Del Bagatto

Minimalist designer rooms adjoin a fabulous bar and restaurant. Located just a short walk from the port.

G2 Via Massimiliano Regis 7, Milazzo locandadelbagatto.com

Casa Rubes

Relaxed, atmospheric B&B in a beautifully converted town house in the heart of Patti's old town.

F3 Via Magretti 127, Patti casarubes.it

Federico Secondo

Understated hotel set in a restored 13th-century palazzo in the centre of Castiglione.

F3 Via Maggiore Baracca 2, Castiglione di Sicilia hotelfedericosecondo.com

NEED TO KNOW

Driving through the village of Savoca

BEFORE YOU GO

Forward planning is essential to any successful trip. Be prepared for all eventualities by considering the following points before you travel.

AT A GLANCE

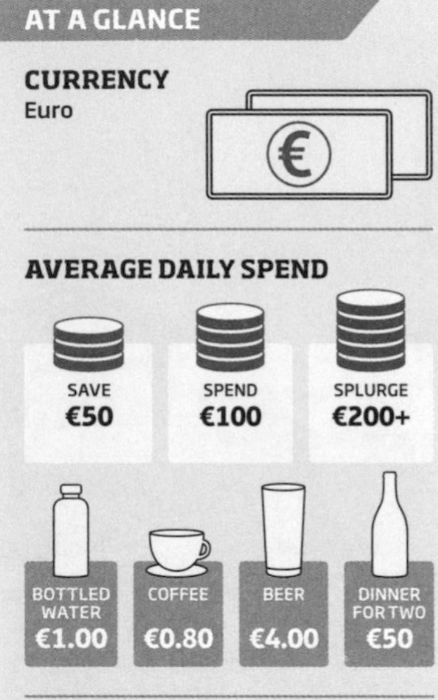

CURRENCY
Euro
AVERAGE DAILY SPEND
SAVE
€50
SPEND
€100
SPLURGE
€200+
BOTTLED WATER
€1.00
COFFEE
€0.80
BEER
€4.00
DINNER FOR TWO
€50

ESSENTIAL PHRASES

Hello	Buon giorno
Goodbye	Arrivederci/Ciao
Please	Per favore
Thank you	Grazie
Do you speak English?	Parla inglese?
I don't understand	Non ho capito

ELECTRICITY SUPPLY

Power sockets are type F and L, fitting two and three-pronged plugs. Standard voltage is 220-230v.

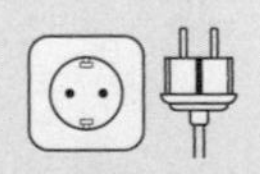

Passports and Visas

EU nationals and citizens of the UK, US, Canada, Australia and New Zealand do not need visas for stays of up to three months. Consult your nearest Italian embassy or check the **Polizia di Stato** website if you are travelling from outside these areas.

Polizia di Stato
W poliziadistato.it

Travel Safety Advice

Visitors can get up-to-date travel safety information from the UK Foreign and Commonwealth Office, the US State Department, and the Australian Department of Foreign Affairs and Trade.

AUS
W gov.uk/foreign-travel-advice
UK
W gov.uk/foreign-travel-advice
US
W travel.state.gov

Customs Information

Limits vary if travelling from outside the EU, so check restrictions before travelling. An individual is permitted to carry the following within the EU for personal use:

Tobacco products 800 cigarettes, 400 cigarillos, 200 cigars or 1 kg of smoking tobacco.

Alcohol 10 litres of alcoholic beverages above 22% strength, 20 litres of alcoholic beverages below 22% strength, 90 litres of wine (60 litres of which can be sparkling wine) and 110 litres of beer.

Cash If you plan to enter or leave the EU with €10,000 or more in cash (or the equivalent in other currencies) you must declare it to the customs authorities prior to departure.

Insurance

It is wise to take out an insurance policy covering theft, loss of belongings, medical problems, cancellation and delays. Emergency medical

care in Italy is free for all EU and Australian citizens. EU citizens should ensure they have an **EHIC** (European Health Insurance Card) and Australians should be registered to **Medicare** to receive this benefit. Visitors from outside these areas must arrange their own private medical insurance before arriving in Italy.

EHIC
W gov.uk/european-health-insurance-card
Medicare
W humanservices.gov.au/individuals/medicare

Vaccinations

No inoculations are needed for Sicily and Italy in general, but bring mosquito repellent, especially if you are travelling during the summer months.

Money

Credit and debit cards are accepted in most shops and restaurants. Prepaid currency cards are accepted in some. Contactless payments are widely accepted. However, it is always worth carrying some cash, as many smaller businesses and markets, especially in more remote areas, still accept cash only. Cash machines can be found at banks, train and bus stations and on main streets in major towns, but they are harder to find in remote areas.

Sicily, like all of Italy's south, is generally slightly cheaper than central and northern Italy. The region suffers from high unemployment rates and a low GDP.

Booking Accommodation

In the summer months accommodation is snapped up fast, and prices are often inflated. In some cities, such as Palermo and Catania, you will be charged a city tax on top of the price for the room (€2 per person per night).

Under Italian law, hotels are required to register guests at police headquarters and issue a receipt of payment *(ricevuta fiscale)*, which you must keep until you leave Italy.

Travellers with Specific Needs

Sicily is not particularly well organized to cater for visitors with disabilities; however, conditions are improving throughout the island. Ramps, lifts and modified WCs are available in an increasing number of places. Visitors travelling by train can request **RFI** (Italian Railway Network) assistance at the Sala Blu of the Messina train station by visiting the website.

W **trenitalia.it**
RFI
W rfi.it

Language

Italian is the official language, but most people still speak Sicilian dialect. The level of spoken English and other foreign languages can be limited, particularly in rural areas, but locals appreciate visitors' efforts to speak Italian, even if only a few words.

Closures

Mondays Some museums and tourist attractions are closed for the day.
Sundays Many shops close early or for the entire day.
Public holidays Schools and public services are closed for the day; shops, museums and attractions either close early or for the day.
Winter Some accommodation establishments and other services in rural areas that cater mainly to holidaymakers close from around October until the Easter school holiday period.

PUBLIC HOLIDAYS

1 Jan	New Year's Day
6 Jan	Epiphany
Mar/Apr	Easter Sunday
25 Apr	Liberation Day
1 May	Labour Day
2 Jun	Republic Day
15 Aug	Ferragosto
1 Nov	All Saints' Day
8 Dec	Feast of the Immaculate Conception
25 Dec	Christmas Day
26 Dec	St Stephen's Day

GETTING AROUND

Whether you are visiting for a short city break or a rural country retreat, discover how best to reach your destination.

AT A GLANCE

PUBLIC TRANSPORT COSTS

CATANIA
€2.50
All-day ticket

PALERMO
€3.50
All-day ticket

MESSINA
€2.70
All-day ticket

TOP TIP
Avoid on-the-spot fines - be sure to stamp your ticket to validate your journey.

SPEED LIMIT

MOTORWAY	DUAL CARRIAGEWAYS
130 km/h (80mph)	**100** km/h (60mph)

NATIONAL ROADS	URBAN AREAS
80 km/h (50mph)	**50** km/h (30mph)

Arriving by Air

Two main international airports serve Sicily: Palermo Punta Raisi and Catania Fontanarossa, both operating international flights. European budget airlines offer flights to Sicily at very reasonable prices.

The smaller Trapani Birgi airport offers connections only to and from Palermo and the islands of Pantelleria and Lampedusa (the latter has a tiny airport linked to Rome, Milan and Verona). The airports on the island connect to Trapani and Palermo airports, and to other mainland towns. A new airport in Comiso serves the Ragusa Syracuse area. For information on getting to and from Sicily's main airports, see the table opposite.

Train Travel

International Train Travel

If you are planning on reaching Sicily by train from abroad, you will first have to cross the whole Italian peninsula which will take at least 14 hours. When buying your ticket, make sure you reserve a seat (or a sleeping compartment), as trains can get very crowded in high season.

Once in Villa San Giovanni, the train is boarded onto a ferry and passengers are asked to get off, even in the middle of night. Make sure to take your valuables with you.

You can buy tickets and passes for multiple journeys around Italy and Europe via **Eurail** or **Interrail**. However, you may still need to pay an additional reservation fee depending on which rail service you travel with. Always check that your pass is valid before boarding.

Eurail
W eurail.com
Interrail
W interrail.eu

Domestic Train Travel

Given the varied and often mountainous topography of Sicily, remote areas are not accessible by train, and the very few train lines in those areas can be slow and unreliable. All the

main train lines in Sicily are run by **Trenitalia**, Italy's main railway operator. Tickets can be bought online and must be validated before boarding by stamping them in machines at the entrance to platforms. Heavy fines are levied if you are caught with an unvalidated ticket.

The island's two main railway routes run between Messina and Syracuse via Catania, and from Messina to Palermo along the northern coast. A secondary line branches from the Messina–Palermo route at Termini Imerese, running southwards to Agrigento. Another line connects Palermo with Trapani. North of Catania, the privately operated **Ferrovia Circumetnea** line runs around Mount Etna, offering a scenic route.

Ferrovia Circumetnea
W circumetnea.it
Trenitalia
W trenitalia.it

GETTING TO AND FROM THE AIRPORT

Airport	Distance to city	Taxi fare	Public Transport	Journey time
Palermo	33 km	€45	Trinacria Express	56 or 72 mins
			Prestia e Comandé	30 mins
Catania	10 km	€18	Alibus	20 mins

ROAD JOURNEY PLANNER

This map is a handy reference for road travel times between Sicily's main towns and cities. The times given reflect the fastest and most direct routes.

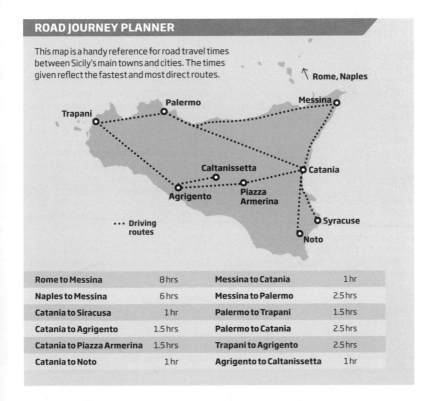

Rome to Messina	8 hrs	**Messina to Catania**	1 hr
Naples to Messina	6 hrs	**Messina to Palermo**	2.5 hrs
Catania to Siracusa	1 hr	**Palermo to Trapani**	1.5 hrs
Catania to Agrigento	1.5 hrs	**Palermo to Catania**	2.5 hrs
Catania to Piazza Armerina	1.5 hrs	**Trapani to Agrigento**	2.5 hrs
Catania to Noto	1 hr	**Agrigento to Caltanissetta**	1 hr

Public Transport

Bus services in Sicilian cities are reliable and user-friendly. In Palermo the transport network is operated by **AMAT**, in Catania by the **AMT** and in Messina by the **ATM**.

Tickets can be bought at tobacconists *(tabaccai)*, news stands *(giornalai)* or from special transport kiosks that also provide transport maps. Tickets are timed and are valid 90 or 120 minutes, and need to be validated in the yellow machines on the bus. Day tickets are usually very cheap and are often the best option.

AMAT (Palermo)
W amat.pa.it
AMT (Catania)
W amt.ct.it
ATM (Messina)
W atm.messina.it

Long-Distance Bus Travel

The three lines – **SAIS**, **AST** and **Etna Trasporti** – cover the entire island, while services such as **Flixbus** and **Eurolines** connect the island to the rest of Italy. Fares are very reasonable. You can usually buy tickets on board for long-haul buses *(pullman* or *corriera)* between towns and cities.

Services often depart from outside main railway stations or from a town's main piazza. In rural areas, check bus stops for timetables and the details of local transport companies.

AST
W astsicilia.it
Etna Trasporti
W etnatrasporti.it
Eurolines
W eurolines.eu
Flixbus
W flixbus.it
SAIS
W saisautolinee.it

Taxis

Taxis are not hailed; take one at an official taxi stand (usually found at the station, main piazza or close to key tourist sights), or reserve one by phone. When you order a taxi by phone, the meter will run from your call.

Only accept rides in licensed, metered taxis. Official taxis are white, have a "taxi" sign on the roof and their official taxi licence number on the doors. Extra charges are added for each piece of luggage placed in the boot, for rides between approximately 10pm and 7am, on Sundays and public holidays, and for journeys to and from the airports. The following companies offer a reliable service:

Radiotaxi Catania
T 095 8833
Radiotaxi Messina
T 090 6505
Radiotaxi Palermo
T 091 8481

Driving

For those eager to discover Sicily's lesser-known parts or its rural areas, travelling by car is the best option. Make sure you have all the necessary documents with you, as traffic police *(carabinieri)* carry out routine checks.

Driving to Sicily

The drive to Sicily from Rome takes around 8 hours and around 6 hours from Naples. Car ferries going across the Strait of Messina leave regularly. Allow 1 hour for the ferry ride, including waiting times and boarding.

Driving in Sicily

If you bring your own foreign-registered car into the country, you must carry a Green Card, the vehicle's registration documents and have a valid driver's licence with you when driving. Many towns and cities enforce a Limited Traffic Zone (**ZTL**). To avoid fines, consult one of the **Urban Access Regulations in Europe** websites.

Tolls are payable on most motorways *(autostrade)*, and payment is made at the end of the journey. Avoid tolls by using the national roads *(strade nazionali)*, or secondary state roads *(strade statali)*. Although less direct, they are often more scenic, allowing you to stop at viewpoints and places of interest en route.

Roads known as white roads *(strade bianche)* have only a gravel surface. These are often narrow and steep, but are usually passable to cars. Always check your route before travelling.

ACI
W aci.it
ZTL and Urban Access Regulations in Europe
W urbanaccessregulations.eu

Car Rental

To rent a car in Sicily you must be at least 21 years old (some renters insist on a minimum age of 25) and have held a valid licence for at least a year.

Driving licences issued by any EU member states are valid throughout Italy. If visiting from outside the EU, you may need to apply for an International Driving Permit (IDP). Check with your local automobile association. Major international car rental agencies have outlets at all main airports and in all major towns and cities in Sicily.

Rules of the Road

Drive on the right, use the left lane only for passing, and yield to traffic from the right. Seat belts are required for all passengers, and heavy fines are levied for using a mobile phone while driving. A strict drink-drive limit is enforced.

During the day dipped headlights are compulsory when you are driving on motorways, dual carriageways and on all out-of-town roads. A red warning triangle, spare tyre and fluorescent vests must be carried at all times, for use in case of an emergency. In the event of an accident or breakdown switch on your hazard warning lights and place your warning triangle 50m (55 yd) behind your vehicle.

For breakdowns call the ACI emergency number (116) or the emergency services. The ACI will tow any foreign-registered vehicle to the nearest ACI-affiliated garage, free of charge if you are a member of a similar, affiliated club.

Hitchhiking

Hitchhiking, or *autostop*, is illegal on motorways, but in more rural areas it is a common way for tourists and backpackers to get around on a budget. Always consider your own safety before entering an unknown vehicle.

Cycling

Sicily's internal roads are fairly quiet and suitable for cycling. There are many scenic routes along the coast and around Mount Etna. However, Sicilian drivers are not used to seeing cyclists on the road, so stay alert at all times. Helmets and high-visibility clothing are not obligatory but wearing them is strongly advised. You can find traffic-free city centres in towns like Syracuse and Ragusa. The website **Sicily Cycling** maps the best cycling routes on the island.

Sicily Cycling
W sicilycycling.com

Bicycle Hire

Social Bike Palermo offers touring and city bikes for rent in Palermo, while **Etna Sicily Touring** rents bicycles in Catania.

Etna Sicily Touring
W etnasicilytouring.com
Social Bike Palermo
W socialbikepalermo.com

Bike Touring

Several companies operate guided and self-guided bike tours. Agencies such as **Ciclofree**, **Sicily Biking Tours** or **Ciclabili Siciliane** offer different types of adventures and excursions, providing you with bicycles and with the added convenience of vans carrying your luggage.

Ciclabili Siciliane
W ciclabilisiciliane.it
Ciclofree
W ciclofree.com
Sicily Biking Tours
W sicilybikingtours.com

Boats and Ferries

Reggio Calabria is the principal mainland port for ferry services to Sicily with **Caronte & Tourist**. **Tirrenia** offers ferries between Palermo, Genoa, and Naples. In summer, car ferries operate between Messina and Naples. Ferry services between the Sicilian islands are well organized and run regularly. Services are offered by several companies, such as **Liberty Lines**, **SNAV** (Societá Navigazione Alta Velocitá), and **Siremar**. Ferries *(traghetti)* and hydrofoils can get quite crowded in summer and might skip some crossings if the weather is bad.

Caronte & Tourist
W carontetourist.it
Liberty Lines
W libertylines.it
SNAV
W snav.it
Siremar
W siremar.it
Tirrenia
W tirrenia.it

Touring Sicily by Boat

Sailing around the Aeolian and Aegadian islands and visiting Sicily's ports is a fabulous way to see some of the island's most breathtaking scenery, including erupting volcanoes.

If you are looking for the ultimate sea vacation, **Sailing Sicily** rents out catamarans and sailboats, complete with a crew of sailors. **Pasqualo** is a great option for small boats to circumnavigate the active volcano of Stromboli. If you are lucky you can see it erupt.

Pasqualo
W strombolidamare.it
Sailing Sicily
W sailingsicily.com

Walking and Hiking

The city centres in many of Sicily's towns are usually compact, with key sites within easy reach of each other. Syracuse, Catania, Palermo, and many more Sicilian towns have large pedestrian areas and are best enjoyed on foot.

Sicily also offers many opportunities for scenic hikes, both in the countryside, on Mount Etna, or in nature reserves, and expert guides are often available to help you plan your route or take you. **Outdoor Active** is a great source for finding your perfect hiking trail. Always make sure you bring enough water, and wear sturdy shoes and a hat, as the sun can be very strong.

Outdoor Active
W outdooractive.com

PRACTICAL INFORMATION

A little local know-how goes a long way in Sicily. Here you can find all the essential advice and information you will need during your stay.

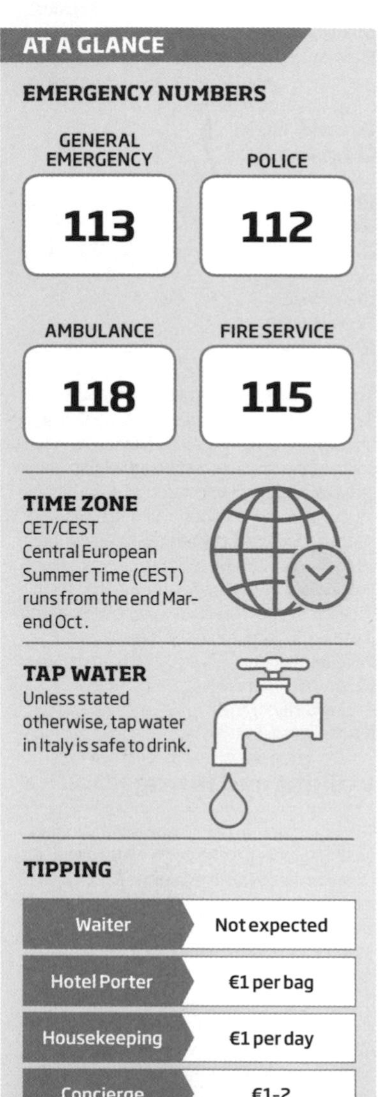

AT A GLANCE

EMERGENCY NUMBERS

GENERAL EMERGENCY	POLICE
113	**112**

AMBULANCE	FIRE SERVICE
118	**115**

TIME ZONE

CET/CEST
Central European Summer Time (CEST) runs from the end Mar–end Oct.

TAP WATER

Unless stated otherwise, tap water in Italy is safe to drink.

TIPPING

Waiter	Not expected
Hotel Porter	€1 per bag
Housekeeping	€1 per day
Concierge	€1–2
Taxi Driver	Not expected

Personal Security

On the whole, Sicily is a safe, unthreatening place for visitors. Bag-snatching scooter drivers are a problem in the big cities and at busy tourist spots, such as the ferry ports and main stations, so hold bags on the inside of the pavement where possible, and try to wear as little jewellery as possible.

Be wary of pickpockets on public transport and in crowded city centres. Also, avoid leaving valuables in your car. However, in smaller towns, villages and rural areas, petty crime is rare.

If you have anything stolen, report the crime within 24 hours to the nearest police station and take ID with you. If you need to make an insurance claim, get a copy of the crime report *(denuncia)*. Contact your embassy if you have your passport stolen, or in the event of a serious crime or accident.

Health

Seek medicinal supplies and advice for minor ailments from pharmacies (*farmacia*). These are marked with a green cross and sell common drugs, without a prescription. *Parafarmacie* have a blue or red cross and sell over-the-counter medicines, toiletries and baby formula, and are open on Saturdays. If you run out of your regular medicine, pharmacists may sell replacements, if you have the original packaging. You can find details of the nearest 24-hour service on all pharmacy doors.

Sicily has a network of first-aid stations. All tourist resorts operate seasonal emergency treatment centres *(guardia medica)*. Hotels will also be able to suggest English-speaking doctors and dentists if required.

Emergency medical care in Italy is free for all EU and Australian citizens *(p234)*. If you have an EHIC card, be sure to present this as soon as possible. You may have to pay after treatment and reclaim the money later.

For visitors from outside of the EU and Australia, payment of medical expenses is the patient's responsibility, so it's wise to arrange comprehensive medical insurance.

Smoking, Alcohol and Drugs

Smoking is banned in enclosed public places and the possession of illegal drugs could result in a prison sentence.

Italy has a strict limit of 0.05 per cent BAC (blood alcohol content) for drivers. This means that you cannot drink more than a small beer or a small glass of wine if you plan to drive. For drivers with less than three years' driving experience the limit is 0.

ID

By law you must carry identification at all times in Italy. A photocopy of your passport photo page (and visa if applicable) should suffice. If you are stopped by the police you may be asked to present the original document within 12 hours.

Local Customs

In some towns and cities you can be fined for dropping litter, sitting on monument steps, or eating or drinking outside churches, historic monuments and public buildings. It is an offence to swim or bathe in public fountains.

Illegal traders operate on the streets of all the cities; avoid buying from them as you could be fined by the local police.

LGBT+ Safety

Homosexuality is legal and widely accepted in Italy; however, some smaller Sicilian towns and rural areas may be less accepting of non-traditional relationships or sexualities, and overt displays of affection may be received negatively.

Visiting Churches and Cathedrals

Strict dress codes apply: cover your torso and upper arms, and ensure shorts and skirts cover your knees. Shoes must be worn. Do not talk loudly or use cameras or mobile devices without first asking permission.

Mobile Phones and Wi-Fi

Wi-Fi is generally available in tourist areas, and cafés and restaurants will usually give you the password for their Wi-Fi on the condition that you make a purchase.

Visitors travelling to Sicily (and Italy in general) with EU tariffs are able to use their devices abroad without being affected by roaming charges. Users will be charged the same rates for data, SMS and voice calls as they would pay at home.

Post

The Italian postal system, Poste Italiane, can be very slow. Stamps *(francobolli)* are sold in kiosks and tobacconists *(tabacchi)*. Letters and postcards can take anything between four days and two weeks to arrive, depending on the destination.

For more urgent mail, go to the post office and ask for insured mail *(assicurata)*, registered mail *(raccomandata)*, or fast mail *(postacelere)*. If speed is of the essence for destinations within Italy, use the postal system's courier service, Paccocelere, or for international destinations use a private courier such as DHL or UPS.

Taxes and Refunds

VAT (called IVA in Italy) is usually 22%, with a reduced rate of 4–10% on some items. Non-EU citizens can claim an IVA rebate subject to certain conditions. It is easier to claim before you buy (you will need to show your passport to the shop assistant and complete a form). If claiming retrospectively, present a customs officer with your purchases and receipts at the airport. Receipts will be stamped and sent back to the vendor to issue a refund.

WEBSITES AND APPS

www.sicilyhistoriesapp.com
Interactive map with historical information about Sicily's sights.

www.enit.it
The Italian tourist board.

www.siciliaoutdoor.org
A useful tool for planning walks and hikes anywhere in Sicily.

www.viamichelin.com
Maps and routes to plan your drives.

INDEX

Index

Page numbers in **bold** refer to main entries.

A

B

C

D

E

N

O

P

T

U

V

W

Z

PHRASE BOOK

IN EMERGENCY

Help!	**Aiuto!**	*eye-**yoo**-toh*
Stop!	**Ferma!**	*fair-**mah***
Call a doctor	**Chiama un medico**	*kee-**ah**-mah oon **meh**-dee-koh*
Call an ambulance	**Chiama un' ambulanza**	*kee-**ah**-mah oon am-boo-**lan**-tsa*
Call the police	**Chiama la polizia**	*kee-**ah**-mah lah pol-ee-**tsee**-ah*
Call the fire brigade	**Chiama i pompieri**	*kee-**ah**-mah ee pom-pee-**air**-ee*
Where is the telephone?	**Dov'è il telefono?**	*dov-**eh**eel teh-**leh**-foh-noh?*
The nearest hospital?	**L'ospedale più vicino?**	*loss-peh-**dah**-leh pee-oovee-**chee**-noh?*

COMMUNICATION ESSENTIALS

Yes/No	**Si/No**	***see/noh***
Please	**Per favore**	*pair fah-**vor**-eh*
Thank you	**Grazie**	***grah**-tsee-eh*
Excuse me	**Mi scusi**	*mee **skoo**-zee*
Hello/good morning	**Buon giorno**	*bwon **jor**-noh*
Goodbye	**Arrivederci**	*ah-ree-veh-**dair**-chee*
Good evening	**Buona sera**	***bwon**-ah **sair**-ah*
morning	**la mattina**	*lah mah-**tee**-nah*
afternoon	**il pomeriggio**	*eel poh-meh-**ree**-joh*
evening	**la sera**	*lah **sair**-ah*
yesterday	**ieri**	*ee-**air**-ee*
today	**oggi**	***oh**-jee*
tomorrow	**domani**	*doh-**mah**-nee*
here	**qui**	***kwee***
there	**la**	***lah***
What?	**Quale?**	***kwah**-leh?*
When?	**Quando?**	***kwan**-doh?*
Why?	**Perchè?**	*pair-**keh**?*
Where?	**Dove?**	***doh**-veh*

USEFUL PHRASES

How are you?	**Come sta?**	***koh**-meh stah?*
Very well, thank you.	**Molto bene, grazie**	***moll**-toh **beh**-neh **grah**-tsee-eh*
Pleased to meet you.	**Piacere di conoscerla.**	*pee-ah-**chair**-eh dee coh-**noh**-shair-lah*
See you soon.	**A più tardi.**	*ah pee-**oo tar**-dee*
That's fine.	**Va bene.**	*va **beh**-neh*
Where is/are ...?	**Dov'è/Dove sono...?**	*dov-**eh**/doveh **soh**noh?*
How long does it take to get to ...?	**Quanto tempo ci vuole per andare a ...?**	***kwan**-toh **tem**-poh chee voo-**oh**-leh pair an-**dar**-eh ah...?*
How do I get to ...?	**Come faccio per arrivare a ...?**	*koh-meh **fah**-choh pair arri-**var**-eh ah...?*
Do you speak English?	**Parla inglese?**	***par**-lah een-**gleh**-zeh?*
I don't understand.	**Non capisco.**	*non ka-**pee**-skoh*
Could you speak more slowly, please?	**Può parlare più lentamente, per favore?**	*pwoh par-**lah**-reh pee-**oo** len-ta-**men**-teh pair fah-**vor**-eh?*
I'm sorry.	**Mi dispiace.**	*mee dee-spee-**ah**-cheh*

USEFUL WORDS

big	**grande**	***gran**-deh*
small	**piccolo**	***pee**-koh-loh*
hot	**caldo**	***kal**-doh*
cold	**freddo**	***fred**-doh*
good	**buono**	***bwoh**-noh*
bad	**male**	***mal**-eh*
enough	**basta**	***bas**-tah*
well	**bene**	***beh**-neh*
open	**aperto**	*ah-**pair**-toh*
closed	**chiuso**	*kee-**oo**-zoh*
left	**a sinistra**	*ah see-**nee**-strah*
right	**a destra**	*ah **dess**-trah*
straight on	**sempre dritto**	***sem**-preh **dree**-toh*
near	**vicino**	*vee-**chee**-noh*
far	**lontano**	*lon-**tah**-noh*
up	**su**	***soo***
down	**giù**	***joo***
early	**presto**	***press**-toh*
late	**tardi**	***tar**-dee*
entrance	**entrata**	*en-**trah**-tah*
exit	**uscita**	*oo-**shee**-ta*
toilet	**il bagno**	*eel ban-yo*
free, unoccupied	**libero**	***lee**-bair-oh*
free, no charge	**gratuito**	*grah-**too**-ee-toh*

MAKING A TELEPHONE CALL

I'd like to place a long-distance call.	**Vorrei fare una interurbana.**	*vor-**ray far**-eh oona in-tair-oor-**bah**-nah.*
I'd like to make a reverse-charge call.	**Vorrei fare una telefonata a carico del destinatario.**	*vor-**ray far**-eh oona teh-leh-fon-**ah**-tah ah **kar**-ee-koh dell dess- tee-nah-**tar**-ree-oh.*
I'll try again later.	**Ritelefono più tardi.**	*ree-teh-**leh**-foh-noh pee-oo **tar**-dee.*
Can I leave a message?	**Posso lasciare un messaggio?**	***poss**-oh lash-**ah**-reh oon mess-**sah**-joh?*
Hold on	**Un attimo, per favore**	*oon **ah**-tee-moh, pair fah-**vor**-eh*
Could you speak up a little please?	**Può parlare più forte, per favore?**	*pwoh par-**lah**-reh pee-**oo for**-teh, pair fah-**vor**-eh?*
local call	**la telefonata locale**	*lah teh-leh-fon-**ah**-ta loh-**kah**-leh*

SHOPPING

How much does this cost?	**Quanto costa questo?**	***kwan**-toh **cos**-stah **kweh**-stoh?*
I would like ...	**Vorrei ...**	*vor-**ray**...*
Do you have ...?	**Avete ...?**	*ah-**veh**-teh...?*
I'm just looking.	**Sto soltanto guardando**	*stoh sol-**tan**-toh gwar-**dan**-doh*
Do you take credit cards?	**Accettate carte di credito?**	*ah-chet-**tah**-teh **kar**-teh dee **creh**-dee-toh?*
What time do you open/close?	**A che ora apre/ chiude?**	*ah keh **or**-ah **ah**-preh/kee-**oo**-deh?*
this one	**questo**	***kweh**-stoh*

that one	**quello**	*__kwell__-oh*
expensive	**caro**	*__kar__-oh*
cheap	**a buon prezzo**	*ah bwon __pret__-soh*
size, clothes	**la taglia**	*lah __tah__-lee-ah*
size, shoes	**il numero**	*eel __noo__-mair-oh*
white	**bianco**	*bee-__ang__-koh*
black	**nero**	*__neh__-roh*
red	**rosso**	*__ross__-oh*
yellow	**giallo**	*__jal__-loh*
green	**verde**	*__vair__-deh*
blue	**blu**	*bloo*
brown	**marrone**	*mar-__roh__-neh*

TYPES OF SHOP

antique dealer	**l'antiquario**	*lan-tee-__kwah__-ree-oh*
bakery	**la panetteria**	*lah pah-net-tair-__ree__-ah*
bank	**la banca**	*lah __bang__-kah*
bookshop	**la libreria**	*lah lee-breh-__ree__-ah*
butcher's	**la macelleria**	*lah mah-chell-eh-__ree__-ah*
cake shop	**la pasticceria**	*lah pas-tee-chair-__ee__-ah*
chemist's	**la farmacia**	*lah far-mah-__chee__-ah*
department store	**il grande magazzino**	*eel __gran__-deh mag-gad-__zee__-noh*
delicatessen	**la salumeria**	*lah sah-loo-meh-__ree__-ah*
fishmonger's	**la pescheria**	*lah pess-keh-__ree__-ah*
florist	**il fioraio**	*eel fee-or-__eye__-oh*
greengrocer	**il fruttivendolo**	*eel froo-tee-__ven__-doh-loh*
grocery	**alimentari**	*ah-lee-men-__tah__-ree*
hairdresser	**il parrucchiere**	*eel par-oo-kee-__air__-eh*
ice cream parlour	**la gelateria**	*lah jel-lah-tair-__ree__-ah*
market	**il mercato**	*eel mair-__kah__-toh*
news-stand	**l'edicola**	*leh-__dee__-koh-lah*
post office	**l'ufficio postale**	*loo-__fee__-choh pos-__tah__-leh*
shoe shop	**il negozio di scarpe**	*eel neh-__goh__-tsioh dee __skar__-peh*
supermarket	**il supermercato**	*eel su-pair-mair-__kah__-toh*
tobacconist	**il tabaccaio**	*eel tah-bak-__eye__-oh*
travel agency	**l'agenzia di viaggi**	*lah-jen-__tsee__-ah dee vee-__ad__-jee*

SIGHTSEEING

art gallery	**la pinacoteca**	*lah peena-koh-__teh__-kah*
bus stop	**la fermata dell'autobus**	*lah fair-__mah__-tah dell __ow__-toh-booss*
church	**la chiesa la basilica**	*lah kee-__eh__-zah lah bah-__seel__-i-kah*
garden	**il giardino**	*eel jar-__dee__-no*
library	**la biblioteca**	*lah beeb-lee-oh-__teh__-kah*
museum	**il museo**	*eel moo-__zeh__-oh*
railway station	**la stazione**	*lah stah-tsee-__oh__-neh*
tourist information	**l'ufficio turistico**	*loo-__fee__-choh too-__ree__-stee-koh*
closed for the public holiday	**chiuso per la festa**	*kee-__oo__-zoh pair lah __fess__-tah*

STAYING IN A HOTEL

Do you have any vacant rooms?	**Avete camere libere?**	*ah-__veh__-teh __kah__-mair-eh __lee__-bair-eh?*
double room	**una camera doppia**	*oona __kah__-mair-ah __doh__-pee-ah*
with double bed	**con letto matrimoniale**	*kon __let__-toh mah-tree-moh-nee-__ah__-leh*
twin room	**una camera con due letti**	*oona __kah__-mair-ah kon __doo__-eh __let__-tee*
single room	**una camera singola**	*oona __kah__-mair-ah __sing__-goh-lah*
room with a bath, shower	**una camera con bagno, con doccia**	*oona __kah__-mair-ah kon __ban__-yoh, kon __dot__-chah*
porter	**il facchino**	*eel fah-__kee__-noh*
key	**la chiave**	*lah kee-__ah__-veh*
I have a reservation.	**Ho fatto una prenotazione.**	*oh __fat__-toh oona preh-noh-tah-tsee-__oh__-neh*

EATING OUT

Have you got a table for ...?	**Avete un tavolo per ... ?**	*ah-__veh__-teh oon __tah__-voh-loh pair ...?*
I'd like to reserve a table.	**Vorrei riservare un tavolo.**	*vor-__ray__ ree-sair-__vah__-reh oon __tah__-voh-loh*
breakfast	**colazione**	*koh-lah-tsee-__oh__-neh*
lunch	**pranzo**	*__pran__-tsoh*
dinner	**cena**	*__cheh__-nah*
The bill, please.	**Il conto, per favore.**	*eel __kon__-toh pair fah-__vor__-eh*
I am a vegetarian.	**Sono vegetariano/a.**	*__soh__-noh __veh__-jeh-tar ee-__ah__-noh/nah*
waitress	**cameriera**	*kah-mair-ee-__air__-ah*
waiter	**cameriere**	*kah-mair-ee-__air__-eh*
fixed price menu	**il menù a prezzo fisso**	*eel meh-__noo__ ah __pret__-soh __fee__-soh*
dish of the day	**piatto del giorno**	*pee-__ah__-toh dell __jor__-no*
starter	**antipasto**	*an-tee-__pass__-toh*
first course	**il primo**	*eel __pree__-moh*
main course	**il secondo**	*eel seh-__kon__-doh*
vegetables	**il contorno**	*eel kon-__tor__-noh*
dessert	**il dolce**	*eel __doll__-che*
cover charge	**il coperto**	*eel koh-__pair__-toh*
wine list	**la lista dei vini**	*lah __lee__-stah day __vee__-nee*
rare	**al sangue**	*al __sang__-gweh*
medium	**a puntino**	*a poon-__tee__-noh*
well done	**ben cotto**	*ben __kot__-toh*
glass	**il bicchiere**	*eel bee-kee-__air__-eh*
bottle	**la bottiglia**	*lah bot-__teel__-yah*
knife	**il coltello**	*eel kol-__tell__-oh*
fork	**la forchetta**	*lah for-__ket__-tah*
spoon	**il cucchiaio**	*eel koo-kee-__eye__-oh*

MENU DECODER

apple	**la mela**	*lah __meh__-lah*
artichoke	**il carciofo**	*eel kar-__choff__-oh*
aubergine	**la melanzana**	*lah meh-lan-__tsah__-nah*
baked	**al forno**	*al __for__-noh*
beans	**i fagioli**	*ee fah-__joh__-lee*
beef	**il manzo**	*eel __man__-tsoh*
beer	**la birra**	*lah __beer__-rah*
boiled	**lesso**	*__less__-oh*
bread	**il pane**	*eel __pah__-neh*
broth	**il brodo**	*eel __broh__-doh*
butter	**il burro**	*eel __boor__-oh*
cake	**la torta**	*lah __tor__-tah*
cheese	**il formaggio**	*eel for-__mad__-joh*
chicken	**il pollo**	*eel __poll__-oh*
chips	**patatine fritte**	*pah-tah-__teen__-eh __free__-teh*

baby clams	**le vongole**	leh **von**-goh-leh
coffee	**il caffè**	eel kah-**feh**
courgettes	**gli zucchini**	lyee dzoo-**kee**-nee
dry	**secco**	**sek**-koh
duck	**l'anatra**	**lah**-nah-trah
egg	**l'uovo**	loo-**oh**-voh
fish	**il pesce**	eel **pesh**-eh
fresh fruit	**frutta fresca**	**froo**-tah **fress**-kah
garlic	**l'aglio**	**lahl**-yoh
grapes	**l'uva**	**loo**-vah
grilled	**alla griglia**	ah-lah **greel**-yah
ham	**il prosciutto**	eel pro-**shoo**-toh
cooked/cured	**cotto/crudo**	**kot**-toh/**kroo**-doh
ice cream	**il gelato**	eel jel-**lah**-toh
lamb	**agnello**	la-**gnel**-lo
lobster	**l'aragosta**	lah-rah-**goss**-tah
meat	**la carne**	la **kar**-neh
milk	**il latte**	eel **laht**-teh
mineral water sparkling/still	**l'acqua minerale gassata/naturale**	**lah**-kwah mee-nair-**ah**-leh gah-**zah**-tah/nah-too-**rah**-leh
mushrooms	**i funghi**	ee **foon**-gee
oil	**l'olio**	**loll**-yoh
olive	**l'oliva**	loh-**lee**-vah
onion	**la cipolla**	lah chee-**poll**-ah
orange	**l'arancia**	lah-**ran**-chah
orange/lemon juice	**succo d'arancia/di limone**	**soo**-koh dah-**ran**-chah/dee lee-**moh**-neh
peach	**la pesca**	lah **pess**-kah
pepper	**il pepe**	eel **peh**-peh
pork	**carne di maiale**	**kar**-neh dee mah-**yah**-leh
potatoes	**le patate**	leh pah-**tah**-teh
prawns	**i gamberi**	ee **gam**-bair-ee
rice	**il riso**	eel **ree**-zoh
roast	**arrosto**	ar-**ross**-toh
roll	**il panino**	eel pah-**nee**-noh
salad	**l'insalata**	leen-sah-**lah**-tah
salt	**il sale**	eel **sah**-leh
sausage	**la salsiccia**	lah sal-**see**-chah
seafood	**frutti di mare**	**froo**-tee dee **mah**-reh
soup	**la zuppa, la minestra**	lah **tsoo**-pah, lah mee-**ness**-trah
steak	**la bistecca**	lah bee-**stek**-kah
strawberries	**le fragole**	leh **frah**-goh-leh
sugar	**lo zucchero**	loh **zoo**-kair-oh
tea	**il tè**	eel **teh**
herb tea	**la tisana**	lah tee-**zah**-nah
tomato	**il pomodoro**	eel poh-moh-**dor**-oh
tuna	**il tonno**	eel **ton**-noh
veal	**il vitello**	eel vee-**tell**-oh
vegetables	**le verdure**	leh vair-**du**-rah
vinegar	**l'aceto**	lah-**cheh**-toh
water	**l'acqua**	**lah**-kwah
red wine	**vino rosso**	**vee**-noh **ross**-oh
white wine	**vino bianco**	**vee**-noh bee-**ang**-koh

NUMBERS

1	**uno**	**oo**-noh
2	**due**	**doo**-eh
3	**tre**	treh
4	**quattro**	**kwat**-roh
5	**cinque**	**ching**-kweh
6	**sei**	**say**-ee
7	**sette**	**set**-teh
8	**otto**	**ot**-toh
9	**nove**	**noh**-veh
10	**dieci**	dee-**eh**-chee
11	**undici**	**oon**-dee-chee
12	**dodici**	**doh**-dee-chee
13	**tredici**	**treh**-dee-chee
14	**quattordici**	kwat-**tor**-dee-chee
15	**quindici**	**kwin**-dee-chee
16	**sedici**	**say**-dee-chee
17	**diciassette**	dee-chah-**set**-teh
18	**diciotto**	dee-**chot**-toh
19	**diciannove**	dee-chah-**noh**-veh
20	**venti**	**ven**-tee
30	**trenta**	**tren**-tah
40	**quaranta**	kwah-**ran**-tah
50	**cinquanta**	ching-**kwan**-tah
60	**sessanta**	sess-**an**-tah
70	**settanta**	set-**tan**-tah
80	**ottanta**	ot-**tan**-tah
90	**novanta**	noh-**van**-tah
100	**cento**	**chen**-toh
1,000	**mille**	**mee**-leh
2,000	**duemila**	**doo**-eh **mee**-lah
5,000	**cinquemila**	**ching**-kweh **mee**-lah
1,000,000	**un milione**	oon meel-**yoh**-neh

TIME

one minute	**un minuto**	oon mee-**noo**-toh
one hour	**un'ora**	oon **or**-ah
half an hour	**mezz'ora**	medz-**or**-ah
a day	**un giorno**	oon **jor**-noh
a week	**una settimana**	oona set-tee-**mah**-nah
Monday	**lunedì**	loo-neh-**dee**
Tuesday	**martedì**	mar-teh-**dee**
Wednesday	**mercoledì**	mair-koh-leh-**dee**
Thursday	**giovedì**	joh-veh-**dee**
Friday	**venerdì**	ven-air-**dee**
Saturday	**sabato**	**sah**-bah-toh
Sunday	**domenica**	doh-**meh**-nee-kah

ACKNOWLEDGMENTS

The publisher would like to thank the following for their kind permission to reproduce their photographs:

Key: a-above; b-below/bottom; c-centre; f-far; l-left; r-right; t-top

123RF.com: Yulia Grogoryeva 33tl; maudis60 159tr; Andreas Zerndl 105br.

4Corners: Antonino Bartuccio 6-7, 99tl, 136t, 190-1, 209br, 218-9t; Massimo Borchi 94bl, / *The Stella sculpture* by Pietr Consagra © DACS 2019 135tr; Claudio Cassaro 124-5t; Stefano Cellai 129cr; Gabriele Croppi 68-9; Giorgio Filippini 166-7t; Paolo Giocoso 140b; Alessandro Saffo 2-3, 19, 74t, 120tl, 138-9t, 160-1, 184-5t, 192-3t, 197br, 198-9, 224-5t.

Addiopizzo Travel: 47cl, 47clb.

akg-images: Eric Vandeville 13cr, 41tr.

Alamy Stock Photo: age fotostock / Hanneke Wetzer 72bl; AGF Srl / Giuseppe Masci 28cla; Per Andersen 26cra; Michael Brooks 39tr, 42br; Paul Brown 22cr; Michele Castellani 217clb; Cavan / Paolo Sartori 51ca; ClassicStock / Charles Phelps Cushing 57bl; Mark Davidson 149bc; Marius Dobilas 146-7t; Peter Eastland / *Street art depicting Marlon Brando as the Godfather* by Christian Guémy (C215) © ADAGP; Paris and DACS; London 2019 40-1b; EmmePi Stock Images 48tl, 62, 64-5; EmmePi Travel 52cr; Giulio Ercolani 90tl, 204cra; F1online digitale Bildagentur GmbH / F. Bilger Photodesign 188b; Faraway Photos 22cl; Tim Graham 20crb; Joan Gravell 226bl; Giulio Di Gregorio 24tl; hemis.fr / Jean- Pierre Degas 24tr, 37br, / Patrick Frilet 163b, / Franck Guiziou 8cl, 43cl, 153tl, 180bl, / Alessio Mamo 99tr; Heritage Image Partnership Ltd / Index / Mithra 56clb; Stephen Hughes 196t; imageBROKER / Bahnmueller 230tl, / Martin Jung 153br, / Olaf Krüger 192cr, / Martin Moxter 208cr, / Karl F. Schöfmann 71br, 92-3b, / White Star / Monica Gumm 48-9b; INTERFOTO / Personalities 55bc; Michael Juno 76tl; Gunter Kirsch 154t; Yadid Levy 75br; Melvyn Longhurst 175cla; MARKA / Martino Motti 167br, / Federico Tovoli 70b; Angus McComiskey 35cla, 228-9t; Antonio Melita 53crb; Sandro Messina 49tr; Gianni Muratore 53tl, 100bc; NAPA 214t; Ville Palonen 41br; Mario Pedone 88br; Chuck Pefley 10clb; PhotoStock-Israel / Ilan Rosen 210cra; Massimo Piacentino 131t; Domenico Piccione 52crb; The Picture Art Collection 55cra, 159br; Giacomo Lo Presti 156b; The Protected Art Archive 54t; M Ramírez 87t; Alex Ramsay 187tl; Realy Easy Star / Rosario Patanè 229br, / Luca Scamporlino 78cr, / Toni Spagone 104-5t, 183tl, 208-9t, 228bc; REDA &CO srl / Michele Bella 50bl, / Riccardo Lombardo 22br, 52cla, / Federico Meneghetti 221tr; Frederic Reglain 68cra, 68bl, 102tl; robertharding / Stuart Black 154bc, / Antonio Busiello 36br, 51b, / Martin Child 12cl, / Matthew Williams-Ellis 20cr, 26tl, 38-9t, 85tr, / Oliver Wintzen 84; Peter Scholey 151cra; Science History Images / Photo Researchers 54cb, 56-7t; Neil Setchfield 192bl; Keith J Smith. 216-7b; Antonio Violi 27tr; WaterFrame_fba 141tc; Westend61 GmbH 220-1b, / Martin Moxter 130b; Jan Wlodarczyk 26-7t, 43br, 179cla; World History Archive 56br; John Zada 25tr.

AWL Images: Giacomo Augugliaro 22t; Hemis 20bl; Stefano Termanini 17t, 108-9, 132-3; Catherina Unger 57tr.

Bye Bye Blues: 44br.

Depositphotos Inc: Alesinya 119t; Romas_ph 102-3b.

Dreamstime.com: Barmalini 33br; Sergiy Beketov 120-1b; Sergio Bertino 172t; Blitzkoenig 151crb; Roberto Caucino 37cl; Marco Ciannarella 42-3t; Andras Csontos 39cla; Digitalalessio 195tr; Dorinmarius 134-5b; Tatiana Dyuvbanova 116-7t; Eddygaleotti 122, 175t, 177bl; Ellesi 56tl, 73t; Emicristea 137br; Erix2005 31c, 123cl; Tamas Gabor 93cb; Stefano Gervasio 10-1b; Giuseppemasci 40tl; Gunold 53clb; Pablo Hidalgo 32tl; Javarman 16c, 55tr, 58-9; Laszlo Konya 89br; Krivinis 164-5b, 176t; Sebastiano Leggio 52cl; Anna Lurye 150-1b; Marsana 163crb; Olgacov 79tl, 202t; Ollirg 49cl, 222b; Michelangelo Oprandi 206-7b, 210cr; Perseomedusa 27cla; Photogolfer 225br; Petr Pohudka 50-1t; Romasph 115t, 205b; Scaliger 55clb; Siculodoc 28-9t, 173cr; Alfredo Steccanella 8cla; Thevirex 194b; Aleksandar Todorovic 101b; T.w. Van Urk 212-3; Stefano Valeri 30-1t, 72-3t, 86bl, 88tl, 106-7, 117clb, 129t, 182bl; Worldfoto 18, 168-9; Andreas Zerndl 162-3t; Zoom-zoom 95br.

Getty Images: 500px / StixLU 4; 500Px Plus / Luca Maccarrone 31ca; 500px Prime / Marco Calandra 211; AFP / Gabriel Bouys 210br, / Ludovic Marin 38bl; Corbis Documentary / Atlantide Phototravel 34-5b, 116clb, / Martyn Goddard 232-3; Corbis Historical / Vittoriano Rastelli 210crb; Corbis News / Stefano Montesi 46-7t; De Agostini / DEA / G. Cappellani 55tl, / A. Dagli Orti 157tl, / G. Dagli Orti 54bl, 55cr, / L. Romano 71tl; DigitalVision / Gary Yeowell 10ca, 20t; EyeEm / Andrea Gurrieri 28-9ca, / Jerry Hoekstra 151br, / Giuseppe Lombardo 13br; Gamma-Keystone / Keystone-France 210bc; Gamma-Rapho / Henri-Alain SEGALEN 29tr; Hulton Fine Art Collection / Mondadori Portfolio / Electa / Vincenzo Negro 204bc; The Image Bank / Atlantide Phototravel /